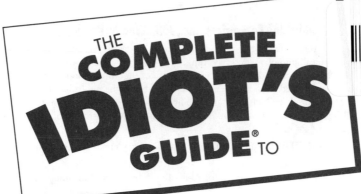

THE
# COMPLETE IDIOT'S GUIDE® TO

D0127837

# 20-Minute Meals

*by Tod Dimmick*

## ALPHA

A member of Penguin Group (USA) Inc.

This is a CWL Publishing Enterprises Book created for Alpha Books by CWL Publishing Enterprises, Madison, WI, www.cwlpub.com.

International Standard Book Number: 0-02-864419-0
Library of Congress Catalog Card Number: 2002113272

04   03        8   7   6   5   4   3   2

Interpretation of the printing code: The rightmost number of the first series of numbers is the year of the book's printing; the rightmost number of the second series of numbers is the number of the book's printing. For example, a printing code of 02-1 shows that the first printing occurred in 2002.

*Printed in the United States of America*

**Note:** This publication contains the opinions and ideas of its author. It is intended to provide helpful and informative material on the subject matter covered. It is sold with the understanding that the author and publisher are not engaged in rendering professional services in the book. If the reader requires personal assistance or advice, a competent professional should be consulted.

The author and publisher specifically disclaim any responsibility for any liability, loss, or risk, personal or otherwise, which is incurred as a consequence, directly or indirectly, of the use and application of any of the contents of this book.

**Publisher:** *Marie Butler-Knight*
**Product Manager:** *Phil Kitchel*
**Managing Editor:** *Jennifer Chisholm*
**Senior Acquisitions Editor:** *Renee Wilmeth*
**Development Editor:** *Nancy D. Lewis*
**Copy Editor:** *Michael Dietsch*
**Illustrator:** *Chris Eliopoulos*
**Cover/Book Designer:** *Trina Wurst*
**Indexer:** *Brad Herriman*
**Layout/Proofreading:** *Becky Harmon, Mary Hunt*

# Contents at a Glance

**Part 1:**    **Meals Done Quick, Done Right**    1

1   Faster and Better    3
*Why 20-minute cuisine is an important part of today's
busy lifestyle.*

2   Ingredients    11
*The basics for the pantry, the fridge, and the freezer.*

3   Methods    23
*A review of cooking methods perfect for 20-minute cuisine.*

4   Equipment    35
*A review of those key pots, pans, tools, and equipment that
make cooking easier.*

5   Practical Secrets    45
*Tips for a fun, tasty, and speedy meal.*

6   In Case of Emergency    55
*How to use "easy timesavers."*

**Part 2:**    **Main Courses**    63

7   Breakfast Time    65
*Delicious tips and recipes for breakfasts that everyone
will enjoy.*

8   Pasta and Pizza    77
*Try my favorite pizza, pasta, and rice recipes, and easy
timesavers that will have you sitting down to a meal quickly.*

9   Seafood    89
*Shine the spotlight—front and center—on easy
seafood preparation.*

10   White Meats    99
*Explore some great ways to make the most out of poultry
and pork.*

11   Richer Meats    111
*Use beef and lamb to make quick, delicious dishes.*

12   Vegetarian    119
*Try some terrific 20-minute vegetarian recipes.*

**Part 3:**    **Make the Meal Complete**       131

13   Show Your Good Side (on the Plate)      133
*Side dishes like rice, pasta, and potatoes balance a
meat-based main course.*

14   Savor the Season: Quick Vegetable Dishes      141
*Here you'll find some terrific, quick vegetable methods
and recipes.*

15   Breads      151
*How you can make bread a part of the 20-minute meal.*

16   Dessert Time!      163
*Quick and delicious desserts are not only possible, they can
be downright easy.*

**Part 4:**    **Theme Cuisine**       177

17   Easy Timesavers      179
*Ingredients, methods, and recipes invaluable for the cook
in a real hurry.*

18   Comfort Foods      191
*Twenty-minute recipes, from appetizers to lightning main
courses, that evoke good feelings.*

19   Ethnic Magic      201
*Recipes and seasoning inspiration from culinary traditions
around the world.*

20   Healthy … and Delicious!      213
*A shortlist of delicious dishes specifically chosen because they
offer high nutrition and often low fat.*

21   Whirlwind Romantic … Food!      223
*Recipes, and historical context, to help prepare a winning
romantic meal.*

22   Entertain, Sane      233
*How the words "entertain" and "20 minutes" belong in
the same sentence!*

23   Leftovers      243
*This chapter focuses on using cooked ingredients to accelerate
a second meal (and sometimes a third!).*

**Part 5:  Behind the Scenes                                           251**

   24  Cyber Soufflé: 20-Minute Cuisine on the Web            253
        *Make the most of the Internet in cooking, without*
        *wasting time.*

   25  Inspiration from Unexpected Places                     261
        *Favorite recipes provide an opportunity for learning and*
        *conversation.*

   26  Wine and 20-Minute Cuisine                             269
        *Food-friendly wines and wine-food pairings.*

   27  The 20-Minute Garden                                   281
        *Growing for the kitchen is an opportunity for flavor,*
        *relaxation, and learning.*

**Appendixes**

   A  Glossary                                               289
   B  References, Resources, and Vendors                     295
     Index                                                  303

# Contents

**Part 1:   Meals Done Quick, Done Right**                                                1

**1   Faster and Better**                                                                 3

Today's Mealtime Reality ................................................................4

Mealtime Is an Oasis in a Busy Week .........................................4

    *Case Study 1—Fatigued Friday* ...............................................5

    *Pasta with Chicken, Mozzarella, and Sweet Red Peppers* ..............5

    *Case Study 2—Manic Monday* ..............................................6

Set Reasonable Expectations ........................................................7

Quality Times Two ......................................................................7

Less Is More ..................................................................................9

Endless Possibilities .....................................................................9

**2   Ingredients**                                                                      11

The Perfect Pantry ....................................................................11

    *Baking: Flour and Meals* .......................................................13

    *Baking: Accoutrements* ..........................................................13

    *Condiments* ...........................................................................13

    *Oils, Marinades, and Vinegars* ............................................14

    *Pasta* ....................................................................................14

    *Rice and Other Starches* .......................................................15

    *Soups* ...................................................................................15

    *Herbs, Spices, and Seasoning Mixes* .......................................15

    *Sweeteners* .............................................................................16

    *Vegetables and Grains* ..........................................................16

The Happy Fridge ......................................................................16

A Friend Named Herb ...............................................................17

The Spice of Life ........................................................................19

Substitutions ...............................................................................21

**3   Methods**                                                                          23

Understanding the Importance of Method ................................24

Culinary "Science" ....................................................................24

Out of the Frying Pan ...............................................................25

    *Quick Stir-Fry Medley* .........................................................27

Onto the Fire ..............................................................................27

    *Grilled Zucchini* ..................................................................29

Into Hot Water .................................................................29
   *Boiled Lobster* ...........................................................30
All Steamed Up .................................................................30
   *Steamed Asparagus* ...................................................31
Broiling to Win Friends and Influence People .......31
   *Garden Broil* .............................................................32
Don't Forget Raw .............................................................32
   *Quick and Cool Cukes* ...........................................33

## 4 Equipment     35

Cookware Items ................................................................35
   *Skillet* .........................................................................36
   *Saucepans* ..................................................................37
   *Large Cooking Pot* ...................................................37
   *Vegetable Steamer* ....................................................38
   *Pizza Stone* ...............................................................38
   *Casserole Dishes* .......................................................38
   *Wok* ...........................................................................38
   *Baking Pans* .............................................................39
   *Fish Poacher* .............................................................39
Kitchen Tools ....................................................................39
Don't Forget the Knives! .................................................41
Hold It: Kitchen Containers ...........................................42
Machinery to Make Life Easier ......................................42
The Freezer Is My Friend ................................................44

## 5 Practical Secrets     45

Fresh Is Quick! .................................................................46
   *Spiced Spinach* ..........................................................47
   *Summer Tomato Platter* ...........................................47
Planned Extras (Never Say "Leftovers") .........................48
Stay Fresh ..........................................................................49
   *Family and Friends* ...................................................49
   *Barry's Taco Salad* ....................................................49
   *Cookbooks* .................................................................50
   *Magazines* .................................................................50
   *Web Cuisine* ..............................................................51
   *Eating Out* ................................................................51
   *Microquick Poached Salmon* ..................................52
   *Spiced Pork Loin Chops* ...........................................53
Magic Sauce ......................................................................53
   *20-Minute Tomato Sauce* ........................................54

**6 In Case of Emergency** 55

Easy Timesavers You Can Buy ...........................................56
  *Lightning Seafood Stir-Fry* .........................................57
Easy Timesavers You Can Make Ahead ...........................57
  *Make-Ahead Lasagna* ..............................................58
Magic Ingredients .........................................................59
  *Case Study: Worn Out Wednesday* .............................59
  *10-Minute Chicken and Herb Pasta* ...........................60
  *How Is It Possible?* .................................................60
  *Tuscan Chicken Breasts* ..........................................60
  *Always Delicious Pasta* ............................................61
Right-Brain Cooking ......................................................61
  *Right-Brain Chicken and Apples* ...............................62

**Part 2: Main Courses** 63

**7 Breakfast Time** 65

Pancakes, Waffles, and Muffins .....................................66
  *Buttermilk Pancakes* ...............................................66
  *Bay View House Sourdough Pancakes* .........................67
  *Cottage Griddlecakes* ..............................................67
  *George Ames's Blueberry Muffins* ..............................68
  *Buttermilk Health Waffles* ........................................69
  *Quick and Healthy French Toast* ................................69
  *Orange French Toast* ...............................................70
Egg Recipes ..................................................................70
  *Scrambled Eggs* ......................................................71
  *Garden Herb Eggs* ..................................................71
  *Eggy Mess* .............................................................72
  *Colette's Bacon and Egg Buttie* .................................73
Breakfast Easy Timesavers .............................................73
  *"Instant" Mixes* .......................................................73
  *Instant Mix Tune-Up* ...............................................74
  *Yogurt* ...................................................................74
  *Breakfast Yogurt* .....................................................75
  *Fruit* ......................................................................75
  *Orchard Fruit Mélange* .............................................75
  *Tropical Fruit Mélange* .............................................76

## 8 Pasta and Pizza 77

Pasta Magic .................................................................77
Favorite Pasta Recipes ...................................................79
  *Spaghetti Carbonara* .................................................79
  *Fettuccini Alfredo* ....................................................79
  *Linguini with Hot Pepper and Oil* ...............................80
  *Penne with Asparagus and Ham* .................................80
  *Baby Spinach and Feta Penne* ....................................81
  *Chicken Chunk Pasta* ...............................................81
  *Rotelle with Mushrooms and Spinach* ..........................82
  *Shrimp Shells* .........................................................82
  *Pasta with Herbs* .....................................................83
Pizza, a Dream Food .....................................................83
  *Basic Pizza Dough* ...................................................84
  *20-Minute Homemade Pizza* ......................................85
  *Cornmeal Wheat Pizza Dough* ...................................86
Favorite Pizza Recipes ...................................................86
  *Feta and Black Olive Pizza* ........................................86
  *Shrimp and Basil Pizza* .............................................87
  *Roasted Red Pepper and Artichoke Pizza* ......................87
Pasta and Pizza Easy Timesavers ....................................88

## 9 Seafood 89

Seafood Seasoning .......................................................90
  *Broiled Soy Salmon* ..................................................91
Grilling and Broiling Recipes ..........................................91
  *Grilled Salmon Steaks* ..............................................92
  *Broiled Halibut Steaks* ..............................................92
  *Sizzling Salmon* .......................................................93
Poaching, Boiling, Simmering, and Steaming Recipes .............93
  *Poached Black Pepper Cod* .........................................93
  *Gorgeous Seafood Stew* .............................................94
Frying and Sautéing Recipes ...........................................94
  *Whisker-Licking Catfish* .............................................95
  *Brewpub Fried Fish* ...................................................95
Baking Recipes .............................................................96
  *Baked Sole* ..............................................................96
Seafood Easy Timesavers ................................................96
  *Microwave Poached Salmon* ........................................97
  *Sole Meuniere* ..........................................................97
  *Quick Seafood Stew* ..................................................98

**10  White Meats**                                                           **99**

   White Meat Seasoning .................................................100
     *Grilled Pork with Cumin and Lime* ...............................*101*
   Grilling and Broiling Recipes ......................................102
     *Rosemary and Garlic Tenderloin* ...............................*102*
     *Veal Scallopini* ...................................................*103*
     *Quick Home-Style Barbecued Chicken* .......................*103*
     *Grampy's Barbecue Sauce* ......................................*104*
     *Chicken Kebabs* ..................................................*104*
   Recipes for Frying and Sautéing ................................104
     *Derek's Buffalo Wings* ...........................................*105*
     *Drumroll Chicken* ...............................................*105*
   The Magic Chicken Breast ........................................106
     *U. B.'s Salsa Chicken* ............................................*106*
     *Aunt Jean's Dijon Chicken* .....................................*106*
     *"Tarragarlic" Chicken* ...........................................*107*
     *Chicken Marsala* .................................................*107*
     *Chive Chicken* ...................................................*108*
   White Meat Easy Timesavers ...................................108
     *Grilled Sweet and Spicy Pork* .................................*109*
     *Brigitte's Speedy Chicken* ......................................*109*

**11  Richer Meats**                                                          **111**

   Richer Meat Seasoning ...........................................111
     *Fleisch Kuchle (Austrian Meat Cakes)* .......................*113*
   Grilling and Broiling Recipes ......................................114
     *Quick Cajun Kebabs* ...........................................*114*
   Frying and Sautéing ...............................................115
     *Beef Wrap* .........................................................*115*
   Wonder Burgers ..................................................115
     *Burgers with a Twist* .............................................*116*
     *Sandra's Easy Meatballs* ........................................*116*
     *Unbelievably Good Chili* ........................................*117*
   Richer Meat Easy Timesavers ..................................117

**12  Vegetarian**                                                            **119**

   How Good Is Vegetarian Food? ...............................120
   Vegetarian Recipe Seasoning ..................................120
     *Red Beans and Rice* ............................................*122*
   Sure-Fire Vegetarian Recipes ..................................122
     *Rosemary's Quick Enchiladas* ...............................*123*

*Butternut Squash Soup* ............................................123
*Make-Ahead Vegetable Lasagna* ...........................124
*Potato and Leek Soup* ...........................................125
Around the World with Flavor ...............................125
*Minestrone Pasta* .................................................126
*Rice Palao* ............................................................126
*Sautéed Greek Mushrooms* .....................................127
*Spiced Vegetable Kebabs* ........................................127
*Unbelievably Good Vegetarian Chili* ......................128
Vegetarian Easy Timesavers ..................................128
*Bill's Arugula Pasta* .............................................129
*Rice Medley* .........................................................129
*Greek Cucumber Dip (Tsatsiki)* .............................130

**Part 3:    Make the Meal Complete                          131**

**13   Show Your Good Side (on the Plate)              133**

Magical Side Dishes ..............................................134
Rice: White, Instant, and Brown ...........................134
*Boiled Rice (Both White and Brown)* .......................135
You Say Potato, I Say … .........................................135
*New and Baking Potatoes* ......................................136
*Boiled New Potatoes* ..............................................136
*Jen's Potato Salad* .................................................136
*Microwave Potatoes* ..............................................137
*Emergency Microwave Baked Potato* .......................137
*Microwave Sliced Potatoes* .....................................137
*Fast and Easy Scalloped Potatoes* ...........................138
*Skillet Potatoes* ....................................................138
*Easy Mashed Potatoes* ...........................................139
Side Dish Easy Timesavers ....................................139
*Brendan's Penne Pasta Salad* .................................139
*Carol Ann's Tortellini Salad* .................................140

**14   Savor the Season: Quick Vegetable Dishes     141**

Salads 101 .............................................................141
*Salad Dressings* .....................................................142
*Salad Favorites* .....................................................143
*Tossed Salad* .........................................................143
*Jean's Oriental Cabbage Salad* ...............................144

*Pear and Walnut Salad* ..............................................................*144*

*Spinach Salad* .........................................................................*145*

Cooked Vegetable Dishes ..........................................................145

*Sautéed Green Beans and Scallions* .........................................*145*

*Pepper Medley* ........................................................................*146*

*Quick Chinese Cabbage Stir-Fry* ...........................................*146*

*Bacon and Cabbage* .................................................................*147*

*Corn and Red Pepper Mélange* ...............................................*147*

*Cheesy Broccoli* ......................................................................*148*

*Sautéed Mushrooms, Olives, and Sun-Dried Tomato Penne* ......*148*

*Onion Rings* ...........................................................................*149*

**15  Breads                                                             151**

Quick Breads .............................................................................152

*Scones* .....................................................................................*152*

*Skillet-Baked Cornbread* ........................................................*153*

*Buttermilk Biscuits* .................................................................*153*

Yeast Breads ..............................................................................154

*Basic White Bread* ...................................................................*155*

*Buttermilk Oat Bread* .............................................................*155*

*Healthy White Bread* ...............................................................*156*

*Rich Breakfast Bread* ..............................................................*156*

*Delicious Whole Wheat* ............................................................*157*

*Wheatena Bread* ......................................................................*157*

*Banana-Oatmeal Breakfast Bread* ..........................................*158*

Bread Easy Timesavers ..............................................................158

Recipes Where Bread Is the Star ...............................................159

*Bruschetta* ..............................................................................*159*

*Jamie's Welsh Rarebit* .............................................................*160*

*Sun-Dried Tomato Canapés* ...................................................*160*

**16  Dessert Time!                                                      163**

It's Not the Pie; It's the Filling ................................................164

*Grampa Phil's Pudding Pie* ....................................................*164*

*Grammalane's Lemon Pie* ......................................................*165*

*Meringue* ................................................................................*165*

*Dad's Baked Fruit* ..................................................................*166*

*Sara's Instant Chocolate Mousse* .............................................*167*

Fruits .........................................................................................167

*Strawberries and Thick Cream* ...............................................*168*

*Poached Pears* .........................................................................*169*

*Warm Apples* ..........................................................................*170*

Cookies ...............................................................170
   *Oatmeal Chocolate-Chip Cookies* ..............................*171*
   *Joe Frankenfield's Brickle* ..................................*172*
Dessert Easy Timesavers ..........................................172
   *Lightning Strawberry Shortcake* ..............................*173*
   *Maple Sundae* ................................................*174*
   *Charles River Mud Pie* .......................................*174*
   *Sabra's Meringue Kisses* .....................................*175*

**Part 4:    Theme Cuisine                                        177**

**17    Easy Timesavers                                           179**
Tortillas ..........................................................180
   *Bacon and Swiss Tortilla Melt* ...............................*181*
   *Joaquin's Tortilla and Scallion Pizza* .......................*181*
   *Tortilla Roma* ...............................................*182*
   *Quick Guacamole* .............................................*182*
   *Nachos* ......................................................*183*
   *Quick Tacos* .................................................*183*
   *Quick Enchiladas* ............................................*184*
Breads .............................................................184
   *Crostini* ....................................................*185*
   *Crostini with Roasted Red Pepper* ............................*185*
   *Hot, Open-Faced Sandwiches* ..................................*186*
   *Mom's Open-Faced Bacon and Tomato Sandwich* ..................*186*
   *Italian Turkey and Sprout Sandwich* ..........................*187*
   *Super Sandwiches* ............................................*187*
   *Tomato and Fresh Mozzarella* .................................*187*
   *Grilled Chicken and Sweet Onion* .............................*188*
   *Lion Eggs* ...................................................*188*

**18    Comfort Foods                                             191**
Appetizers .........................................................192
   *"Uncle" Marcia's Cheese Puffs* ...............................*192*
   *Hot Artichoke Dip* ...........................................*192*
Comfort in a Bowl ..................................................193
   *Chicken, Spinach, and Rice Soup* .............................*193*
Nostalgia Menu .....................................................194
   *Tuna Melts* ..................................................*194*
   *Grilled Ham and Swiss* .......................................*195*

*Quick Grilled Cheese Dipping Sauce* ..........................195

*Grilled Cheddar Chicken Sandwich* ..........................196

*Grilled Brie and Mushroom Sandwich* ..........................196

*Pasta* ..........................197

*Penne à la Vodka* ..........................197

*John Q's Mac and Cheese (with Slight Variation)* ..................198

*Fried Vegetables* ..........................198

*Fried Red Peppers* ..........................198

*Roasted Vegetables* ..........................199

*Fried Tomatoes* ..........................199

**19   Ethnic Magic**                                                **201**

Expand Your ... Spice Rack ..........................201

*Highland Eggs* ..........................202

*Chicken and Shrimp Paella* ..........................203

*Lightning Chicken Curry* ..........................204

*Real Greek Salad* ..........................205

*Black Bean and Corn Stew* ..........................206

*Hummus Platter* ..........................207

*Beef and Broccoli Stir-Fry* ..........................207

Nuts About 20-Minute Cuisine ..........................208

*Za's Peanut Sauce and Rice* ..........................208

*Korean-Style Fried Rice* ..........................209

*Derek's Nutty Chicken Stir-Fry* ..........................209

Ethnic Easy Timesavers ..........................210

*Thai Couscous Salad* ..........................210

*Bacon, Eggs, and Rice* ..........................211

*Down Under Burger* ..........................211

**20   Healthy ... and Delicious!**                                  **213**

Low Fat Does Not Mean Tasteless ..........................214

Nutritious and Quick ..........................214

*Whole-Wheat Penne with Summer Squash,
Tomato, and Mushroom* ..........................215

*Freddie's Spanish Eggs* ..........................216

*Baked Acorn Squash* ..........................216

*Broiled Lemon Rosemary Chicken* ..........................217

*Chicken and Paprika Cream* ..........................217

Low Fat and Quick ..........................218

*Chicken, White Bean, and Vegetable Stew* ..........................219

*Anya's Turkey Salad* ..........................220

*Country Potato Chowder* ......................................220
*Broiled Zucchini* ......................................221
*Pasta with Broiled Tomatoes and Garlic* ...............221

## 21 Whirlwind Romantic ... Food! 223

What Is It About Food That Inspires Romance? ......223
Luxurious Meals ......................................225
*Bowties with Sherry Pepper Cream* .................225
*Romantic Veal* ......................................226
*Anya's Smoked Salmon Penne Pasta* ...............227
*Paul's Quick and Easy Mac and Cheese* ...........228
Romantic Easy Timesavers ...........................228
*Fondue* ......................................229
*Muffy's Pumpkin Mousse* ...........................229
*Pan-Broiled Bacon, Scallops, and Rice* ...........230
*Eggs for Two, Scrambled with Sun-Dried Tomato
and Sweet Onion* ......................................231

## 22 Entertain, Sane 233

Fast and Fabulous ......................................234
Recipes for Fast Appetizers ...........................235
*Jean's Mexican Dip* .................................235
*Derek's Curry Ball* .................................236
Recipes to Please the Toughest Crowd ...............236
*Tuna Broccoli Pasta Salad* ...........................236
*Quick and Easy Angel Hair Pasta with Shrimp and Feta* ...237
*Stir-Fried Orange Beef* .............................238
*Ham and Swiss Casserole* ...........................239
*Spicy Mayonnaise* .................................239
*Dorst Family Crab Cakes* ...........................240
Why Not Make Some Things Ahead of Time? ......240
*Marcia's Shrimp Mold* .............................241
*Friedkin Family Salmon Mousse* ...................241
*Cold Poached Salmon* .............................242

## 23 Leftovers 243

Rice Dishes ......................................244
*Chicken, Tomato, and Rice* ...........................244
*Salsa Rice* ......................................245
*Stir-Fried Teriyaki Beef, Pea Pods, and Rice* ......245

|  |  |  |
|---|---|---|
| *Curried Rice* | | 246 |
| *Rice with Mozzarella, Bacon, and Scallions* | | 246 |
| Pasta Recipes | | 247 |
| *Skillet-Broiled Double Cheese Casserole* | | 247 |
| *Romano Pasta* | | 248 |
| *Black Tie and a Red Dress* | | 248 |
| *Penne with Sweet Sausage and Tomato Sauce* | | 249 |
| *Lamb and Feta Orzo* | | 250 |

**Part 5:   Behind the Scenes                                          251**

**24   Cyber Soufflé: 20-Minute Cuisine on the Web              253**

| | |
|---|---|
| The Newest Kitchen Appliance ... Your Mouse | 253 |
| À La Carte Web | 255 |
| *General Recipe Sites* | 255 |
| *Healthy Cooking and Vegetarian Sites* | 255 |
| *Comfort Food* | 256 |
| Selected Site Reviews | 256 |
| *Sites Focused on Quick Cooking* | 256 |
| *General Recipe Sites* | 257 |
| *Miscellaneous* | 257 |

**25   Inspiration from Unexpected Places                         261**

| | |
|---|---|
| It's a Tradition! | 261 |
| A New Haircut and Old-Country Recipes | 263 |
| *Italian Farmhouse Vegetable Stew* | 264 |
| *Minestrone* | 265 |
| *Minestra* | 266 |
| Cuisine Can Take You Down Memory Lane | 266 |
| *Sautéed Scallops* | 267 |
| *Grapes Rockefeller* | 267 |
| *Baked Cherry Miel* | 268 |

**26   Wine and 20-Minute Cuisine                                 269**

| | |
|---|---|
| Wine Guidelines | 269 |
| *Pairings* | 270 |
| *Types of Wine* | 272 |
| Food and Wine Menus | 273 |
| Favorite Wines | 275 |

**27  The 20-Minute Garden                                   281**

Nature's Recipe ..............................................................281
The Dirt on Sure Winners ...........................................283
  *Fresh Tomato Salad* .................................................*284*
  *Sautéed Herbed Summer Squash* ...........................*284*
  *Sautéed Garden Beans* ..............................................*285*
  *Chard with Balsamic Vinegar* ...............................*285*
  *Flower Bed Salad* .....................................................*286*
  *Rhubarb Sauce* ..........................................................*286*
  *Fresh Herb Pizza* ......................................................*287*
  *Ratatouille* ...............................................................*288*

**Appendixes**

**A  Glossary                                                    289**

**B  References, Resources, and Vendors                         295**

**   Index                                                      303**

# Foreword

If you've ever wondered *"How* do I cook?" then *The Complete Idiot's Guide to 20-Minute Meals* is for you! This book, written for the beginning home cook who wants to learn the basics, is also appropriate for the experienced home cook who seeks a handy repertoire of delicious, fast, and easy meals that utilize a wide variety of ingredients and culinary techniques. This new book is a source of reference and inspiration and will become an important tool for today's busy cooks.

Tod Dimmick is your friend in the kitchen, and his upbeat tone is welcoming: You'll want to invite him to your table, too! Especially, you'll learn that his shared knowledge runs from equipment, ingredients, recipes, and methods all the way to wine, entertaining, and cooking from a kitchen garden, with a profusion of other topics in between.

As an example, his chapter on "romantic food" contains recipes that would surprise even the most jaded palate. After all, who would shy away from Bowties with Sherry Pepper Cream or Anya's Smoked Salmon Penne Pasta? Certainly not me!

In addition, Tod is a family man: He knows the ins and outs of trying to get dinner on the table on a busy weeknight, because he is both the chef and one of the diners. So dear reader, you know his advice has been tested from every practical angle. He writes from experience, and a lot of it.

Finally, Tod has taken the "What's for dinner?" question a step further (and this is a significant step, most often omitted from other cookbooks). He also seeks to answer the even more contemporary question: *"Why* should I cook?" For Tod, cooking brings myriad benefits, and this view shines through every recipe, quotation, and tip in this book.

"Cooking is an opportunity," writes Dimmick in the Introduction. And with this book in hand, you will agree. Cooking from his recipes, along with his guidance, is fun, pleasurable, and creative. You learn at your own pace. The variety of recipes offered never leaves you in the mealtime doldrums. Preparing a meal allows you to control ingredients and nutrition. And the result is an array of fast, easy, and tasty recipes for home-cooked meals!

Tod's philosophy gets readers back to the root of cooking: people. A meal shared brings people together and brings meaning beyond the food served. As Tod says of family cooks: "You've inspired countless smiles, laughter, family bonding, and warm friendships. That's a great feeling, and, for me, that's probably the most important reason I enjoy preparing a meal."

Mara Reid Rogers

Mara Reid Rogers is an award-winning, professional freelance author and author of eight cookbooks. She is also the co-host of the travel and cuisine radio show "The Midday Dish with Mara Reid Rogers" on WJON-AM 1240 Information Radio (www.wjon.com).

# Introduction

Cooking is an opportunity.

Preparing a meal is a chance to learn. It's an opportunity to create. It's an opportunity to experiment and have fun. All of that is compelling, but there's much more to a meal. A meal is, or should be, about relaxation, about family, and about time together. Throughout history the symbol of a family has been the dinner table, the one reliable place where we all used to gather. By coming together, we feel a part of a group, we feel more whole, and we "fuel up" in a sense broader than simply ingesting calories.

The frenetic pace of life today threatens to short-circuit the time-honored benefit of a meal together. We think cooking takes too much time, and look for alternatives perceived as quicker, such as convenience foods or even take-out. Although that's not bad in moderation, as a regular lifestyle that approach to food not only sacrifices time together as a family, it also sacrifices control over what we eat, and sometimes a healthy balance to our diet.

This book is first about dispelling the notion that cooking a tasty, nutritious meal must be a time-consuming process. We'll review all the basics, from ingredients to equipment to cooking methods, and then embark on an ingredient-by-ingredient, theme-by-theme series of examples of what I call "20-minute cuisine," all to prove that quick cooking is not only possible, but downright easy.

I also make the case throughout that, with basic methods and principles in mind, cooking offers a lifelong chance for learning and creativity. Here's a chance to have fun with eating, something we've got to do tonight anyway! That's part of my argument that we should all look at cooking not as a *chore*, but as an *opportunity*.

Finally, again through example and illustration, I make the case that cooking is about people, and how, through your efforts as a cook, you can help bring your family and friends together.

Several appendixes help fill out the wealth of cooking information in this book, from great books and publications about cooking to the Internet, a new and exciting area of support for the busy cook.

Twenty-minute cuisine is a chance to learn, to have fun, to create, and to bring people together. That's a lot of responsibility for a meal. But believe me, the ingredients do most of the heavy lifting.

I hope you find this book helpful as both a reference and as inspiration. Give some of these recipes a whirl: Once you get started, amazing things start to happen!

## How This Book Is Organized

The book is divided into five parts:

**Part 1, "Meals Done Quick, Done Right,"** explores the elements of the successful kitchen, from tools to spices, herbs, and the ingredients for the perfect pantry. We then review cooking methods critical for 20-minute cuisine. When you're through with this section, you'll be ready to cook.

**Part 2, "Main Courses,"** digs right in to recipes and tips for preparation of quick, tasty entrees. We'll focus on all the key ingredients, from pizza and pasta to seafood, vegetarian, and meat dishes.

**Part 3, "Make the Meal Complete,"** examines other parts of a great meal, from potatoes to vegetables, and from breads to desserts.

**Part 4, "Theme Cuisine,"** takes the topic of 20-minute cuisine and, through that lens, looks at some of the many ways to make cooking fun. We relax into comfort foods, take a tour of quick cuisine around the world, get the skinny on healthy (but quick) cooking, look at romantic meals, and more.

**Part 5, "Behind the Scenes,"** explores the many elements of a meal that don't go on the plate, yet impact how much pleasure you take from what you prepare. We'll tell the secrets of using the web for cooking, discuss wine and food, and more. As this section draws to a close, you'll see just why, and how, a tasty, delicious meal is not only fun to prepare, but also a terrific opportunity to bring family and friends together.

## Extra Morsels

In each chapter, I've included a number of helpful hints, small boxes with information related to the topic at hand. Here's what to look for:

**Flare-Up**

A sudden, unexpected fire when cooking. More than a few cooks have stories to tell about singed eyebrows from flare-ups. Here, a flare-up is an alert about a common misunderstanding, mistake, or potential hazard.

**Cook's Glossary**

Words and phrases that might be used in cooking or in recipes.

**Cuisine Context**

Information about food, or background that helps cooking make sense ... and even more fun.

**Cook to Cook**

Tips and secrets, *from one cook to another,* on how to make something simpler, quicker, faster, and easier.

## Acknowledgments

Cooking is about learning from people and working with people. Separate the mechanics from the people (the reason we cook), and cooking becomes a dry subject indeed. This project involved cooking of the *good kind,* and many people were involved.

This work would not have been possible without the help of several dear friends (and skilled cooks) who provided inspiration, guidance, and invaluable recipe-testing time. They include Jean Burke (Boston Test Kitchen), Anya Dorst (Northwest Test Kitchen), Anne and Derek Footer (West Coast Test Kitchen), and Marcia Friedkin (Gotham City Test Kitchen).

Thanks also to Mary Ellen Ames, Janet Bailey, Za Barron, Brigitte Boeck-Chenevier, Sandra DiMartino, Italo DeMasi, Freddie Dimmick (Mom), Dave Dimmick (Dad), Rosemary Driscoll, Mark Footer, Barry Friedman, Sabra Flood, Diane Frankenfield, Joe Frankenfield, Colette and Peter Grant, Carol Ann Ryan, Brendan Sheehan, and many others for inspiration and recipe suggestions.

Finally, thanks to my sons Spencer (7) and Kurt (4) who agreed to try most of what I produced, and actually said they liked *some* of it. To my wife Jen, who did try everything, read most everything, and supported the whole process. I love you. And to Elaine Early, who was there throughout to watch the kids and keep things sane. *Sort of.*

## Special Thanks to the Technical Reviewer

*The Complete Idiot's Guide to 20-Minute Meals* was reviewed by an expert who double-checked the accuracy of what you'll learn here, to help us ensure that this book gives you everything you need to know about 20-minute cooking. Special thanks are extended to Bill Malloy.

## Trademarks

All terms mentioned in this book that are known to be or are suspected of being trademarks or service marks have been appropriately capitalized. Alpha Books and Penguin Group (USA) Inc. cannot attest to the accuracy of this information. Use of a term in this book should not be regarded as affecting the validity of any trademark or service mark.

# Part 1

## Meals Done Quick, Done Right

If, in this book, we're building an understanding of 20-minute cuisine, this part is the foundation of that house. Here we review the basics—what we need to get started: ingredients, methods, and equipment. We'll list the basics for the pantry, fridge, and freezer. We'll talk about herbs and spices, the magic dusts that add flavor and interest to a meal. We'll cover cooking methods perfect for 20-minute cuisine, such as broiling, grilling, and frying. I'll start us with some quick recipes, just the tip of the culinary iceberg of material floating beneath the surface of this book. Our task is made much easier with the right tools: To fry, one needs a frying pan. In this part, we review those key pots, pans, tools, and equipment that make cooking easier and help speed you on your way.

# Faster and Better

## In This Chapter

- ◆ The role of a meal in busy lives
- ◆ Quality and taste
- ◆ Familiar mealtime "case studies"
- ◆ Setting mealtime targets ... and achieving them

Part of the reason that people give up on cooking is because they're afraid to get started. It's intimidating to look at the multitude of possible ingredients, seasonings, and cooking methods, and picking out one unique combination to execute right here, tonight. It's hart to visualize doing "all that" in a short period of time, especially after a tiring day. That's where preparation—and this book—come in.

It always takes longer to do something the first time—from driving, to your job, to cooking—that's called a learning curve. This book is designed to make that curve as short as possible.

In each section, you will find step-by-step guidance in getting started, from the perfect pantry to creative stretching (of the meal, that is). The goal is twofold. First, we're going to, together, assemble all the tools you need to get home and get in motion. These tools include the knowledge of how things go together, so that just *knowing* that there is a pork tenderloin waiting in the fridge is inspiration to create something.

That sense of inspiration leads to the second goal, to change your outlook on cooking. Easy to say, slightly harder to do! Nevertheless, to change meal preparation from a grudging chore to an opportunity to create is a critical perception, because it helps us *want* to cook. With that outlook, preparing a meal becomes a soothing segue from the day at the office to an evening with the family ... made special by something that you have put together for them. What a difference!

# Today's Mealtime Reality

Once upon a time, Mom spent the afternoon preparing the family meal. At least that's how the story goes. Time was no issue, because after all, what could be more important than preparing dinner? These days, no matter how many adults are in the household, they're probably all working. Working long hours. Because of this, the time available to make a meal is shrinking toward zero.

To cope with this time crunch, busy people turn to fast food, instant meals, or the Same Old Thing (I call this the "Chicken Nuggets from Hell" syndrome). It's a sad state, because these alternatives are often more expensive, and certainly less healthy, than a tasty home-cooked meal. Even worse, fast food tends to dull the taste buds, and turn your attitude toward food from one of anticipation and pleasure to a necessity, a fuel stop.

How did we get here? It's simple, really. All of us are busy, and all of us have the same minutes in a day. Because learning is time-consuming, many of us fall into routines that, while they might conserve time, shield us from anything new. Take it from a guy who served his wife chili for seven days in a row early in his marriage, variety makes everyone happier.

Fast, tasty, healthy meals are not only possible, they're easy ... with a bit of knowledge and preparation. The purpose of this book is to enable a practical and fun approach to 20-minute *cuisine*.

> **Cook's Glossary**
>
> A **cuisine is** a style of cooking. *The Complete Idiot's Guide to 20-Minute Meals* is all about 20-minute cuisine— delicious, quick, and fun.

# Mealtime Is an Oasis in a Busy Week

But before diving into detail, I'll make the case that these 20 minutes can be so much more than simply "cooking." A slightly different perspective creates new energy and enthusiasm ... and a requirement suddenly becomes fun. A meal serves several purposes, after all. Of course food is fuel: We all have to eat. But mealtime, at least until this frenzied day and age, has always been the one part of a busy day when people come together, whether it be as friends or as family.

*But how is a good meal possible in only 20 minutes?* Through efficient use of time and a little bit of advance planning. Here are just two examples.

## Case Study 1—Fatigued Friday

At the end of a long week, I want to relax and enjoy the feeling of the weekend. The last thing I want to do is spend hours in the kitchen. On a night like this, speed is more important than ever, yet at the same time the meal has got to have a touch of class. After all, I want to start the weekend off right. Let's see … a little pasta and some tasty ingredients.

# Pasta with Chicken, Mozzarella, and Sweet Red Peppers

Prep time: 5 minutes  •  Cook time: 15 minutes  •  Serves 4 to 6

Olive oil for cooking

1 large onion, coarsely chopped

1 lb. boneless, skinless chicken breasts, sliced thin

2 sweet red peppers, seeds and stem removed, diced

½ lb. mozzarella cheese, shredded

1 tsp. dried oregano

1 tsp. dried basil

½ tsp. ground cumin seed

1 lb. rotelle (or other shaped pasta), cooked

Parmesan cheese to top

Salt and pepper

Tossed salad

Italian bread

Heat oil in a large sauté pan over medium-high heat. Sauté onions for five minutes. Add chicken and sauté until browned on all sides, about five minutes. Add red pepper. Sprinkle with mozzarella, oregano, basil, and cumin seed. Stir and sauté for five minutes. Toss with the pasta, top with Parmesan cheese, salt, and pepper to taste, and serve with tossed salad and Italian bread.

### Cook's Glossary

**Parmesan cheese** is an aged, hard, flavorful Italian cheese served grated or shredded on a multitude of dishes starting with pasta, its soul mate on the table. Grated has been around for a long time on grocers' shelves. Now shredded Parmesan, usually sold in reclosable bags, is available in most grocery stores.

We sat around the table and enjoyed our pasta with salad and a glass of wine. A simple, satisfying, and delicious meal helped the frustrations of the week suddenly seem far away and unimportant.

The secret? All ingredients are on hand, the meal is simple yet tasty, and the cooking methods are quick and reliable. That's 20-minute cuisine.

## Case Study 2—Manic Monday

Last Monday night, my family came home tired and hungry. My dad showed up just about dinnertime (his timing is always perfect). Time: 6:45. At 7 we sat down to a dinner of homemade *lasagna*, tossed salad, bread, and a glass of Chianti (milk for the kids).

Once again, the meal created an atmosphere of a small celebration, we relaxed and enjoyed the evening. I've learned that this feeling is a gift I can give to my family through food, and I feel doubly appreciative.

The secret? On Sunday I assembled a lasagna (recipe to come in Chapter 6!), put it in the oven, and set the bread machine in motion. That's also 20-minute cuisine.

Come Monday, all I needed to do was reheat servings, slice the bread, and put together a salad. If it's summertime, my salad comes right out of the garden, but in New England where I live, there's not much *Mesclun* in March, so supermarket salads are the name of the game.

That lasagna could last for the week in a pinch, although for variety I like to plan a couple of meals from it and then freeze the rest in serving-size portions for a couple of weeks later, when I'm ready to see my old friend again. The bread serves double-duty with Sunday dinner, and leftovers become part of delicious toast at breakfast time. Lasagna is just one of many dishes that lend themselves well to advance preparation. Your work is done, and you can dazzle the visiting friend (or dad) with a delicious meal. That's also 20-minute cuisine.

It's our choice whether we view the time we spend on food as a chore or a pleasure. Something to endure, or something to anticipate, and I suspect most of us are ready for a little more pleasure. For many people, a great deal of joy comes from creating something for the table. It might be something new (learning), revisiting an old friend (lasagna), or a new twist on an old favorite, but regardless of the content, the result is satisfaction.

**Cook's Glossary**

**Lasagna** is a rich, layered pasta dish with lasagna noodles, usually interspersed with tomato sauce, mozzarella cheese, and ground beef, although variations are infinite and fans will go to the mat to defend their favorite. **Mesclun** is a mix of salad greens, usually containing lettuce and assorted greens, such as arugula, cress, endive, and many others.

Taking that 20 minutes we've got to spend anyway, even if it used to be driving to the local drive-thru, and trying something new, is to suddenly change that daily time from coping to living.

# Set Reasonable Expectations

To keep sane, it's important that 20-minute cuisine avoids involving a mad dash. As a parent of young children, I am well aware that frenzy is often the name of the game, but at mealtime there are many tricks we can use to keep the schedule, and heart rate, under control. My experience is that a successful meal is made possible through planning, preparation, and *reasonable expectations*. Accordingly, on these pages you will find that:

- ◆ We're not going to attempt multiple-step menus, because just reading the recipe could take 20 minutes.
- ◆ We'll keep things simple in terms of preparation and clean up.
- ◆ We'll suggest plenty of *Easy Timesavers*; prepared or partially prepared ingredients that give you a quick start.
- ◆ We'll avoid recipes with large numbers of ingredients, in the interest of saving time. (An exception are dishes, like our friend lasagna, that take longer to prepare, but because they can be made in advance, more than make up for the time investment with their quick use down the road.)
- ◆ We'll also avoid expensive or hard-to-find ingredients. (Lemongrass might be interesting at the restaurant, but we'll leave it there.)
- ◆ We'll focus on our objective, quick preparation, so that we can enjoy our meal.

Even with these parameters in mind, we have a world to explore. Picture asparagus sautéed in butter with tarragon. Linguini tossed with garlic, olive oil, scallops, and lemon. Warm rhubarb sauce over vanilla ice cream. All these are quick and simple to make, yet serve them and—after the silence of appreciative eating—you're likely to hear comments like "delicious," "elegant," or even "gourmet." What a concept!

# Quality Times Two

For our purposes here, the quality of the food we eat can be considered in two ways:

- ◆ The ingredients in a meal
- ◆ The nutritional value

One of the great satisfactions of preparing a meal is control over what goes in each dish. This might sound simple, but think for a minute about fast food. When you prepare a meal, you know what goes in it. I know I sleep just a bit better knowing what I feed to people I care about.

Quality also affects taste, and taste affects how we enjoy a meal. We would all rather have fresh warm bread than stale, a crunchy carrot over a limp old one, and as for old chicken, well, you get my point. Fresh is good, and fresh is under your control when you're in charge of a meal. For anyone who is a gardener, the quintessential pleasure of summer is a fresh, ripe tomato, just picked from the vine. The flavor is incredible, and just can't be duplicated by an unripe fruit that has traveled by truck or plane from the other side of the planet.

> **Cook to Cook**
>
> As I write this, one major fast food chain is running a national advertisement questioning the "mystery meat" in some unnamed fast food produced by another chain. For most of us, not only is the meat a mystery, but so are the preservatives, salt, sugar, flavor enhancers, fat, and all sorts of other wonderful things that we'd probably rather not know about.

Control over content requires a bit of background knowledge on nutrition. While this book is explicitly about cooking, it is perhaps useful to start with *what to cook!* The following figure is the updated food pyramid from the Food and Drug Administration (FDA), which provides some basic guidance. How this guidance translates to your daily diet is up to you.

*The Food Pyramid.*

*(Food and Drug Administration website www.nalusda.gov/fnic/Fpyr/pyramid.gif)*

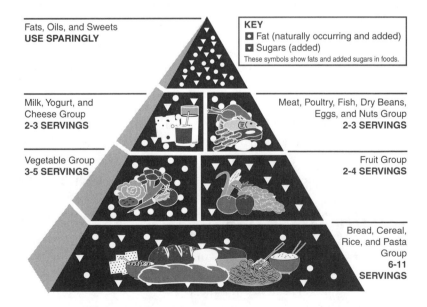

Fats, Oils, and Sweets
**USE SPARINGLY**

**KEY**
◼ Fat (naturally occurring and added)
▽ Sugars (added)
These symbols show fats and added sugars in foods.

Milk, Yogurt, and Cheese Group
**2-3 SERVINGS**

Meat, Poultry, Fish, Dry Beans, Eggs, and Nuts Group
**2-3 SERVINGS**

Vegetable Group
**3-5 SERVINGS**

Fruit Group
**2-4 SERVINGS**

Bread, Cereal, Rice, and Pasta Group
**6-11 SERVINGS**

# Less Is More

At some high-end restaurants, patrons expect to be pampered. They seek out unusual hors d'oeuvres, exotic salads, entrees from Bulgaria, desserts from France. They're paying for the careful blending of spices and herbs, for subtle seasonings and dishes that took three people an hour to prepare. A gourmet meal at such a place will cost a lot, and if it is prepared well, it might even be worth it. Will we be able to replicate such a meal with our limited time and budget? Not likely.

Increasingly, however, new types of gourmet restaurants are appearing on the scene. Epitomized by Chez Panisse in Berkeley, California, under the deft hand of chef Alice Waters, this type of restaurant insists on quality and freshness—in fact, it's their reason for existence. Although the occasional exotic ingredient works its way into the menu (after all, it wouldn't be "high end" without some rather unusual elements), the focus is on incredibly fresh ingredients prepared in somewhat unusual ways. Think squash ravioli with fried sage, or asparagus with ginger. Visitors seek creativity and quality, not necessarily expensive ingredients. Perhaps ingredients readily available at a good farm stand, prepared in a slightly different way.

We will be able to come a lot closer to this type of cuisine than to a recipe that uses imported truffles and caviar. This restaurant operates on the passionate belief that with the freshest possible ingredients your meal cannot go wrong. And while you and I might not have access to the same producers as Alice Waters, I'll bet we do know a great farm store, a place where in season the peas are crisp and sweet, where the tomatoes are a meal by themselves. These flavors are sublime, and they beg to be served with a minimum of preparation and distracting seasonings so that their own flavors can shine through. Fresh can be easy, quick, and delicious. Fresh requires less work, and gives more flavor. Less is more.

# Endless Possibilities

Even in 20 minutes there's an awful lot of potential. We'll go into a great deal of detail later on, but let me give you one example. My mother-in-law said she would love to see some discussion of what to do with a chicken breast. What a terrific suggestion.

A chicken breast to a cook is like a blank canvas to an artist; the possibilities are endless. The ubiquitous meat can be broiled, grilled, sautéed, pan-seared, even poached or steamed. Each treatment, *absent any seasoning at all*, still results in a slightly different taste result. Then engage in some creative seasoning, perhaps one or more of the following: salt, pepper, oregano, thyme, cumin, paprika, cayenne pepper, nutmeg, even cinnamon, and a completely different experience emerges.

How about a marinade? Or perhaps a wine sauce, a cream sauce, a *reduced* broth, bursting with concentrated chicken flavor? Or cubes of chicken as an element in a pasta or rice dish, in a stir-fry, as part of a tomato sauce or a stew?

It would not be much of a stretch to say we could fill this guide with nothing but recipes for chicken breasts. Of course, to preserve your sanity (and mine!), we'll explore other ingredients, but I hope it's entertaining to consider the number of permutations you could achieve simply from this one ingredient, almost all of them fitting within the so-called "limits" of 20-minute cuisine. The same variety is possible with other meats (beef, pork, turkey), many vegetables (visualized marinated grilled zucchini), and mushrooms. As you can see, the possibilities are indeed endless, so in this book we're in the fortunate position of limiting our suggestions to only the best!

> **Cook's Glossary**
>
> To **reduce** is to heat a broth or sauce to remove some of the water content, resulting in more concentrated flavor and color.

## The Least You Need to Know

- Fast, tasty, healthy meals are not only possible, they're easy … with a bit of knowledge and preparation.
- A meal is the one part of a busy day when people come together, whether it be as friends or as family.
- With the freshest possible ingredients your meal cannot go wrong.
- Even in 20 minutes, there's an awful lot of potential.

# Chapter 2

# Ingredients

## In This Chapter

- Ingredients to get started
- Herbs and seasonings
- Essentials and a few things for fun
- To substitute or not to substitute, that is the question

With a common base, we start from a point where most of the recipes that follow are within reach. Here are the basics, ingredients for the pantry, the fridge, and the spice rack.

As we go, we'll start to explore not only the ingredients themselves, but combinations and serving suggestions. With this what-goes-with-what knowledge, you'll be armed and dangerous … at least in a culinary sense!

## The Perfect Pantry

A well-stocked *pantry* is a huge timesaver for the busy cook, as well as a potential source of inspiration. It's an area of the kitchen where you can conveniently reach all the basic ingredients necessary to prepare 20-minute cuisine.

### Cook's Glossary

A **pantry** is a storage space (a small room, a closet, a series of shelves) for basic cooking ingredients. To a cook, a pantry might be the favorite room in the house!

This inventory is *not* intended to dictate every food item in your house; rather it provides a suggested building-block list of items to be used for the meals suggested in this book. (Your boxes of chocolate are safe.)

Wherever possible, I suggest ingredients that are whole grain, low fat, and generally nutritious. I've found that food prepared with these ingredients just plain tastes better, not to mention lending peace of mind from eating healthy.

For my pantry I lined a closet with shelves and labeled each shelf with the type of ingredient. My categories are listed here. Feel free to use them or create your own.

The following is a list related to 20-minute cuisine:

◆ Baking: flours and meals

◆ Baking: accoutrements

◆ Condiments and sauces

◆ Oils and vinegars

◆ Pastas

◆ Pasta sauces

◆ Rice and other starches

◆ Soups

◆ Spices and herbs (more on this later in the chapter)

◆ Sweeteners

◆ Vegetables and grains

The following are other pantry categories: breakfast cereals, crackers, drinks (bottled), fruits, sweet snacks, and savory snacks.

### Cuisine Context

Preparing your pantry might feel like you are creating grocery store aisles in your house, but the resulting organization enables efficiency and speed when it comes to cooking crunch time.

By no means should you feel obligated to copy these precise designations, but feel free to use them as a start. Each section varies in size. As is probably immediately evident, the contents of a person's pantry say a lot about the person! These items should be available at any supermarket or online. For recommended vendors, see Appendix B. For the purpose of consistency, I've called the storage location a "shelf," although it might be a cabinet, a drawer, a bin, or something else in your kitchen.

## Baking: Flour and Meals

This shelf is the lifeblood of any bread maker.

### The Baking: Flour and Meals Shelf

| Essential | Fun |
| --- | --- |
| White flour | Specialty flours (buckwheat, rye, etc.) |
| Whole-wheat flour | Whole-grain blends |
| Bread crumbs | Pancake and waffle mixes (Easy Timesaver!) |
| Cornmeal | |
| Oatmeal | |
| Cake mixes (Easy Timesaver!) | |
| Pudding mixes (Easy Timesaver!) | |

## Baking: Accoutrements

Other items that are used in baking.

### The Baking: Accoutrements Shelf

| Essential | Fun |
| --- | --- |
| Chocolate chips | Buttermilk powder |
| Bakers chocolate | Confectioner's sugar |
| Vanilla | Chopped almonds |
| Baking powder | Chopped walnuts |
| Baking soda | |
| Cooking spray (such as canola spray) | |
| Corn Starch | |

## Condiments

Condiments add flavor and texture to a dish. Often, like spices, a little goes a long way. Here are condiments to have on hand:

◆ Kosher salt

◆ Salad dressing or mix

- ◆ Capers
- ◆ Salsa
- ◆ Olives (Kalamata, the rich Greek black olive, are my favorite.)
- ◆ Catsup

## Oils, Marinades, and Vinegars

Kitchen liquids that assist in the actual cooking process as well as add flavor.

### The Oils, Marinades, and Vinegars Shelf

| Essential | Fun |
|---|---|
| Extra virgin olive oil | Balsamic vinegar |
| Red wine vinegar | Walnut oil |
| Canola oil | Peanut oil |
| Worcestershire sauce | "Hot" oil (oil infused with hot pepper) |
| Soy sauce | |
| Teriyaki sauce | |
| Hot pepper sauce, such as Tabasco | |

## Pasta

With pasta, there's no "Essential" vs. "Fun." It's all fun. Consider whole-wheat pasta if you can find it; it has a unique, rich, nutty taste. Try different manufacturers of pasta, as ingredients and taste vary. Otherwise, your favorite shape will do fine.

### Pasta

| Adult Favorites | Kid Favorites |
|---|---|
| Spaghetti | Rotelle |
| Linguini | Gemelli |
| Shells | Holiday shapes |
| Angel hair | Macaroni and cheese (Easy Timesaver!) |

## Rice and Other Starches

A critical element in recipes from across the globe, rice is a "must have" for the pantry:

- Basmati (California basmati is great, no washing required)
- White quick-cooking
- Arborio

Other hearty types of rice, such as brown and wild rice mixes, are terrific, but they take longer than 20 minutes to cook!

## Soups

These basics are useful for many recipes:

- Low-salt chicken broth
- Beef broth
- Vegetable broth
- Cream of mushroom, cream of celery, and cream of chicken soups—the heart of many recipes for leftover poultry.

## Herbs, Spices, and Seasoning Mixes

With the following seasonings in your pantry, you will be equipped to prepare all the menus described in this book, and many more besides. Lots more on these later in this chapter in the section, "A Friend Named Herb."

- Allspice
- Basil
- Bay leaf
- Caraway seed
- Cardamom
- Cinnamon
- Chili powder
- Cloves
- Coriander
- Dill
- Ginger

- Marjoram
- Nutmeg
- Paprika
- Peppercorns
- Oregano
- Red pepper
- Rosemary
- Sage
- Tarragon
- Thyme

**Cook to Cook**

Herbs have been used for centuries for seasoning and a variety of medicinal uses (some real, some imagined). They also add, it should be noted, flavor and interest *without* fat or calories.

## Sweeteners

Items to sweeten thing up a bit:

- Brown sugar (light brown is fine)
- Honey
- Molasses
- Refined sugar

## Vegetables and Grains

These staples form the foundation of many a terrific dish.

### Vegetables and Grains

| Essential | Fun |
|---|---|
| Cannellini beans | Pearl barley |
| Corn | Mushrooms |
| Kidney beans | Roasted red peppers |
| Chick peas | Sun-dried tomatoes |
| Refried beans | Lentils |
| Split peas | |
| Canned tomatoes | |
| Tomato sauce | |
| Tomato paste (small, 4-ounce cans) | |
| Sauerkraut | |

# The Happy Fridge

The fridge is a place of magic for the 20-minute cook for two reasons:

- It is the holding tank for accessories and main ingredients kept fresh and ready to be used at a moment's notice.
- It is the storage vault for large weekend-prepared dishes, our fail-safe way to ensure quick and tasty meals during the week.

The following table lists those items you'll find useful for cooking and assembling 20-minute cuisine. As with the pantry, this inventory is *not* intended to dictate every food item. I'll leave the particular kind of breakfast juice up to you.

## Fridge Items for 20-Minute Cuisine

| Accoutrements/Seasonings | Main Ingredients |
| --- | --- |
| Dijon mustard | Cottage cheese |
| Olives | Plain yogurt |
| Salsa | Sour cream |
| Mayonnaise | Cheddar cheese |
| Lemon juice | Mozzarella cheese |
| Barbecue sauce | Meats (your favorites) |
| Butter | Vegetables (your favorites) |
| Dill pickles | Fruits (your favorites) |
| Yeast (often kept in the fridge) | |

# A Friend Named Herb

Food is about flavor. From the simple delight of a chicken grilled in its own juices to the rich layers of the same meat sautéed with a mélange of mushrooms and wine, flavor is what brings us in and gives us pleasure. The *source* of flavor might be the main ingredient itself (think of a rich fish), or the main ingredient might serve as a willing platform for a combination of added flavors. The *characteristic* of an herb is often a fragrant or pungent smell, and a parallel effect on the food. Some herbs are used also for their color, such as saffron, which lends a deep yellow hue.

Here are some of the characteristics of each recommended pantry herb:

- **Basil.** A flavorful, almost sweet, resinous herb delicious with tomatoes and in all kinds of Italian or Mediterranean-style dishes.
- **Caraway.** A spicy, distinctive seed used for bread, pork, cheese dishes, and cabbage dishes. It actually helps reduce stomach upset, which is why it is often paired with, for example, sauerkraut.

**Cook to Cook**

In the United States, where dozens of cultural influences mingle, we face both a challenge and a dazzling seasoning opportunity. Ingredients that might otherwise never meet are now featured together in high-end restaurants (think hoisin and bourbon, cherry and kiwi, cumin, and salmon).

- **Chili powder.** Actually a mixture, but so commonly used I'm treating it as an herb, chili powder is usually made with hot peppers, cumin, and oregano. It provides the base "blast" for a flavorful chili, but that is only the beginning. (Perhaps chili burgers? Stay tuned.)

- **Chives.** An easy onion flavor to add interest to any dish. Well, maybe not apple pie.

- **Coriander.** A rich, warm, spicy herb used in all types of recipes, from African to South American, from entrees to desserts.

- **Dill.** A slightly sour, unique flavor that is perfect for eggs, cheese dishes, and of course vegetables (pickles).

- **Marjoram.** A sweet herb, similar to oregano (actually a cousin), also used in Greek, Spanish, and Italian dishes.

- **Oregano.** A fragrant, slightly astringent herb used in Greek, Spanish, and Italian dishes.

- **Parsley.** A fresh-tasting green leaf, adding color and interest to just about any savory dish.

**Cuisine Context**

Herbs lend their names to many a recipe. In this book you'll find Tarragarlic Chicken, Herbed Pasta, and Rosemary and Garlic Lamb Chops, just to name a few. Each is distinctive, and many are complementary to each other. As with any combination, however, be it people, chemicals in the lab, or herbs, some combinations work better than others.

- **Red pepper.** Hot yet rich, crushed red pepper, used in moderation, brings flavor and interest to many savory dishes.

- **Rosemary.** A pungent, sweet herb used with chicken, pork, fish, and especially lamb. A little of it goes a long way.

- **Sage.** The lemon rind, fruity scent, and "sunny" flavor is a terrific addition to many dishes. My favorite: Scrambled eggs.

- **Tarragon.** A sour-sweet, rich smelling herb just perfect with seafood, vegetables (asparagus especially), chicken, and pork.

- **Thyme.** Minty, zesty leaves are used in a wide range of recipes.

Although the following table shows some general guidelines on ingredients and herb matching, keep in mind that inclusion of one herb might push out another. Throughout this book you'll note that recipes (with one or two interesting exceptions) comply with these guidelines. I'll do my best to show, through usage examples, what works and what doesn't. Prepare several of these recipes, and very quickly you'll get a sense for what works.

## Herb Usage Chart

| | Vegetarian | Seafood | Chicken | Pork | Beef and Lamb | Vegetables |
|---|---|---|---|---|---|---|
| Basil | xx | x | xx | | xx | |
| Caraway | x | | | x | | |
| Chili | xx | x | xx | x | xx | x |
| Chives | xx | xx | xx | xx | x | x |
| Coriander | x | x | x | x | x | x |
| Dill | xx | xx | xx | | | |
| Fennel | xx | x | x | x | x | xx |
| Marjoram | x | x | xx | xx | xx | x |
| Parsley | xx | xx | xx | xx | xx | xx |
| Red pepper | xx | x | xx | xx | xx | xx |
| Rosemary | xx | xx | x | xx | xx | xx |
| Sage | x | | x | xx | xx | x |
| Tarragon | x | | xx | x | x | x |
| Thyme | xx | xx | xx | xx | xx | xx |

*XX = Best Match; X = Works*

### Cuisine Context

Many herbs have a long and rich history connected to the cuisine of a particular region of the world, and to the area itself. I've been told that smell is closely related to memory, and certainly that connection works for me when I think of certain herbs. I will never forget a trip to Crete years ago, walking over the dusty hillsides amidst the pungent smell of oregano bushes. To this day, when I smell oregano, I think of that trip. Lavender and rosemary have similar associations with France. The cuisine of each region often features local herbs, and over time these dishes have evolved to a perfect match that visitors can use as a standard. When we use herbs in our own cooking, it's always fun, and sometimes useful, to think about the sources of these flavors.

# The Spice of Life

Spices have been used by creative cooks for thousands of years. Generally the seeds, seed pods, shells, or even woody parts (cinnamon bark) of plants, spices are characterized by intense flavors and aromas. If herbs bring a fresh "green" flavor, spices bring an intense "brown" one. Spices play an important role in regional cuisine as well (think cardamom with the Middle East, cinnamon with the Far East) where they tend to be strongly represented in warmer climates where spices do not spoil or, occasionally, where their strong flavors mask otherwise bad food.

Here are some spice characteristics:

- **Allspice.** Named for its flavor echoes of several spices (cinnamon, cloves, nutmeg), allspice is used in many desserts and in rich marinades and stews.
- **Cardamom.** An intense, nutty-smelling spice used in baking and coffee.
- **Cinnamon.** Sweet, rich, yet spicy, cinnamon is commonly used in baking (apple pie!), but can also be used for delicious and interesting entrees.
- **Cloves.** The smell of cloves makes many people think of holiday ham; our culture has thrown the two of them together. The sweet, strong, almost wintergreen flavor is used in baking and with meats such as ham.

- **Ginger.** Flavors of citrus and a floral smell make this a terrific addition to many savory and sweet dishes (Ginger Carrots!).
- **Nutmeg.** A sweet, fragrant, musky spice used primarily in baking.
- **Paprika.** A rich, warm, earthy spice that also lends a rich brown-red color to many dishes.
- **Peppercorns.** Biting and pungent, freshly ground pepper is a must for many dishes, adding an extra level of flavor and taste. To give examples would be to run through most of the savory recipes in every cookbook you've ever seen.

**Cook to Cook**

For cooks, herbs are generally the leaves of flavorful plants characterized by fresh, pungent aromas and flavors, such as parsley, sage, rosemary, and thyme.

**Cook to Cook**

Quick benefits from a combination of herbs and spices can be achieved with seasoning blends from a specialty spice company. With names like Southwest Seasoning, Beef Rub, and Cajun Chicken and Fish Spice, their suggested usage is clear, and you're one step closer to being done. For a list of some of my favorite spice vendors, see Appendix B.

This list of spices is a general guideline for what works. With a bit of experience, you'll start to recognize matches made in heaven.

Spices send ripples throughout your dish; a little bit can go a long way. As with herbs, there are matches that work well, and there are matches to avoid. For a hot chili fan, for example, fiery pungent cumin is indispensable; but in that big savory batch there's probably not more than a tablespoon of the powerful spice.

## Spice Usage Chart

| | Vegetarian | Seafood | Chicken | Pork | Beef | Vegetables |
|---|---|---|---|---|---|---|
| Allspice | X | | X | X | X | |
| Cardamom | X | | X | XX | XX | X |
| Cinnamon | X | | X | X | X | X |
| Cloves | | | | X | X | |
| Ginger | X | X | X | X | X | X |
| Nutmeg | X | | X | X | XX | X |
| Paprika | X | X | XX | X | X | X |
| Pepper | XX | XX | XX | XX | XX | XX |

*XX = Best Match; X = Works*

# Substitutions

A substitute teacher is brought to class when the regular teacher is missing. Just like with school, in the kitchen there are terrific substitutes … and one or two to avoid. Fortunately, however, substitutions are rather intuitive: Successful substitutions stem from exchanging like with like. Here are a few guidelines:

◆ **Main ingredients.** As an example, pork, a mild white meat, might go well in a dish calling for chicken. If every other ingredient is kept constant the resulting dish will taste quite similar. On the other hand, inserting a completely different variable is likely to result in a different dish entirely … substituting bluefish for chicken, for example (grin).

◆ **Seasonings.** Substitutions can also be made between herbs and some spices with similar flavor and texture. That's where some basic knowledge is important. Among the herbs, those that contribute a distinctive but not overpowering flavor, sage, oregano, basil, rosemary, for example, can be experimented with freely. Others such as cilantro, which lend a strong, possibly overpowering flavor, should be substituted with caution. It's probably fine to use basil in place of cilantro in a recipe, but not the other way around.

**Flare-Up**

Cilantro lends a strong flavor, and should only be substituted for other herbs with caution, lest it overpower your helpless entrée.

♦ **Fats and oils**. These are necessary elements in many methods of cooking, such as sautéing or frying, and in many baking recipes. While I'm a big fan of the flavor of butter, I'm not a fan of cholesterol and saturated fat. As a result, when preparing a recipe that calls for butter, I often use canola or olive oil. Yes, both of these oils are largely fat; however, vegetable fats tend to be unsaturated and lower in cholesterol; they taste great; and the doctor is happy.

The implicit message, when you know that sage and oregano go well with both chicken and pork, is you're going to be safe substituting pork in a recipe originally calling for chicken. You'll find freedom and pleasure in exploring different combinations, and you'll make better use of what you happen to have on hand in the pantry or the fridge. Just go easy on the bluefish.

## The Least You Need to Know

♦ A well-stocked pantry is a huge timesaver for the busy cook, as well as a potential source of inspiration.

♦ Food prepared with healthy ingredients just plain tastes better, not to mention the peace of mind from eating healthy.

♦ Food is about flavor; it's what brings us in and gives us pleasure. Quality ingredients, herbs, and spices are the magic that bring this flavor to the table.

♦ Don't be afraid to substitute, but remember that successful substitutions stem from exchanging like with like.

# Chapter 3

# Methods

## In This Chapter

- A method to the madness
- Frying, stir-frying, and sautéing
- On fire and in hot water
- Steaming mad, broiling, and rubbed raw

A "method" is how to do something according to a plan. For a meal, a method is a particular way of preparing a dish. There are many cooking methods, so here I've picked out those that lend themselves most readily to 20-minute cuisine: frying, stir-frying, sautéing, boiling, broiling, steaming, and grilling.

We'll review each of the methods in detail, but first the context. In this and the chapters that follow, you'll find many recipes that provide specific ingredients, prescribe a method of preparation, and suggest ways to manipulate the individual ingredients (filet, baste, chop, and so on).

These individual recipes are prescriptions, but keep in mind the possibilities of substitutions to alter recipes to your taste, and to give you more freedom to use ingredients you actually have on hand. (Just in case I give you a recipe requiring Mongolian Warbler eggs and you've only got plain old chicken eggs in the fridge.) Although cooking is both an art and a science, I'll also provide a practical "what goes with what" guide. Freedom is one thing, out of control is another … a teaspoon chili powder can ruin a perfectly good apple pie!

# Understanding the Importance of Method

In spite of the number of recipes in this book, they all follow a few basic methods. Add perhaps casseroles, including how to make lasagna, and you've got general groupings that cover every recipe in this book.

Take this thought a step further: Once you've tried several stir-frying recipes, for example, you'll notice that although the ingredients differ, the size of the pieces, the ratio of liquid to solids, the time required to cook, and the frequency you need to stir are all very similar. With that in mind, the next time you break out the wok, perhaps you might think: "I don't have the specific items for recipe XYZ, but I do have broccoli, pork, onions, mushrooms, and soy sauce. Why don't I …" Bingo! You've just taken advantage of your knowledge of "method" to create your own dish.

### Cuisine Context

With the universe of recipes out there in print, online, and in people's little recipe boxes, it's more manageable, perhaps, to think of them all as belonging to a limited set of recipe families. If you have a good grasp of a couple of members of one family (cooking with a wok), chances are you'll be fine with other similar brethren in the future, perhaps even a few you create on your own!

# Culinary "Science"

Textbooks have been written about the science of cooking. After all, in many ways a kitchen is a laboratory. The cook induces controlled reactions to selected solids and liquids through the introduction of heat, cold, acids, and alkalines. These reactions change the nature of these solids (otherwise known as food) and make them edible. Put that way, it can seem like pretty dry stuff. You might not be actively thinking "science" when you're steaming broccoli, but regardless, you're changing cellular structure.

A bit of basic knowledge, however, helps understand why things happen the way they do, and knowledge is power. Here are just a few "reactions" that affect 20-minute cuisine. More will surface as we proceed:

◆ Adding salt to your water for cooking pasta raises the boiling temperature. Why is that useful? Higher temperature means that your pasta will cook more quickly. A bit of salt in the water adds flavor as well, although this method might not be appropriate if you're watching your sodium intake.

◆ Baking soda is a chemical compound (sodium bicarbonate) that helps make muffins and pancakes rise through a reaction—with acid in other ingredients— to release carbon dioxide bubbles and cause a quick rise. What you're cooking is actually being "inflated."

◆ Yeasts are actually alive and release carbon dioxide as a by-product of just plain living. They take a little longer to do their stuff for foods such as breads. To start to grow, they need all the things that you provide when you fire up the bread machine: food (flour), moisture, and heat. Sourdough makes perhaps the most dramatic use of yeast. It is the sour (yeast) that not only raises the bread, but lends that wonderful chewy texture and rich flavor.

◆ You've probably noticed that fresh greens, like lettuce, wilt if left out too long. It's probably intuitive, but nevertheless interesting science to explore why. A leaf is made up of a multitude of tiny cells, each holding, among other things, water. When all the cells are full, a leaf is firm and crispy. When the cells lose some of their water, they wilt. If the wilting hasn't gone on too long, it can be reversed by soaking the leaves in water for a while, then drying them off in a salad spinner. Voilà—crispy lettuce.

> **Cook to Cook**
>
> A terrific book about the science of cooking is *The Inquisitive Cook* by Ann Gardiner and Sue Wilson. Another one to check out is *The Complete Idiot's Guide to Cooking Techniques and Science* by Sarah Labensky, CCP, and Jim Fitzgerald, Ph.D., CCP.

# Out of the Frying Pan

Frying, stir-frying, and sautéing are among the quickest and most reliable cooking methods. They are the favorite ways to prepare meals for many people, from pan-fried catfish in the South to clams in New England.

◆ Frying usually involves a heavy, flat frying pan, or skillet, and requires a fat of some kind, such as butter or oil. If done right, frying serves the purpose of rapidly heating the food while sealing in the juices.

◆ Stir-frying has many definitions. For our purposes, stir-frying refers to cooking with a wok (a large, thin-walled, bowl-shaped metal pan that heats rapidly using a gas flame). This method cooks extremely rapidly, and due to the shape of a wok lends itself extremely well to dishes comprised of small pieces and a sauce or liquid that coats everything (stir-fried pork and vegetables with soy sauce). If you don't have a wok, a skillet or frying pan will also serve.

◆ Sautéing is very similar, using a sauté pan or frying pan to cook food. The difference is that the temperature is lower, and that you give the food a bit more time to cook. Vegetables such as onions, for example, are perfect for sautéing. They turn a wonderful caramel color, soften, and gain a sweetness that is the alter ego of the sharp, raw original.

The fat or oil used for frying and sautéing is important for several reasons:

◆ Different fats and oils have different cooking temperatures. Butter, for example, burns easily, affecting the flavor. For low to medium temperature frying (many of the frying recipes in this book) olive oil works fine, although for higher temperature frying, canola oil is better (I've recommended canola in those recipes). There are many other oils, but I've limited most recipes to olive and canola because they cover almost everything, and it keeps the oil issue simple.

◆ Different fats and oils bring different flavors. Butter brings a wonderful, rich, well, "butter" flavor that is sublime on a wide variety of foods, from seafood (think scallops) to green beans. Olive oil brings a variety of flavors (there are different types of olive oil) ranging from fruity and light to rich and almost nutty. Canola oil is one of the most neutral oils, allowing the flavor of the food to shine through.

**Cuisine Context**

Some studies have even shown olive oil may be related to longer life!

◆ Different fats and oils have different health issues. While the view on butter varies according to the latest medical journal, the consensus is to limit the intake of saturated fat (the primary fat in butter) to reduce potential health problems. Olive and canola oils are composed primarily of unsaturated fats, which in moderation are considered to actually bring health benefits.

The effect of fats and oils in cooking is to accelerate the cooking process while sealing in juices. One of the potential hazards is that, because food cooks quite rapidly, it can be overcooked, which hurts flavor and texture of the food.

The following is a "hot list" of items that are perfect for frying, stir-frying, and sautéing:

- **Frying.** Fish, chicken breasts, hot sandwiches, hamburger, and sausages.
- **Stir-frying.** Shellfish, chicken pieces, pork pieces, sweet peppers, fish pieces, broccoli, and mushrooms.
- **Sautéing.** Onions, broccoli rabe, sweet peppers, poultry, cooked pasta, and veal.

The potential list is massive; these are just some of my favorites. Many of these are interchangeable, scallops can easily be fried as well as stir-fried, for example.

## Quick Stir-Fry Medley

Prep time: 5 minutes  •  Cook time: 14 minutes  •  Serves 4

(*Note:* The broccoli pieces will have a little crunch. If you like your broccoli soft, cook a minute or two longer.)

| | |
|---|---|
| 3 TB. canola oil | 2 cups broccoli, broken into bite-size pieces |
| 1 small onion, diced | 1 red sweet pepper, cut into bite-size pieces |
| 1 lb. pork, cut into bite-size pieces (boneless pork chops work well) | 3 to 4 TB. soy sauce |

Heat a wok or skillet with oil over medium heat. Add onion. Cook, stirring, for four minutes. Add pork pieces. Cook, stirring, for five minutes or until pork pieces are cooked through. Add broccoli, red pepper, and soy sauce. Cook for another five minutes, and serve over white rice. For added flavor, add hot oil with soy sauce.

# Onto the Fire

Grilling is perhaps the oldest method of cooking food. Who can imagine how long ago people started to cook with fire? (*Pass me another hunk of wooly mammoth steak.*) Fast, simple, and messy, we humans love this method of cooking.

Lately, physicians warn of health problems related to excess charring and ash in our food (the by-product of overzealous grilling), but that caution aside, it is a flavorful part of quick cooking. In New England where I live, grilling is often confined to the warmer months, but our family loves the flavor so much that I'll be out on the porch in February grilling a halibut steak. In 20 minutes, of course.

A grill is a tremendously flexible tool, and many food items can be cooked on one. Our limitation for the purpose of 20-minute cuisine, however, is that we should use a gas grill. A gas grill heats quickly, enabling us to fit a meal into the necessary time. (A charcoal grill, in my experience, takes at least 15 to 20 minutes to heat up … and that's at its fastest.)

The table that follows shows the usual suspects for grilling, as well as just a few of the more unusual items.

## Great for Grilling

| Usual Suspects | Added Fun |
| --- | --- |
| Beef and hamburgers | Corn |
| Chicken | Thanksgiving turkey |
| Seafood steaks | Seafood filets |
| Sausages and hot dogs | Scallops and clams |
| Pork | Vegetables (zucchini squash and onions) |

The trick with the more unusual items is to use creative helpers:

♦ The whole turkey, for example, was my brother's pride and joy last Thanksgiving. (I'll only call this "20-minute" cuisine because of the number of meals we ate afterward with no time at all, because the turkey was already done!) He used the rotisserie on his gas grill to constantly turn the bird. Highly skeptical, the rest of us watched, wondering if the result would be a ruined turkey and a pizza Thanksgiving. Instead, we found it succulent, moist, and delicious, with a flavorful, crispy skin. We'll be doing that again.

♦ If you have the choice, fish steaks (halibut steaks, for example) hold together beautifully on the grill. Some hefty seafood filets, however, such as a nice slice of salmon, can be cooked straight on the grill. To avoid losing your flaky prize into the ashes below, wrap the fish in aluminum foil completely to protect it from disintegration. (Note that the result here is more like steaming your fish, because the charcoal flavor will not penetrate foil.) Another alternative is to cook the fish, skin side down, on the grill, and then flip it onto a small piece of foil to finish cooking on the other side. To lift the fish, slide the grill spatula under the foil.

**Flare-Up**

When grilling vegetables, use large enough pieces to manipulate on the grill top without slipping through (if your heart is set on grilled peas, you'd better use foil), and drizzle the pieces with oil to keep them from drying.

- Vegetables are easy to grill. Long sticks of zucchini, for example, drizzled with oil and sprinkled with herbs, salt, and pepper are a terrific accompaniment to a summer meal.

# Grilled Zucchini

Prep time: 5 minutes  •  Cook time: 6 minutes  •  Serves 4

3 small zucchini, sliced lengthwise into quarters (4 long pieces per squash)

⅓ cup extra virgin olive oil

2 cloves garlic, chopped

2 tsp. dried basil

Salt and pepper

Heat the grill. Put zucchini slices in a small bowl that can be covered. Mix olive oil with chopped garlic in another bowl. Pour over the zucchini. Cover and shake to coat. Sprinkle with basil, salt, and pepper. Lay pieces on the heated grill crosswise to the grill wires, to minimize risk of a piece slipping through. Cook three minutes per side, and serve.

# Into Hot Water

Boiling food is a time-honored cooking method, from cooking eggs in a green leaf over a fire to boiling entire banquets in a giant cauldron in medieval times. Today's taste preferences seem to veer away from boiled food, perhaps because of the tendency of boiling to mute or dull flavors of many items that are not self-contained (like an egg or a lobster). Most of the recipes in this book focus on other cooking methods, but it would be remiss to not salute the boiling pot, and of course point out a few indispensable boiled items, without which the world would be a lesser place:

- New potatoes
- Lobster
- Corn on the cob
- Rice
- Hard-boiled eggs
- Artichokes
- Hot dogs (of course)

# Boiled Lobster

Prep time: 5 minutes   •   Cook time: 12 minutes   •   Serves 2

2 gallons water (If you're near the ocean, clean seawater adds flavor and cooks more quickly—remember the higher temperature of salty water.)

2 (1 to 1¼ lbs.) lobsters, live and kicking

3 TB. salt, if not using seawater

1 stick butter, melted while the lobsters are cooking, and served in a heated bowl

Bring water to a rapid boil in a large cooking pot (I use my 16-quart pot to avoid any mess). Lower lobsters into the water head first, close the lid, ignore the scraping sounds on the side of the pot, and set your timer for 12 minutes. At the end of this time, remove the red wonders from the pot and serve. Again if you're near the sea, serving bright red lobsters on a platter of washed dark green seaweed is a sight to behold.

What part of a lobster to eat first is a matter of passionate debate, but indisputably the best parts are the two large claws and the tail. The claws will be best opened with a nutcracker, breaking the claws near their base and pulling the meat out with a small fork or your fingers. The tail can be broken off just behind the large body shell, slit with a knife, and the meat worked out. In both cases, dip the meat in the melted butter and enjoy a quick delicacy. Serve with a crisp dry sauvignon blanc, a tossed salad with wine vinegar and olive oil, and fresh bread. You'll talk about the meal for months.

# All Steamed Up

Steaming is one of my favorite cooking methods because of its speed and minimal impact on flavor and texture of food. The method is particularly appropriate with ingredients that bring a delicate flavor. Fresh vegetables, such as pea pods, broccoli, green beans, and many others are perfectly suited to steam cooking, as they have subtle, delicious flavors that are lost to more aggressive heat.

**Cook to Cook**

Fresh snap beans—steamed until just cooked but still slightly crispy and topped with butter, a sprinkling of tarragon, and salt—are one of the pleasures of summer.

Another "hot list" of foods, this time vegetables just perfect for steaming:

- Peas and snow peas
- Broccoli
- Cut corn
- Asparagus
- Summer squash

Although I particularly enjoy steaming vegetables, I've found that poultry, pork, and many kinds of seafood (steamed clams!) are also beautiful matches with this form of cooking. Steaming is quick, does not require the use of any fats or oils, and enables precise control over doneness. Because added ingredients are not generally necessary, flavor is again enhanced.

## Steamed Asparagus

Prep time: 5 minutes    •    Cook time: 6 minutes    •    Serves 4

1 bunch (about 1 lb.) fresh asparagus, washed, unappetizing stem ends removed, then each stalk cut in half and separated into two piles, heads and stems

Butter or margarine for serving

1 tsp. dried tarragon

1 tsp. chives

Salt for serving

Heat water in the steamer to boiling. When boiling, add stem pieces of asparagus and cook for three minutes. Then add head end pieces, and steam for four minutes. Test with a fork for softness. If necessary, steam for one to two minutes longer. Remove to serving plates, top with butter, and sprinkle with tarragon, chives, and salt to taste. Delicious!

# Broiling to Win Friends and Influence People

Broiling combines some of the best elements of grilling and baking. Under high heat, food turns crispy and brown, cooks quickly and evenly, and can gain a nice "grilled" flavor. Food can be broiled with a minimum of added fat or oil, so that broiled dishes have less fat than the same ingredients fried or stir-fried.

The following is a "hot list" of items just perfect for broiling:

- Fish steaks (such as halibut or swordfish)
- Beef (London broil)
- Poultry (our friend the chicken breast)
- Fruit (I'm not kidding; visualize broiled pears)
- Vegetables (huge range, think of tomatoes, eggplant, and zucchini)

**Flare-Up**

The potential downside is that cooking under high heat is very drying, so carefully watch what you're cooking!

# Garden Broil

Prep time: 5 minutes • Cook time: 6 minutes • Serves 4 to 6

2 large, ripe tomatoes, sliced thickly

1 large, peeled eggplant, sliced thickly

2 zucchini squash, striped (half peeled, so that the squash has a zebra look), sliced thickly

¼ cup extra virgin olive oil

Basil (fresh leaves are perfect, 1 tsp. dried will do)

¼ cup Kalamata olives

Kosher salt

Preheat the broiler. Arrange sliced tomatoes, eggplant, and sqash in a single layer on a greased cookie sheet, and drizzle with olive oil. Broil under high heat for three minutes or until surface of vegetables begins to bubble and crisp. Flip each piece and broil for two to three more minutes. Serve over rice, drizzle with more olive oil, and top with basil, olives, and salt.

# Don't Forget Raw

Funny thing about preparing a good meal; the word *cooking* doesn't necessarily mean that you have to "cook" anything. Many fruits and vegetables, and even some fish and meat (sushi and steak tartare) taste better when they're not changed by heat. Several are actually ruined by heat. (I've yet to meet a cooked cucumber that I've liked. Perhaps there's culinary wisdom behind the expression "cool as a cucumber.")

**Cuisine Context**

There are a number of vegetables that are magical when *barely* cooked, so that they retain their snap and fresh flavor, like asparagus.

The following is a list of items just perfect without cooking:

- ◆ Fresh mushrooms
- ◆ Vegetables of many kinds (carrot, celery, spinach, zucchini, cucumber)
- ◆ Most fruits

Fruits and vegetables are healthy and delicious and occupy a lot of real estate on that FDA Pyramid (see Chapter 1). If they taste great with minimum preparation and bring all these other benefits, fresh and raw deserve a place of honor in 20-minute cuisine.

# Quick and Cool Cukes

A fun variation on a salad. Even the kids eat them. (Tell them these are pickles.)

Prep time: 5 minutes    •    Serves 4

2 small cucumbers, peeled and sliced into
¼-inch sections

½ cup cold water

½ cup vinegar

½ tsp. dried dill or 1 TB. fresh dill

3 ice cubes

Arrange cucumbers slices in a 12-inch shallow bowl or pie plate. Pour water and vinegar over slices, sprinkle with dill, and add the ice cubes. This 20-second cuisine will disappear in about 20 seconds.

With these basic cooking methods under our belt, so to speak, we should begin to have some perspective on what type of ingredient lends itself to what type of cooking. Fresh, delicate ingredients, such as vegetables and seafood, often are most appropriate for relatively delicate methods of cooking, such as steaming. Richer, heartier ingredients, such as many types of meat, on the other hand, stand up to more aggressive heat such as grilling.

Now with cooking methods in mind, we turn to the equipment appropriate for each of these methods.

## The Least You Need to Know

♦ Although there are many recipes in this book, they all follow a limited number of basic methods: frying, stir-frying, sautéing, boiling, broiling, steaming, and grilling.

♦ Food prepared with healthy ingredients just plain tastes better, not to mention providing peace of mind from eating healthy.

♦ Frying, stir-frying, and sautéing are among of the quickest and most reliable cooking methods.

♦ Cooking with the assistance of water (steaming and boiling) enables quick preparation and, in the case of steaming, preservation of delicate flavors.

♦ Grilling and broiling enable quick cooking with the welcome addition of wonderful smoky flavors.

♦ The word *cooking* doesn't necessarily mean that you have to "cook" anything.

**4**

# Equipment

## In This Chapter

- ◆ Pots, pans, and then some
- ◆ Kitchen tools and knives
- ◆ Use technology to get you there, fast
- ◆ Freezer for convenience

Anyone who has spent some time leafing through a kitchenware catalog or browsing in a home store knows there are many choices when it comes to equipment for the kitchen. The challenge is limiting your purchases to what you really need. Not only do you need to consider how much money you might end up spending, but also where you will store everything once you have it (let alone find it when you need it). The truth is, a few carefully chosen items can do what you need with a minimum investment of time and money. This chapter reviews the few, simple, invaluable implements and equipment you should have for preparing 20-minute cuisine.

## Cookware Items

As you may have already surmised from the chapter on cooking methods, there is a close relation between method and equipment; to fry one needs a frying pan. Important cookware items needed for 20-minute cuisine include the following:

- A large *skillet* with a lid and spatter screen
- A small skillet
- A large saucepan with a lid (4 quart)
- A medium saucepan with a lid (2 quart)

- A large cooking pot (that holds 2 to 3 gallons of water)
- A vegetable steamer
- A pizza stone
- A large casserole or baking dish with lid
- A medium casserole dish
- A baking pan
- A muffin pan

**Cook's Glossary**

A **skillet,** or frying pan, is generally a heavy, flat metal pan with a handle, designed to cook food over heat, from a stovetop to a campfire.

Other fun things to support quick cooking include the following:

- A fish poacher
- A wok (if you have a gas cooktop)

To be prepared for 20-minute cuisine, not to mention having your kitchen well equipped for most tasks, the sections that follow outline the basics … a much shorter list.

## Skillet

A skillet is the workhorse of the 20-minute kitchen. The larger one is large enough to handle an entire meal, from breakfast to dinner. It's an important part, maybe *the* most important part, of the 20-minute cookware arsenal.

A good skillet must have the heft to stand up to hard repeated use, but even more importantly, it must be able to distribute heat evenly. A poor-quality skillet heats unevenly and burns food, whereas a sturdy, well-made frying pan will gradually rise to the appropriate temperature and stay there.

**Cook to Cook**

I've used high-end skillets and inexpensive bargain store skillets, and to me the secret of success can be summed up in one word: mass.

There is no doubt that high-end cookware manufacturers have mastered the art of heft, but there's no monopoly. A solid, cast-iron frying pan (like grandma used to cook with) can be just what the doctor ordered. I have two skillets for specific uses:

- ◆ **Skillet 1.** Use with breakfast foods, such as pancakes.
- ◆ **Skillet 2.** Use with savory dinner items, including such generally nonbreakfast items as garlic, onions, and hot peppers.

Cast iron will sometimes hold flavors, regardless of cleaning effort, and the hint of garlic in griddlecakes is not a great thing. The large skillet can hold an entire dinner with leftovers to spare.

The small skillet serves as a member of the flavor brigade, typically working in concert with other kitchen tools. I use the small skillet, for example, to sauté onions to a golden softness before using them as a topping on whole-wheat pizza, or to brown ingredients to be subsequently added to a stew or chili. Again mass is the magic word, because even heating is critical to successful frying and sautéing.

A large spatter screen is a terrific idea for skillet cooking, because there will be times when you will want to cook without a lid, but would prefer not to remember your meal through spatters on the ceiling.

## Saucepans

Saucepans also bring essential aid to the basic kitchen. Although I've suggested 2- and 4-quart sizes, there's an infinite range available. As the name implies, they are perfect for preparing sauces, from basic pasta sauce to wine reductions to cream sauces. They will hold soups, steam vegetables (with a steam insert or steam top), and perform a myriad other functions. Consistent with all cookware, the watchword is quality and durability; you want saucepans that will stand up to daily aggressive use.

## Large Cooking Pot

A large cooking pot (I make good use of my 16-quart behemoth) is kitchen magic for many cooks. The pot over the fire, a romantic image of the "good old days" comes to mind, where the pot was never really empty, but gradually evolved as different ingredients were added to the stew. Today we empty the pot, of course, but that makes it no less useful. Boiled food, such as corn and lobsters, just aren't possible without a good-size pot.

For the person who plans ahead to save time, a large pot is a critical vehicle for savory stews, chili, and soups. A large batch can be assembled and cooked, and then eaten over the course of the week, or frozen for a busy rainy day.

**Cook's Glossary**

A **vegetable steamer** is either an insert for a large saucepan, or a special pot with tiny holes in its bottom designed to fit on another pot with boiling water.

## Vegetable Steamer

A *vegetable steamer* takes two main stovetop forms: as an insert for a large saucepan, and as a special pot with tiny holes in its bottom designed to fit on another pot with boiling water. The insert is generally less expensive. It resembles a metal poppy flower that expands to touch the sides of the pot, with small legs to hold the food to be steamed above boiling water. Either way, steaming is a very quick-cooking method that preserves flavor and texture, and has a secure spot in the 20-minute cuisine kitchen.

## Pizza Stone

A pizza stone is the secret for the knowledgeable pizza chef. Preheated with the oven (I cook pizza at 450°F), the stone cooks a crust to a delicious crispy pizza parlor texture. It also holds heat well, so that a pizza removed from the oven on the stone will stay hot for as much as half an hour at the table. A pizza stone is also terrific for baking other kinds of breads that benefit from that crisp hearth texture, such as focaccia.

## Casserole Dishes

Casserole dishes are primarily used in baking. They hold liquids and solids together and keep moisture around ingredients that might otherwise dry out. Most recipes that call for a casserole dish require longer than 20 minutes, so the rationale for inclusion in this list is that a large casserole can be used for a dish that will dispense a delicious meal several times. Several recipes in this book call for using a casserole dish, starting with lasagna in Chapter 6.

## Wok

A wok is a wonderful tool for quick cooking. Unfortunately, it is only suitable for use on a gas cooktop, unless you purchase an electric version, which may not have the important capability of rapid heating characteristic of a wok over a gas flame. Large enough to hold an entire meal, different enough to inspire interest, a wok brings fun to a meal.

## Baking Pans

Baking pans round out the 20-minute kitchen. They also are versatile and can be used for tasks ranging from baking potatoes to chicken, from cookies to croutons. Cake pans are of course used for cakes, whether from scratch or from a mix (remember Easy Timesavers!). Related tools, such as cookie sheets, are also a nice addition; however, in a pinch the cake pan will do the job. The usage of a muffin pan is primarily limited to muffins, although there are a few creative uses I've found for savory muffin-shaped entrées.

## Fish Poacher

For a seafood lover, a fish poacher is a great member of the 20-minute kitchen. A poacher is a long, rectangular pot with a separate metal basket designed to hold a fish inside the pot, either above boiling water for steaming, or in simmering liquid for poaching. They come in varying sizes up to 24 inches, although an 18-inch version will cover all but the largest meals. The method is quick and easy, resulting in a delicious, flaky fish that disappears in minutes from our dinner table.

# Kitchen Tools

Now that you've got that big skillet, you need something to stir the scallions, measure the marjoram, and flip the flapjacks. Important tools for 20-minute cuisine include the following:

- **Wooden spoons.** Three, of varying lengths, will be enough to start with.
- **Spatulas.** Both a good-quality, sharp-edged spatula, and a coated, nonstick spatula will be very useful for flipping those pancakes and turning those medallions.
- **Rubber spatulas.** These are the magic wands of cookery. For those of you who can't stand waste, this handy tool enables you to save every last bit of sauce from the pan and frosting from the bowl.
- **Pasta spoon.** One of those long-handled spoons with teeth for gripping pasta is very useful for life with pasta.

**Flare-Up**

If you have a nonstick skillet, a coated, nonstick spatula (or a wooden one) will prevent damage to the surface.

**Cook to Cook**

I've heard busy cooks comment that they can never get enough measuring cups and spoons. When you need that ⅓ cup measure, and it's in the dishwasher, the argument for an extra is pretty compelling. The cost is not great, and the time savings is valuable.

- ◆ **Measuring cups for dry and wet ingredients.** The user-friendly 20-minute kitchen should have two sets of nested measuring cups for dry ingredients (flour, oatmeal, nuts, and so on). Sets of measuring cups usually include ¼ cup, ⅓ cup, ½ cup, and 1 cup. The kitchen should also have at least two glass measuring cups for liquid ingredients. These cups come in 1- and 2-cup sizes; I find the 2 cup to be the most practical and versatile. Glass measuring cups are graded along the side to indicate all amounts less than the 2-cup capacity and are used for all liquids, from water and milk to oils and sweeteners.

- ◆ **Measuring spoons.** The same "have an extra on hand" rationale applies to measuring spoons; the busy cook will always need an extra teaspoon. Measuring spoons typically include ⅛ teaspoon, ¼ teaspoon, ½ teaspoon, 1 teaspoon, ½ tablespoon, and 1 tablespoon.

- ◆ **Colander and a large kitchen sieve.** Pasta often saves a meal, and, unless you've got strong arms and a steady hand to pour off boiling water from the pot, a colander is necessary to make pasta happen. The colander's junior cousin, the sieve, can also be used for rinsing vegetables, fruits, and meats, and straining liquids to remove unwanted larger particles.

- ◆ **Wire whisk.** For sauces, eggs, dry mixtures, and liquid, a whisk is a simple and effective mixing tool.

- ◆ **Garlic press.** Here's another item where you get what you pay for (I've destroyed several), so look for a solid press, where the pivoting press head won't break.

- ◆ **Box grater** (the kind with different size holes on each side). This is very useful for creating small to tiny pieces of an ingredient, from vegetable shavings to grated parmesan.

- ◆ **Lime squeezer.** This is an unusual yet practical tool for the 20-minute cook. It takes a half a lime (and fits some lemons) and presses out all of the juice. In marinades and sauces, lime juice is a tasty, memorably fresh ingredient. A lime squeezer is also indispensable for making the perfect margarita.

- ◆ **Salad spinner.** A simple gadget perfect for anyone who loves fresh greens and salads. It enables you to thoroughly rinse or soak your greens to clean them and renew their crispness, and then rapidly spin off the excess water.

- **Kitchen shears (scissors).** These display their usefulness in unexpected places. They are valuable for cutting herbs, vegetables, flowers, and even pizza (to avoid harming a pizza stone).

- **Peeler.** Many fruits and vegetables require a peeler to remove inedible or un-appetizing skin.

- **Melon scoop.** While this recommendation may seem esoteric, a melon scoop provides a quick and easy way to prepare a dessert or salad.

- **Can opener.** This device is critical for anyone who uses ingredients from cans. There are manual and electric can openers, but I recommend purchasing an electric one. They are typically not expensive ($10 to $15).

- **Timer.** If not built into your oven or microwave, you will need a reliable timer to clock your creations.

- **Corkscrew.** For the wine lover, this is as important as a skillet for the cook. Better get two.

# Don't Forget the Knives!

Knives are a critical investment for the kitchen and one place where I heartily recommend a splurge to the high end. I've used cheap knives as well as more expensive versions, and from experience can say that you get what you pay for. That said, you do not need to invest $500 in a complete set that may contain items you'll rarely use.

These knives, whether in a block or in the drawer, are worth the investment:

- **Chef's knife.** A sturdy knife with a straight (nonserrated) blade used for everything from chopping vegetables to slicing meat. These versatile knives come in a variety of sizes, from 6 to 12 inches.

- **Paring knife.** A short (usually 3- to 4-inch blade) straight-edged knife used for delicate cutting, peeling, coring, and paring.

- **Bread knife.** A long (8- to 10-inch), serrated knife designed to easily cut through bread.

- **Knife sharpener.** There are two general types, manual sharpeners and electric. Both work well, though electric sharpeners are more expensive and quicker.

### Cook to Cook

I've included a knife sharpener in this list because a knife is only as useful as its cutting edge. (At least one part of that late-night TV knife ad is correct.)

A knife block is a great idea if you invest in quality knives, not only for safety but also to help preserve the knife edge, and keeping a knife from scraping against other cutlery. There are many choices, from the familiar stand-on-the-counter version to flat blocks (magnetized) that hold about six knives and fit in a drawer (or can be hung on wall).

# Hold It: Kitchen Containers

This broad category covers storage as well as serving containers and is intended to round out the checklist of nonelectric items for your 20-minute kitchen. I'm not including crockery (plates, cups, serving platters, and so on), which I'm assuming you already have. In my kitchen, I make ongoing use of several containers that make quick, convenient cooking and serving easy.

Few things are more graceful or satisfying than a simple wooden bowl. It can be used for serving salad or fruit, for chopping nuts, or for any number of other tasks. Mixing bowls are similar multitaskers, from mixing cakes and other batters to serving grapes. Finally, Plastic containers are the workhorse of the practical kitchen. These inexpensive, durable cups and bowls can be used for everything from single ingredients (egg whites) to entire dishes (chili), and can go from the fridge to the microwave. Most home stores sell a collection of these containers, which should include several of each of these sizes: 1 cup, 2 cup, 4 cup, and 6 to 8 cup.

With these in hand (or at least in the drawer), you'll never be at a loss for what to do with that gorgeous leftover kebab. In the chapters that follow, we'll go over some inventive uses for these leftovers, that enable a delicious meal in *much less* than 20 minutes the second time around.

# Machinery to Make Life Easier

I'm assuming that most readers have a fridge, a microwave, an oven, and a stove. If you don't, there are ways around the challenge, but they'll involve more gadgets. Follow manufacturers instructions carefully for using any electric appliance, particularly if its use calls for operation when you're not at home to prevent any risk of accident or fire (for example, a bread machine or Crock Pot). Helpful machines for 20-minute cuisine include the following:

- ◆ **Rice cooker.** A rice cooker is a simple, pot-shaped device that is useful for its simplicity and speed. You can cook rice on the stove, of course, but it requires a bit more attention to avoid burning. A rice cooker requires that you add rice, water, and then forget about it, as most have an auto shut-off function that switches to "warm" when the rice is done.

◆ **Bread machine.** This might seem like a strange choice for a quick meal. After all, just making dough takes up to an hour and a half, and most bread cycles are over two hours. Today's bread machine, however, minimizes the time that you must take, to something on the order of five minutes to add the necessary ingredients. Most machines come equipped with a timer, so that a few minutes in the morning means that a fresh, warm loaf of bread is waiting for you when you get home from work. That yeasty bread smell permeating the house is added magic.

◆ **Mixer.** There's a lot of choice in the type of mixer you use, from the reliable, inexpensive hand beater to the art deco Kitchenaid that does the work for you. For preparing batters, cakes, and so on, you'll need to decide how much work you want to do and how much you want to spend.

◆ **Blender.** A sturdy blender makes short work of ingredients that need to be liquefied and blended, from soups to fruit drinks.

◆ **Food mill.** This will assist with everything from shredding cheese for your pizza to shredding the onions to go on top to pureeing the sauce.

◆ **Electric kettle.** Although I primarily use this handy European import to heat water for coffee in the coffee press, the electric kettle also serves other purposes.

**Flare-Up**

Setting up the bread machine in advance works extremely well as long as you follow the manufacturers directions, and are especially careful to choose recipes with ingredients that will not spoil over an eight-hour day in the machine, such as milk and eggs.

**Cook to Cook**

Boiling water with the electric kettle takes much less time than with the stovetop, and in a pinch is a huge help for extra quick pasta or hot dogs.

◆ **Crock Pot/slow cooker.** This is another device that might seem counterintuitive, a slow cooker takes up to eight hours to slowly cook a meal. Again the magic is in the time required on your part: A few minutes in the morning means dinner is ready when you get home.

◆ **Gas grill.** For grilled food lovers seeking to work within 20-minute boundaries, a good gas grill is a worthwhile investment. Charcoal, unfortunately, just takes too long to heat.

◆ **Toaster.** The ideal breakfast machine, turning last night's bread into the perfect vehicle for butter and jelly, alongside coffee and juice.

◆ **Popcorn maker.** I'd have trouble making the case that this is practical and necessary, but boy is it useful to have around when the kids need a quick snack.

# The Freezer Is My Friend

Years ago, I "borrowed" a large chest freezer from my parents, and it has proven to be another indispensable aid for the busy cook for two reasons related to storage and advance preparation. Part of the hassle of quick cooking is ensuring that the necessary main ingredients are all on hand when you need them. The freezer helps to address that challenge by enabling storage of quantities of base ingredients.

In my freezer I have supplies of separately frozen chicken breasts, pork chops, hamburgers, and other items that, after a quick microwave defrosting, have me off and running. Then when I've prepared a large dish, I go back to the freezer with serving-size containers of lasagna, or chili, or stuffed peppers, ready to be thawed out and used at a moment's notice. I also use the freezer to store tomato sauce made fresh from the garden; it is not only quickly accessible but extends the use of garden produce year round. (I still haven't gotten around to returning the freezer to my parents.)

## The Least You Need to Know

- Stovetop cookware must have the heft to stand up to hard repeated use, but even more important, it must be able to distribute heat evenly.
- A solid cast-iron frying pan and a large saucepan are two essential items for the 20-minute kitchen.
- A kitchen equipped with carefully chosen tools and knives (enough for what you need to do, but not so much as to overwhelm) enables quick, efficient preparation of a tasty meal.
- The right machinery can make your life easier.
- A collection of storage containers means that every timesaving ingredient that can be used later has a home in your fridge.

# Practical Secrets

## In This Chapter

- ◆ Fresh ingredient incentives
- ◆ Never say "leftovers"
- ◆ Fresh sources of inspiration
- ◆ 20-Minute Tomato Sauce

Part of successful 20-minute cuisine is in the approach. Treat it as fun, as an opportunity (and really believe it!), and suddenly the whole thing is something to anticipate rather than to dread.

In this chapter, we start by picking favorite ingredients, taking a look at leftovers, and picking up new tips and tricks for the kitchen. Finally, I share one or two of my favorite recipes, including a tomato sauce that might just be the most useful recipe I've ever used ….

# Fresh Is Quick!

One of the greatest benefits of 20-minute cuisine is that there's no time to ruin natural flavors. We have every incentive to take advantage of the characteristics inherent in using fresh ingredients:

- ◆ Flavor
- ◆ Texture
- ◆ Ease of preparation
- ◆ Speed of preparation
- ◆ Health

Think for a moment about fresh-picked tomatoes or carrots, fresh peas right from the garden or the farm stand, crisp garden lettuce with dark soil still clinging to its roots. Packaging and shipping methods are improving, but for the foreseeable future just about any vegetable or fruit, locally produced, will taste infinitely better than the distant cousin with jet lag from a flight originating halfway across the country (or the globe).

Regarding seafood, who wouldn't agree that the freshest fish tastes the best and is certainly the most appealing? The same applies to many other meats. (Some forms of beef, though, do indeed taste better after aging.) Fresh ingredients have delicious flavors that would be lost to long cooking, so the best way to treat them is to serve them raw, or cook them through a gentle method such as blanching (partially boiling), steaming, or sautéing. Each of these methods, used in moderation, results in fresh produce that is easy to eat, yet preserves that fresh snap and garden flavor.

Here are two recipes that make the most of fresh vegetable flavors.

**Cook to Cook** _____

With the following Spiced Spinach recipe, gentle steaming and interesting seasoning result in a dish that will add fun to any meal. For a fresh tomato lover, the Summer Tomato Platter recipe is irresistibly delicious, even romantic. One bite and you're on the terrace of your Tuscan villa, looking out over the olive groves.

# Spiced Spinach

Prep time: 5 minutes  •  Cook time: 5 minutes  •  Serves 4

One bunch fresh spinach, rinsed, with un-appetizing stem ends removed

Pinch nutmeg

¼ cup cream or milk

Salt to taste

Steam spinach over boiling water for two to three minutes until just wilted. After steaming, sprinkle with a little nutmeg, drizzle with cream, and salt to taste.

Delicious with grilled sausages, fresh bread, and a glass of Cotes du Rhone red wine.

**Cook's Glossary**

A **pinch** (maybe the oldest cook's measure around?) is the amount of a substance that can be held between your thumb and forefinger.

And one of my favorites requires no cooking at all:

# Summer Tomato Platter

Prep time: 5 minutes  •  Serves 4

2 large fresh tomatoes, sliced thickly (about ½ inch)

1 handful fresh basil leaves

½ lb. fresh mozzarella cheese (comes in brine), sliced in ¼-inch medallions

Good-quality extra virgin olive oil

Kosher salt

Arrange tomato slices in a single layer on a large platter. Place one basil leaf on each tomato slice, then a piece of mozzarella. Drizzle platter with olive oil and sprinkle with salt.

With fresh Italian bread, this is delicious, and a meal in itself. *No extra charge for the Italian countryside.*

# Planned Extras (Never Say "Leftovers")

Many meal entrees can be built to last. Even better, making more leverages your effort. For a minimum of extra preparation time, the cook obtains extra meals that can take only as much time to heat as the oven or microwave require. Even so, a great many people are gun-shy when it comes to *leftovers*. Common reasons for this are concern that food will spoil, that leftovers are less appetizing than food prepared on the spot, that leftovers are somehow déclassé, and that people will turn up their noses at someone who eats leftovers. Nothing could be farther from the truth! Many dishes are just as good the next day, and some are even better the second time around.

### Cook's Glossary

A **leftover** is extra food not eaten at a meal. "Leftovers" are also a frame of mind. To some people they are somehow lessened in value, like a new car the minute you drive it off the lot. To many others, leftovers are a time-aving opportunity to take prepared ingredients to explore a new way of serving.

Regarding spoilage, keep in mind that if a dish requires high heat to prepare, harmful organisms will be reduced or eliminated. Be sure, of course, to store prepared food properly, in the refrigerator or freezer, depending on how long you want to keep it, and if refrigerated, consume food within a few days. Exceptions include some vegetable and seafood dishes where a critical attribute is fresh flavor and texture, qualities that will not be preserved in the fridge. (I did once try leftover grilled calamari as a sandwich the next day, but I'd rather not talk about it.) Regarding déclassé, well, if famous TV chefs can promote leftovers, so can us mere mortals. A lot of us were also brought up with a strong practical streak, and there is a lot of satisfaction from leftovers; they make the most of your time, and nothing is wasted.

Although most dishes will do fine the next day, here's a hot list of cool leftovers that a purist will insist taste even better the second time around:

- Barbecued chicken
- Lasagna and other pasta dishes
- Stews and rich soups
- Chili

A bit of extra time invested in one of these flavorsome dishes repays by enabling a 10-minute meal the next night. And the next night, too, if you want.

# Stay Fresh

Experienced cooks know that there are many resources for inspiration when it comes to any style of cooking, and 20-minute cuisine is no exception. The more you cook, the greater your own experience comes into play, and yet it is always critical to keep expanding and learning. Variety might be the spice of life, but it sure spices up cooking, too! Terrific sources of inspiration include the following:

- Family and friends
- Cookbooks
- Magazines
- The web
- Eating out

## Family and Friends

Some topics serve as a sort of universal glue, that just about anyone has in common with the next person, so it's something they can talk about. Sports ("How 'bout them Yankees?") and weather ("Nice day, eh?") come to mind, and food is right up there on the list. Most people have to eat, usually every day. You might be surprised how many people you know take a more-than-casual interest in creative cooking.

# Barry's Taco Salad

Prep time: 8 minutes   •   Cook time: 8 minutes   •   Serves 4

| | |
|---|---|
| 1 lb. ground beef | 8 oz. shredded cheddar cheese |
| 1 can creamed corn | ½ head shredded iceberg lettuce |
| 1 envelope taco mix | 1 large tomato, chopped |
| 1 (10-oz.) package tortilla chips | |

Brown ground beef in a large frying pan over medium heat. Drain fat. Turn off heat and mix in can of creamed corn and taco mix. Layer the following in a large bowl: tortilla chips (crushed by hand), ground beef mix, cheddar cheese, lettuce, tomatoes. Repeat layers until all ingredients are used (usually two or three layers). Garnish with sour cream, black olives, salsa, and serve with (what else) Dos Equis beer.

## Cookbooks

Although usually intended to be a practical resource, cookbooks are a subject of passion for many people. There are hundreds, maybe thousands, out there on topics from seafood to desserts, from African to Spanish, from quick recipes to meals that require two-day preparation. For every type of cookbook there's a type of person who buys it, from the person who really just wants a practical guide for how to make *X*, to others (and there are a lot of them) who actually don't cook but read for pleasure! Many people collect cookbooks and have a library devoted to cuisine that, well, makes me hungry.

> **Cuisine Context**
>
> For every type of cookbook there's a type of person who buys it, from the person who really just wants a practical guide to others (and there are a lot of them) who actually don't cook but read the books for pleasure!

I assume that as a reader of a book on 20-minute cuisine, your time is limited and you're thus more likely to need the practical end of the spectrum. In Appendix B, I've listed my favorite cookbooks in this area—books that are often both practical and fun to read.

## Magazines

Magazines bring a double-edge chef's knife to the busy cook: They provide inspiration yet sometimes overwhelm. I love reading them, but I have to force myself to keep reality in mind. Some glossies will present an idyllic tableau of recipes (and photographs of beautiful people cooking these recipes) that tend to veer away from the messy reality of the kitchen. As they say on the sports car ads, "This was conducted by professional drivers on a closed track. Do not attempt this at home."

With a touch of realism in mind, however, many are pure pleasure to read, from *La Cucina Italiana* (visualize dinner in Florence) to *Cooks Illustrated* (packed with how-to information and no advertising). These magazines form the backbone of my much-anticipated "vacation reading literature" bag. Other favorites include the following:

- *Saveur.* A general interest yet sophisticated magazine devoted to food and wine.
- *Cooking Light.* A popular magazine devoted to healthy cuisine and lifestyle.
- *Bon Appetit.* Food, wine, and travel laid out with opulent photography and a terrific "too busy to cook" section.

## Web Cuisine

Over the past two years, I've managed a website devoted to reviewing and recommending web resources related to fine food. I've reviewed hundreds of sites on every cooking-related topic from Afghan to Slow Food, and I can tell you that the web offers one of the most exciting developments related to cooking in years. To give you a sense of the potential, I invite you to visit two sites:

- **vivisimo.com.** Vivisimo is a new and exciting search engine based on a concept called "clustering"; it groups its findings according to common themes. To get a sense of the potential, type in the search box "Italian Recipes" (or French, or Russian, or any style that interests you), then sit back and watch what happens.

> **Cook to Cook** ___
> You will find a huge range of sites, neatly categorized on the left of your screen, all related to Italian recipes in some way. I'm not suggesting you visit all of these sites (I know your time is limited), but through this simple test I hope you'll get a sense of the potential of the web.

- **epicurious.com.** This is one of the major cooking-related sites on the web, maintained by the publishers of *Gourmet* and *Bon Appetit* magazines. From the home page, click the button next to the Recipe Search box titled "Advanced." On this screen, you will see the range of possibilities for searching out a recipe. For example, you can do a specific search for recipes that involve sautéing, chicken, and mushrooms. If in your pantry you find that you have three ingredients you'd like to use, type those in and see what comes up. The flexibility is astounding … and this is only one site of many.

I've listed more of my favorite food-related websites in Appendix B and provide some detailed guidance on how to use them in Chapter 24.

## Eating Out

Reading about food is one thing, tasting it is another; so, eating out is an irreplaceable source of inspiration for the busy cook. Keep in mind that many restaurant owners, for whom revenue depends on "table turnover," are just as focused on speed as we are. Many of the menu items you'll find in such restaurants can be adapted for the home kitchen.

After trying something in a restaurant, I am often tempted to bring a lesson home and try new ways of preparing an ingredient I know and love. On a family vacation in Scotland, a chef prepared an entire poached salmon for a dinner party. Resplendent on a bed of fresh herbs and lemons, the fish was a beautiful, dramatic sight, and a simple, new, and delicious way to prepare a fish I already knew I loved. I've started to poach salmon, and other fish, at home as a result of this experience. With 20-minute cuisine in mind, I was even more delighted to learn that poaching and the microwave work hand in hand. I not only have a quick and delicious method, I get to bring back memories of a terrific trip.

# Microquick Poached Salmon

Prep time: 5 minutes   •   Cook time: 6 minutes   •   Serves 4

4 salmon filets, about 1½ lbs. total

2 TB. olive oil

1 TB. white wine

1 TB. lemon juice

1 tsp. capers

1 TB. water

2 TB. sour cream

Fresh parsley

Salt and pepper

Put filets in a medium casserole dish with a microwave-safe cover. Combine oil, wine, lemon juice, capers, and water. Pour mixture over fish, and turn to coat. With the cover on, microwave on high for six minutes, turning dish halfway through. Check for doneness, and heat until cooked through. When finished, remove filets to serving plates. Add sour cream to remaining liquid in dish, mix to creamy consistency, and pour over fish. Garnish with parsley and season to taste with salt and pepper.

If a restaurant dish is appealing, look not only at the specific recipe (if the chef will share), but try to guess the herbs and spices used. Sometimes the learning is not because of the main ingredient, but because of a unique way it is treated. Lemon/cumin and honey/paprika are two simple combinations used to season a meal that I promptly took home to try.

# Spiced Pork Loin Chops

The pork in this recipe can be grilled or broiled. This example uses broiling as the suggested method.

Prep time: 5 minutes    •    Cook time: 8 minutes    •    Serves 4

**Marinade:**                                         2 TB. honey

2 TB. canola oil                              1 lb. center cut pork loin chops, sliced thin

1 tsp. ground cumin seed              Salt and pepper

1 tsp. paprika

Preheat the broiler. Mix oil, cumin, paprika, and honey. Place pork slices on a baking sheet, pour marinade over, and turn to coat. Season with salt and pepper. Arrange slices in a single layer on the sheet, and broil under high heat for four minutes. Turn and broil an additional four minutes, or a bit longer until cooked through.

Serve over rice with buttered green beans and your favorite chilled white wine.

# Magic Sauce

There is nothing more convenient and powerful than having a great tomato sauce up your sleeve, well … not literally. I call the following 20-Minute Tomato Sauce recipe "magic" because it is so versatile. From pizza and pasta to stir-fry and stews, this chunky sauce will add character and flavor.

We'll refer to this sauce several times through the following chapters. With this sauce as a base, delicious pizza, pasta, chili, and many other dishes are within quick reach. I like to make a big batch and freeze a container for later … when I don't have the time to prepare it from scratch.

# 20-Minute Tomato Sauce

Prep time: 5 minutes • Cook time: 15 minutes • Serves 4

| | |
|---|---|
| 3 TB. olive oil | 2 TB. tomato paste |
| 1 large onion, chopped | 1 tsp. dried oregano |
| 2 cloves garlic, crushed | 1 tsp. dried basil |
| 1 (28-oz.) can plum tomatoes, chopped, liquid preserved | 1 tsp. salt |
| | ½ tsp. sugar |

Add olive oil to a large sauté pan. Sauté onions over medium heat for three minutes. Add garlic and cook for an additional four to five minutes. Add tomatoes, liquid, tomato paste, oregano, basil, salt, and sugar and cook, stirring, for 8 to 10 minutes.

To use this sauce in a quick, tasty meal, cook a pound of your favorite pasta while stirring the sauce. You may be tempted, when preparing this sauce, to add other ingredients, from new herbs (rosemary, sage) to cooked hamburger or a number of other hearty ingredients. Go for it. Serve plates of pasta topped with sauce and Parmesan cheese, accompanied by a garden salad and fresh bread, and the stage is set for a great little meal.

## The Least You Need to Know

- Twenty-minute cuisine can take full advantage of fresh, healthy ingredients.
- With no extra effort or time, many meal entrées can be made larger to cover a second meal.
- Friends and family can be a rich source of cooking ideas … all while having a great conversation.
- A good tomato sauce enables many terrific meals.

# Chapter 6

# In Case of Emergency

## In This Chapter

- ◆ Purchase versatile timesavers
- ◆ Make your own timesavers
- ◆ Magic ingredients
- ◆ Right-brain cooking

This chapter begins to explore some of what makes cooking fun; approaches and ingredients that require creativity and a bit of invention. We start with the practical side, what I call "Easy Timesavers," which are prepared ingredients that accelerate a tasty meal. We look at how to use timesavers one can purchase from the store, and others to make to store in the fridge or the freezer. We'll look at ingredients and prepared foods that can work quick culinary magic for your meal. We'll discuss a topic near and dear to my heart, the concept of "right brain cooking"; using creativity and having fun with ingredients that just happen to be on hand. Oh yes, you'll also find my recipe for lasagna, one of the ultimate make-ahead timesavers, and the quintessential comfort food.

# Easy Timesavers You Can Buy

The premise of this book is that busy people need to prepare a meal in 20 minutes. That premise does not mean, however, that any of us is guaranteed the luxury of a whole 20 minutes, and I say this with only the slightest irony. For that reason, many of the following chapters feature not only "from scratch" 20-minute recipes, but a section on comparable Easy Timesavers methods and recipes that take full advantage of pre-pared foods, marinades, and other timesaving tricks. This is the arsenal of the intelligent, busy cook who knows how to find quality ingredients for a meal on a double-quick schedule. They include things like the following:

♦ Prepared salads made possible by improved packaging that keeps produce fresh

♦ Marinated entrees, ready to cook without additional seasoning (Teriyaki Pork Tenderloin and Barbecued Ribs)

♦ Cooked entrees (those beautiful roasted chickens behind the grocery store deli)

♦ Ingredient mixes, such as Trader Joe's frozen Seafood Mix (similar mixes are available in the frozen food section of many grocery stores), just perfect for quick prep of a seafood stew or pasta

♦ Pre-prepared pizza crust, enabling quick pizza with a homemade taste

♦ Pre-prepared seasoning mixes

Many more specific suggestions follow, each intended to provide an even quicker timeline for a meal without sacrificing taste or quality.

The enemy of quick cooking, it should be noted, is the all-too-human desire to make things overcomplicated. Of course we all want to explore new cuisines and new ways of cooking, but a common misconception is that to make good food, one must use multiple ingredients and multiple steps. In many cases the opposite is true: Simple preparation of quality ingredients allows delicious fresh flavors to shine through. In this sense, 20-minute cuisine has great potential. Use quality ingredients, follow simple methods, and take advantage of the possibilities.

**Cook to Cook**

Save extra freezer space for storage of quick items that go from freezer to table in minutes.

Partially pre-prepared foods such as ingredient mixes and pizza dough also deserve freezer space, allowing storage of quick items that go from freezer to table in minutes.

This delicious and quick dish takes advantage of frozen vegetables and frozen seafood mixes available at your grocery store.

# Lightning Seafood Stir-Fry

Prep time: 5 minutes • Cook time: 14 minutes • Serves 4

2 TB. canola oil (For added zing, add a few drops of hot oil.)

1 large onion, chopped

1 TB. chopped garlic

1 (1-lb.) pkg. seafood mix

1 (1-lb.) pkg. frozen pea pods

1 (6-oz.) can water chestnuts

3 TB. soy sauce

Heat oil in a wok over medium-high flame and cook onions and garlic for two minutes. Add seafood mix and cook over high heat for five to eight minutes or until seafood is cooked. Add frozen pea pods, water chestnuts, and soy sauce. Cook, stirring, for four minutes or until just done (slightly crispy pea pods are the goal). Serve over rice.

# Easy Timesavers You Can Make Ahead

My freezer has a section with busy days in mind. In that section are minestrone soup, lasagna, stuffed peppers, meatloaf—the kinds of things that I listed previously as ideal for leftovers. Some of it has a plan in mind (eat tonight). Others are for those days when everything goes crazy, and we're late, tired, and a bit cranky.

I can't predict the future, but I can guess that there are time's when I'll need not just good food quickly, but *good food instantly*. In the following chapters you'll also find Prepare Ahead selections. Some of these selections in volve preparing ingredients in large quantities to cover future use (without taking any extra time at all). Others involve making an entire entrée in large quantities that are ready quickly, or even immediately, when you need them and don't have time to do anything more than fire up the defrost on the microwave.

**Cuisine Context**

It's an irony of life that on a day when we most need a good, relaxing meal, we're least likely to get it. Unless we're prepared. When a bit of extra time *is* available, therefore, try to capitalize by preparing for such busy days.

Just to be clear about my idea of "make ahead," these dishes likely take a bit more time to cook (therefore, better to make on, say, Sunday night), but then take almost no time to heat and serve later. Lasagna, featured here, is a good example. It takes a bit more than 20 minutes to put together and then needs to cook for about an hour. (Still, your actual work time stays reasonable.) The dividends come the next day (and the next, and the next …).

The secret to lasagna is layers; essentially meat, cheese, sauce, and pasta (plus anything interesting you like to slide in there). They're put into the large baking/casserole dish alternately. Here's my favorite, with spinach to add flavor and color.

# Make-Ahead Lasagna

Prep time: 20 minutes   •   Cook time: 60 minutes (unattended)   •   Serves 8 to 10

| | |
|---|---|
| 3 TB. olive oil | 1 lb. lasagna noodles |
| 2 medium onions, chopped | 1 batch 20-Minute Tomato Sauce |
| 1 lb. ground beef | 1 (2-lb.) container ricotta cheese |
| 1 tsp. salt | 1 (10-oz.) pkg. frozen spinach, thawed and drained of excess water |
| ½ tsp. ground black pepper | |
| 1 tsp. oregano | 1 lb. mozzarella, shredded |
| ½ tsp. crushed red pepper | ⅓ cup Parmesan cheese |

Preheat the oven to 350°F. In a large saucepan, heat olive oil over medium heat. Add onions, and sauté for five minutes. Add ground beef, salt, pepper, oregano, and red pepper. Cook, stirring, for about eight minutes, until browned and cooked through. While beef is cooking, boil water for lasagna noodles over high heat in a large cooking pot and cook noodles to al dente (still slightly firm). Remove from water and rinse with cold water to stop softening.

In a large casserole or baking dish, layer as follows:

> Enough sauce to cover bottom
>
> One layer noodles
>
> Half the ricotta
>
> Half the spinach
>
> Half the mozzarella
>
> Half the remaining sauce

Repeat, starting with pasta. Reserve ½ cup mozzarella to put on top. Top with Parmesan cheese and remaining mozzarella. Bake for 45 to 55 minutes, until top is bubbly and any protruding noodles are crispy. Remove and let rest for 10 minutes. Then eat, refrigerate, or cut for the freezer. A masterpiece awaits.

Lasagna is just one of many dishes that lend themselves well to advance preparation. If you've got some stored away in the fridge or the freezer, your work is done, and you can afford to relax and even dazzle the visiting friend (or dad) with a delicious meal. That's smart 20-minute cuisine.

# Magic Ingredients

Several key ingredients lend themselves naturally to advance preparation, don't require any extra time to make a larger batch, and accelerate your meal the next night. Primary suspects include the following:

- ◆ Pasta
- ◆ Rice
- ◆ Potatoes
- ◆ Cooked meats

With each of these ingredients, making extra gives the opportunity to serve it again, often in a completely different and fun way (no same old thing night after night).

## Case Study: Worn Out Wednesday

Tonight we're home at 6:45, and I have to head out in 45 minutes to a meeting. At 7 P.M., we sit down (after shouting to the kids to come) to a meal of steamed green beans, 10-Minute Chicken and Herb Pasta, and sliced bread.

The secret? The previous night we had eaten Gemelli pasta with tomato sauce, and I had used the entire box to gain leftovers. The night before that we had eaten Tuscan Chicken, and at that meal as well I had made extra. Those two ingredients enabled a quick, satisfying meal that capitalized on work I had already done.

**Cook to Cook**

Two pre-prepared ingredients, from previous dinners, enable a quick, satisfying meal that capitalizes on work already done.

The easy and quick preparation of 10-Minute Chicken and Herb Pasta is thanks to the extra quantities you prepared earlier of the key ingredients.

# 10-Minute Chicken and Herb Pasta

Prep time: 5 minutes  •  Cook time: 5 minutes  •  Serves 4

2 TB. olive oil

1 onion, chopped

1 clove garlic, chopped

¾ lb. (approximate) cooked chicken, cut into 1-inch pieces (Refer to recipe for Tuscan Chicken Breasts that follows.)

¾ lb. (approximate) cooked pasta; small shapes work best, although spaghetti will serve (Refer to the recipe for Always Delicious Pasta that follows.)

1 tsp. dried basil

½ tsp. crushed red pepper

1 TB. dried parsley

Salt and pepper to taste

Parmesan cheese

Heat oil in a large frying pan, add onion and garlic, and cook over medium heat for five minutes. Add chicken, pasta, basil, red pepper, and parsley, and heat for another five minutes, stirring. Season with salt and pepper, topped with Parmesan cheese. Serve with steamed vegetables and a glass of dry white wine for a simple, tasty meal.

## How Is It Possible?

How much time is required to prepare those key ingredients? Tuscan Chicken Breasts and Always Delicious Pasta take very little time, and in the course of enjoying two meals you make this meal *possible*.

# Tuscan Chicken Breasts

Prep time: 5 minutes  •  Cook time: 10 minutes  •  Serves 8

⅓ cup + 2 TB. olive oil

Juice of ½ lime

2 to 3 lbs. boneless, skinless chicken breasts

1½ tsp. oregano

1 tsp. rosemary

Salt and pepper

Heat ⅓ cup olive oil in a large frying pan over medium heat. While the pan is heating, mix remaining olive oil and lime juice in the measuring cup or in a bowl. Put chicken breasts in a large bowl, and pour lime juice and olive oil mixture over. Turn breasts to coat. Sprinkle with oregano, rosemary, salt, and pepper. Add breasts to pan and cook, approximately five minutes per side or until a cut through the thickest breast shows complete cooking. Serve with rice and fresh vegetables (steamed carrots work well).

# Always Delicious Pasta

Note that most previously cooked meats can be added to this sauce.

Prep time: 5 minutes    •    Cook time: 15 minutes    •    Serves 4, twice

**Sauce:**

2 cups tomato sauce (See the "Magic Sauce" section in Chapter 5; this can be made in 20 minutes while you cook the pasta. Simply add sage and bay leaf to the recipe.)

½ tsp. sage

1 bay leaf

1 lb. pasta, uncooked

Parmesan cheese

In a small saucepan, heat tomato sauce and mix in sage and bay leaf. Simmer while the pasta cooks.

In a large pot, bring salted water to boil for pasta (accelerate if necessary with the electric kettle). Cook pasta to your preferred texture, drain, and serve on individual plates topped with tomato sauce (remove the bay leaf) and Parmesan cheese. A tossed salad alongside, and this is a meal.

# Right-Brain Cooking

My wife and I have had many discussions about where cooking ideas come from (or any other idea, for that matter). I've heard it said that the left brain is the source of skills in mathematics and logic, whereas the right brain is the reservoir of creativity and artistry (apologies to the professionals for oversimplifying!).

By this logic, the precise following of a recipe might be considered "left brain," while the opposite, perhaps an aversion to following a recipe, might be called a "right-brain" approach. This discussion led us to the concept of a right-brain cook, a chef who might use general guidelines, but who will not hesitate to strike out to new cooking territory, to experiment with new ingredients and new methods. To try new combinations. To boldly go where no cook has gone before … (okay, enough already).

So now it's time to browse the fridge and the pantry. Let's see … in the fridge, a package of chicken breasts (don't go home without them). Vegetables: I've got onions and kale in the garden. Fruits? We've got a Granny Smith apple and some raisins. Let's give this a whirl ….

**Cuisine Context**

The right-brain cooking concept fits perfectly in this chapter because of situations in which we all find ourselves occasionally; it's time to eat, and in spite of best intentions, ready ingredients for a "normal" meal are just not there.

# Right-Brain Chicken and Apples

Prep time: 5 minutes   •   Cook time: 15 minutes   •   Serves 4

2 TB. olive oil

1 onion, chopped

2 cloves garlic, chopped

1 lb. chicken breast, cut into ½-inch pieces

½ tsp. ground ginger

1 tsp. oregano

½ tsp. rosemary

1 bunch kale (Cabbage, chard, and frozen or fresh spinach are great substitutes.)

¼ cup raisins

1 Granny Smith apple, cored and cut into ½-inch pieces

In a large skillet, heat oil over medium heat. Add onions and garlic and cook for five minutes. Add chicken pieces, ginger, oregano, and rosemary and cook, stirring and turning the pieces, for six to eight minutes, or until cooked through. Add kale and raisins and cook for three minutes, until greens are wilted. (If using frozen spinach, microwave-thaw and squeeze dry.) Finally, add apple pieces and cook for one minute.

Serve immediately with salt and pepper. Verdict from wife and houseguests: "delicious." Aw, shucks.

## Flare-Up

Keep in mind that creativity must build on a base of knowledge of what goes with what. Otherwise, it's entirely possible to make something inedible or just plain strange.

This recipe works, and works well, and in the absence of an emergency (the requirement to eat, and this was our motivation to invent), we would never have discovered it. Of course it is important to keep in mind that creativity must build on a base … knowledge that ginger goes with chicken and apples, for example.

## The Least You Need to Know

♦ Easy Timesavers are prepared foods, marinades, and other timesaving tricks that form the arsenal of the intelligent, busy cook.

♦ With a bit of extra time, consider preparing for a busy day by making an oversize entrée. It lurks in your fridge or freezer, and when you need it, it's there—*quick*.

♦ Several key ingredients, including pasta, rice, potatoes, and cooked meats, lend themselves naturally to advance preparation, don't require any extra time to make a larger batch, yet accelerate your meal the next night.

♦ Try right-brain cooking; use your imagination and have fun with ingredients at hand … you may discover something new!

# Part 2 Main Courses

Part 2 is all about mealtime basics—the main courses that anchor our expectations and set the tone for the rest of the meal. Each chapter covers a basic main course theme, including such mainstays as breakfast, pizza and pasta, seafood, vegetarian dishes, and meat dishes.

# Chapter 7

# Breakfast Time

## In This Chapter

- Start the day right ... and quick
- Sure-fire breakfast recipes
- When you don't have even 20 minutes

Breakfast brings both opportunity and, let's be honest, time pressure. During the working week, if you're like me, 20 minutes is too much time to spend making breakfast. For this reason I won't try to talk you out of breakfast staples that I use myself: breakfast cereals, bagels, and so on. For off-the-shelf breakfast foods we get speed and convenience. If we're careful, we also can find nutrition. There are cereals out there that are made with whole grains and a minimum amount of sugar ... and still taste great.

With a few minutes of preparation, however, you earn an added level of taste and nutrition over pre-prepared breakfast foods. I'm talking in this case about bacon and eggs (and other egg dishes), pancakes, and one of my favorite breakfasts, toast made from good bread, spread with butter and jelly.

Add a few more minutes, and, at least for me, we're talking about time I save for a weekend morning where the stopwatch isn't running. Then pancakes, waffles, French toast, muffins, and more on the agenda; homemade, delicious breakfasts that are healthy and surprisingly quick, and take advantage of skillet cooking (or the waffle iron), or quick oven baking (muffins). For these dishes, the Easy Timesaver "make ahead" principle applies.

# Pancakes, Waffles, and Muffins

The quintessential country breakfast, pancakes, waffles, and muffins are hearty and delicious, and keep you going until a late lunch. These selected favorite recipes are quick, yet flavorful enough to become favorites.

## Buttermilk Pancakes

Prep time: 5 minutes • Cook time: 15 minutes • Serves 4, twice

| | |
|---|---|
| 1 TB. oil for cooking | 1½ tsp. sugar |
| 1 cup eight-grain flour | 1½ tsp. baking soda |
| 2 cups white flour | 2 eggs |
| ½ cup buttermilk powder | 2 cups milk |
| ½ tsp. salt | 3 TB. canola oil |

### Cook to Cook

Don't forget about the convenience of having a "second breakfast" of pancakes in the fridge. While the original pancakes might have taken a bit more than 20 minutes to make, the second serving, clocking in at 4 minutes (microwave heating time), more than makes up the difference. With double-dip recipes like this, we have a lot more menu flexibility.

Preheat large skillet or griddle over medium heat and add oil. Turn oven to "warm" and put in your serving plates. Mix eight-grain flour, white flour, buttermilk powder, salt, sugar, and baking soda in a large bowl. Add eggs, milk, and oil. Mix until lumpy (not too smooth). Using a ¼ cup measure to spoon batter, pour four pancakes, each about three inches in diameter. When bubbles appear in the batter, pop, and stay open (after about two minutes), flip the pancake, cook for an additional minute and a half, and slide these finished cakes into the oven. Repeat until batter is gone.

Serve with margarine or butter and warm maple syrup (with juice and coffee alongside) for a breakfast to remember all week.

# Bay View House Sourdough Pancakes

Hearty pancakes with a hint of sourdough.

Prep time: 5 minutes   •   Cook time: 15 minutes   •   Serves 4, twice

Oil for the griddle

2 cups Sour Starter (See Chapter 15 for the recipe.)

1 cup whole-wheat flour

½ tsp. salt

1 tsp. baking soda

1 cup milk

1 egg

1 TB. canola oil

Preheat large skillet or griddle over medium heat and add oil. Warm serving plates in the oven, along with a container for finished pancakes as you cook. Mix Sour Starter, flour, salt, and baking soda in a bowl. Add milk, egg, and oil. Mix until lumpy. Follow cooking directions from the Buttermilk Pancakes recipe.

**Cook to Cook** _____

Pancakes, waffles, French toast, and muffins can all be made as large batches on the weekend, earning quick and delicious seconds during the week.

# Cottage Griddlecakes

Hearty and creamy in the same griddlecake!

Prep time: 5 minutes   •   Cook time: 15 minutes   •   Serves 4, twice

Oil for the griddle

1 cup white flour

1 cup wheat flour

⅓ cup cornmeal

⅓ cup buttermilk powder

1 tsp. baking soda

½ tsp. salt

3 TB. sugar

2 eggs

3 TB. canola oil

1⅔ cup water

⅔ cup cottage cheese

Preheat large skillet or griddle over medium heat and add oil. Warm serving plates in the oven, along with a container for finished pancakes as you cook. Mix white flour, wheat flour, corn-meal, buttermilk powder, baking soda, salt, and sugar in a bowl. In a separate bowl, whisk eggs, oil, and water. Add liquid to flour mixture, mix until lumpy, then stir in cottage cheese. Follow cooking directions from the Buttermilk Pancakes recipe.

# George Ames's Blueberry Muffins

This large batch will last for two meals. Enjoy once on the weekend—30 minutes—and then get the second meal instantly during the week!

Prep time: 5 minutes  •  Cook time: 25 minutes  •  Serves 6 to 8

| | |
|---|---|
| 4 cups flour | 2 eggs |
| 6 tsp. baking powder | 2 cups milk |
| 2 tsp. salt | ¾ cup melted shortening |
| 6 TB. sugar | 2 cups blueberries |

Preheat oven to 425°F. Mix flour, baking powder, and salt in a large bowl. In another bowl, mix blueberries and sugar. In a large glass measuring cup or separate bowl, whisk eggs until they start to get foamy. Add milk and melted shortening (which can be melted in the microwave). Pour liquid mixture into the bowl with dry ingredients, mixing and stirring until combined but still lumpy. (Don't mix until smooth; that actually will inhibit cooking.) Mix in blueberries. Spoon mixture into greased muffin pans, and bake for 24 to 28 minutes or until done. Delicious!

### Cuisine Context

For George Ames's Blueberry Muffins, don't expect the overly sweet modern-day bakery-style muffins. These authentic treats are designed to showcase the berries, not the sweet tooth. They're biscuitlike in flavor, with a tart spike from the blueberries. If your sweet tooth prevails, add more sugar to the recipe.

# Buttermilk Health Waffles

A touch of cornmeal adds crunch and bite to these hearty waffles.

Prep time: 5 minutes • Cook time: 15 minutes • Serves 6 to 8

2 cups white flour

⅓ cup whole-wheat flour

⅓ cup cornmeal

1 tsp. baking soda

¼ tsp. salt

3 eggs

⅓ cup vegetable oil

1 cup + 2 TB. buttermilk (*Alternative:* Use 1¼ cups water and ¼ cup buttermilk powder with the dry ingredients.)

Preheat waffle iron. Warm serving plates in the oven, along with a container for finished waffles as you cook. Mix white flour, whole-wheat flour, cornmeal, baking soda, and salt in a bowl. In a separate bowl, whisk eggs, oil, and buttermilk (or water, if using buttermilk powder). Pour liquid slowly into dry mixture, stirring until lumpy. Pour about ⅓ cup batter into the center of the waffle iron (use more batter on the next one if this is not enough). Cook until the waffle is crisp and light brown. This will vary according to individual machines, I've assumed an average of three to four minutes each.

# Quick and Healthy French Toast

A slight twist on the old standby, and the perfect way to finish off that loaf of bread.

Prep time: 5 minutes • Cook time: 15 minutes • Serves 4

2 TB. canola oil

3 eggs

1 cup milk

½ tsp. salt

3 TB. sugar

8 slices bread (can be from a pre-sliced loaf, or, if using an uncut loaf, cut into ½-inch thick slices)

3 TB. wheat germ

Spread oil in a large skillet preheated over medium heat. In a bowl, whisk eggs, milk, salt, and sugar. Keep the bowl next to the heated skillet. Dip a slice of bread in egg-and-milk mixture, allowing it to be covered but not completely soaked. Quickly move to the skillet. Sprinkle each slice with wheat germ on the "up" side before flipping. Flip after two to three minutes, cook for an additional two to three minutes or until done. Serve with butter and warm maple syrup.

# Orange French Toast

The tang of citrus and the sweetness of syrup make this a memorable breakfast.

Prep time: 5 minutes   •   Cook time: 15 minutes   •   Serves 4

| | |
|---|---|
| 2 TB. canola oil | ½ tsp. salt |
| 3 eggs | 2 TB. sugar |
| ⅓ cup orange juice | 1 tsp. ground cinnamon or baking spice mix |
| ⅔ cup milk | 8 slices bread (can be from a pre-sliced loaf, or, if using an uncut loaf, cut into ½-inch thick slices) |
| 2 tsp. grated *zest* from orange or lemon peel | |

Spread oil in a large skillet preheated over medium heat. In a bowl whisk eggs, orange juice, milk, zest, salt, sugar, and cinnamon. Keep the bowl next to the heated skillet. Dip a slice of bread in egg-and-milk mixture, allowing it to be covered but not completely soaked. Quickly move to the skillet. Turn after two to three minutes, cook for an additional two to three minutes or until done. Butter and a dusting of confectioner's sugar accentuates the citrus flavor, although I'll never object to warm maple syrup, either.

### Cook's Glossary

**Zest** consists of small slivers of peel, usually from a citrus fruit like lemon, lime, or orange. Lemon zest is used in many recipes to add a tart taste of citrus. A zester is a small kitchen tool used to scrape lemon zest off a lemon (a grater, one of my recommended kitchen tools, also works fine).

# Egg Recipes

I've heard more than one person say that an egg is the perfect breakfast food. Maybe even the perfect *food*. It comes in its own container, it's easy and fast to cook, it keeps you going until lunch, and it's just packed with nutrition.

For a while our family avoided them because of one too many articles on fat and cholesterol, but now I read that eggs aren't so bad after all. I must be reading too much. Just make sure you're comfortable with the knowledge that when you eat eggs, you're eating fat along with other components.

Eggs can be prepared not just for breakfast, but for any meal of the day.

# Scrambled Eggs

Prep time: 4 minutes   •   Cook time: 6 minutes   •   Serves 4

3 TB. canola or olive oil

6 eggs

½ cup milk

Salt and pepper

Preheat a large skillet over medium heat and add oil. In a bowl, whisk eggs and milk. Pour mixture into the heated skillet, and allow to cook for a minute. Stir slowly, allowing the solid pieces to move so that the liquid mixture touches the heated pan and solidifies. Continue stirring, slowly, until eggs reach the desired consistency.

Serve with salt and pepper. A bite of scrambled eggs with crisp toast is one of the wonders of the morning.

**Cook to Cook**

Beware of high heat, which cooks eggs too quickly, sacrificing texture. The more you cook eggs, the drier they will get.

# Garden Herb Eggs

Prep time: 5 minutes   •   Cook time: 7 minutes   •   Serves 4

3 TB. canola or olive oil

6 eggs

⅔ cup milk

½ cup shredded cheddar (or other) cheese

1 tsp. dried basil

1 TB. chives

Salt and pepper

Preheat a large skillet over medium heat and add oil. In a bowl, whisk eggs, milk, cheese, basil, chives, salt, and pepper. Pour mixture into the heated skillet and cook per instructions for Scrambled Eggs.

# Eggy Mess

Prep time: 5 minutes • Cook time: 7 minutes • Serves 4 to 6

| | |
|---|---|
| 3 TB. canola or olive oil | 1 ham steak, cubed |
| 1 large onion, chopped | 1 large tomato, chopped |
| 6 eggs | 1 tsp. dried basil |
| ⅔ cup milk | Salt and pepper |
| ½ cup shredded cheddar (or other) cheese | |

Preheat a large skillet over medium heat and add oil. Sauté onion for five minutes. While onion is cooking, whisk eggs, milk, cheese, ham, tomato, basil, salt, and pepper in a bowl. Pour mixture into the heated skillet, and cook per instructions for scrambled eggs.

### Cook to Cook

I've written the Eggy Mess recipe based on the last time I made it, but the dish is, by definition, a work of "art" based on your own fridge and your own taste. It is just perfect for a group of hungry people with a sense of adventure.

While the platform—the egg-and-milk mixture—remains the same, the cast changes frequently. I've made Eggy Mess with mushrooms, olives, and feta (sort of a "Greek eggs"), with hot salsa (Mexican eggs), and many other variations. The point is that with experimentation, you'll develop your own favorite! Have a favorite vegetable? Consider creating your own recipe!

Served to us by friends in Scotland, the following too-easy British breakfast staple has successfully invaded our kitchen. Yes, it does resemble a fast-food breakfast sandwich. (I wonder where those fast-food places got this great idea.) Yes, it is also delicious.

## Colette's Bacon and Egg Buttie

Prep time: 5 minutes  •  Cook time: 10 minutes  •  Serves 4 to 6

½ lb. good-quality bacon, thickly sliced
(Canadian bacon works the best; it's thick,
almost like a ham steak.)

8 soft bread rolls or biscuits, split

Butter for spreading

8 eggs

Salt and pepper

In a large skillet, cook bacon over medium heat until crispy. Remove and distribute pieces between the buttered rolls. In heated skillet, cook eggs in bacon fat to your preferred degree of doneness. (My favorite is over easy, with a barely runny yolk.) As eggs finish cooking, move them to sandwich rolls on top of bacon. Season with salt and pepper.

In Scotland, you might find people seasoning this sandwich with "brown sauce," which is similar to zesty barbecue sauce. For something close, you might try barbecue or Worcestershire sauce, or even mustard, on this breakfast treat. Uncanny how quick yet delicious these are.

# Breakfast Easy Timesavers

Here are several alternatives for breakfast when you don't even have 20 minutes:

- ◆ Instant pancake and waffle mixes
- ◆ Yogurt
- ◆ Fruit
- ◆ Instant hot cereals

**Cook to Cook**

For a mix that requires only added water, look for "complete" on the box—the milk and egg solids are already there, in dried form.

## "Instant" Mixes

Most supermarket shelves have several pancake and waffle mix options. For a lightning-fast standby, I always have on hand a box of mix that requires only added water. Most of these mixes work well, although I can never resist doctoring them up just a bit for health and taste (and cranky individualism).

Here's one sure-fire way to add a little something extra to the mix:

# Instant Mix Tune-Up

Cottage cheese adds a rich creamy texture. Wheat germ adds a nutty flavor. Delicious!

Prep time: 3 minutes • Cook time: 15 minutes • Serves 4, twice

½ to ¾ cup *cottage cheese*

¼ cup wheat germ

1 (3-cup) batch prepared pancake mix (water already added)

*Optional:* Fresh fruit such as blueberries, raspberries, or sliced banana

**Cook's Glossary**

**Cottage cheese,** the curds from skim milk, is a by-product of milk production. Its mild flavor and creamy texture make it a tempting addition to pancake and other mixes.

Stir cottage cheese and wheat germ into prepared batter. Blueberries and raspberries can be simply stirred in or added to the batter in the pan to minimize crushing, but bananas always work better if they are added to the batter just after it is poured into the pan and begins to cook. Place each piece of banana carefully, several to a pancake, and flip when bubbles around the side of the piece of fruit appear. Serve with butter and syrup.

## Yogurt

Years ago, my wife and I spent two weeks in Greece. Every country has its own interpretation of breakfast food, and where we were, breakfast meant yogurt. It was made from the livestock that roamed the hills around the town, and I swore I could taste the dried herbs of the countryside in the creamy mix. Yogurt was sold plain, so we bought things to mix: local honey, raisins, and fresh fruit of all kinds. The yogurt was out of this world delicious, and we began to wonder why. We finally figured out (the labels were in Greek) that the large, prominent "10" on the label must refer to fat content: 10 percent fat. It figures.

Still, we found that plain yogurt can be used to create a beautiful thing, even at home where we could avoid the fat. Here's just one example of a compelling yogurt. Like with eggs, the varieties are limited only by your imagination.

# Breakfast Yogurt

Prep time: 4 minutes    •    Serves 4

1 (32-oz.) container plain yogurt (Nonfat, low-fat, or whole milk—your choice!)

¼ cup honey (Adjust to suit your sweet tooth or lack thereof.)

¼ cup wheat germ

1 cup blueberries

Stir together yogurt, honey, wheat germ, and blueberries; serve into bowls; and enjoy.

## Fruit

No discussion of breakfast is complete without bowing to the fruit bowl, the source of many lightning-fast, tasty, and healthy breakfasts. My approach to fruit for breakfast is to minimize preparation and time, and take full advantage of fresh flavors. With this in mind here are two of my favorites. There's nothing sacred about mixing and matching fruits, so look at these as quick, simple, and tasty *starting points*.

**Cook to Cook**

This might sound a bit strange as a recommendation for breakfast, but a small drizzle of Amaretto liqueur over a bowl of fresh fruit works flavor-enhancing magic. A *very* small amount.

# Orchard Fruit Mélange

Prep time: 10 minutes    •    Serves 8

1 bunch grapes

2 apples, peeled, cored, and chopped into grape-size pieces

½ cantaloupe, carved into balls with a melon baller

½ pint pitted cherries

Juice of ½ lemon

In a large bowl (a glass bowl is a nice touch for viewing all the fruit), mix grapes, apples, cantaloupe, and cherries. Drizzle with lemon juice.

# Tropical Fruit Mélange

Prep time: 10 minutes  •  Serves 8

2 bananas, peeled and sliced into ¼-inch rounds

1 can (or about 12 oz. fresh) pineapple chunks

½ pint blueberries

½ muskmelon, carved into balls with a melon baller

Juice of ½ lemon

Mix bananas, pineapple, blueberries, and muskmelon in a large bowl, drizzle with lemon juice, and serve.

We've all heard the notion that "breakfast is the most important meal of the day," yet too many people lose the breakfast habit because of the perception that the morning meal takes too much time. Even 20 minutes to prepare breakfast is just too much time for many busy families.

I hope, through this chapter, you've seen that a great breakfast is not only possible in 20 minutes, it's possible in *much less* time than that. With the right ingredients, from fruit to eggs to toast, a simple, nutritious meal is just a few minutes away. And with a bit more time (maybe even a full 20 minutes on a Saturday morning), there's a huge range of breakfast treats, from pancakes to waffles, just waiting to make your weekend special.

## The Least You Need to Know

♦ During the working week, even 20 minutes can be too much time to spend making breakfast. Focus on those dishes that are either lightning fast, or capitalize on work you've already done (a double batch of muffins covering two meals).

♦ Eggs are a 20-minute cuisine platform; to understand the basic method of preparing eggs is to be able to start creating your own variations.

♦ Throw your own ingredients into the mix: Doctoring up "instant" mixes adds flavor and fun.

♦ Yogurt, fruit, and toast are standbys ready to enable a fast, healthy breakfast.

# Chapter 8

# Pasta and Pizza

## In This Chapter

- ◆ America's favorite foods
- ◆ Sure-fire pasta and pizza recipes
- ◆ Easy timesavers

Pizza and pasta hold a place of honor at the dinner table of people across the land. Quick cooking and easy, these dishes are an important part of the busy cook's repertoire. From homemade dishes (most of this chapter) to pre-prepared sauces for pasta (I use them, too!), you'll find many variations in these pages.

In this chapter, we'll explore some of my favorites. As you'll see, these ingredients are incredibly flexible, serving has platforms for ingredients from vegetables and seafood to meats and (of course) cheese. These dishes are just a bit out of the ordinary, are easily prepared quickly, and will add a touch of fun and flavor to the evening meal.

## Pasta Magic

Pasta is magic. Most people like it, and in fact, a lot of people will describe pasta as their favorite food. Its genesis might be Italy, but its enthusiastic adoption in this country, and its multiple methods of preparation, have made pasta an American tradition. From basic pasta with tomato sauce (the most common, and perhaps, the most authentic) to pasta tossed with pear and gorgonzola (a bit more unusual), a pasta dish willingly changes its stripes for any occasion.

Pasta characteristics make it uniquely valuable to the 20-minute cook:

◆ Convenience

◆ Kid-friendliness

◆ Flexibility

◆ One-dish meal

### Flare-Up

While most types of pasta cook in less than 20 minutes (usually 8 to 14 minutes) some take longer. When you're in a hurry, be sure you're using one of the quicker-cooking types!

### Cuisine Context

I have friends who make pasta from scratch—using an electric pasta machine—even for a quick weeknight meal. (The simplest pasta dough recipe requires only eggs and flour. Hmm, that would make a good holiday present one day ....)

### Flare-Up

For the 20-minute cook I would not recommend a manual pasta machine, which can require 20 minutes to just do the cranking, without even starting to cook.

In its simplest form, a meal of spaghetti with tomato sauce (the recipe we discussed in Chapter 6), is the very definition of an Easy Timesaver. Pasta usually takes from 6 to 15 minutes to cook (depending on the type you buy; fresh pasta cooks much more quickly than dried), well within our 20-minute parameters. Until you want to use it, it sits quietly in the pantry, requiring no refrigeration, and with a sell-by date of sometimes a couple of years down the road.

Supermarkets take up whole aisles with pasta sauce needing only a quick heating, so there's no shortage of choice there either. Busy families, of course, know all this. The challenge isn't showing people the benefits of pasta (which we already know!) but, instead, providing some interesting enhancements to an old favorite.

Pasta is one of a very few dishes that my kids will always get excited about (grilled crispy salmon skin is another—go figure), so a pasta meal is a regular feature in our household. I'm not sure where they get their preferences (must be the same place as other kids), but they'll try to insist on plain pasta, with Parmesan, and, being good parents, we'll insist that pasta only comes with sauce. And that they can only have more if they finish their salad. The games we play as parents ....

The appeal of pasta is not only its simplicity but, ironically, its variety. This is one of the true magic ingredients that will willingly frame other flavors and textures and only improve in the process. Pasta can be served with tomatoes and many other kinds of vegetables. Pasta can be divine with seafood, from shrimp and scallops to fish. Lighter meats, richer meats, cheeses, cream; they're all welcome to the pasta party.

# Favorite Pasta Recipes

I've listed some of my favorites here. Each recipe, based on one pound of dried pasta, will make a batch sufficient for two meals (Easy Timesavers!). Please note that all these recipes are based on similar cooking methods. After making a few of these, the method will start to feel natural. Feel free to experiment with your own variations!

## Spaghetti Carbonara

This classic's golden color comes from the eggs.

Prep time: 5 minutes  •  Cook time: 15 minutes  •  Serves 4 to 6

¾ lb. bacon

1 lb. spaghetti

¾ cup Parmesan cheese, shredded

¼ cup sour cream

2 eggs, well beaten

Salt and pepper

Set a large pot to boil with water for pasta. In a skillet, cook bacon until crispy, dry on paper towels, and crumble. Cook spaghetti. When spaghetti is done, drain, put back in the pan, and quickly toss with crumbled bacon, Parmesan cheese, sour cream, and eggs. (The hot pasta cooks the eggs.) Season with salt and pepper and serve to rave reviews.

## Fettuccini Alfredo

Sour cream gives this recipe a creamy, tangy richness.

Prep time: 5 minutes  •  Cook time: 15 minutes  •  Serves 4 to 6

1 lb. spaghetti

1 cup sour cream

3 TB. butter

¾ cup Parmesan cheese, shredded

Salt and pepper to taste

Cook spaghetti. When done, drain and toss with sour cream, butter, and Parmesan cheese. Salt and pepper to taste. It's delicious and quick, and you can tell the kids it's macaroni and cheese.

# Linguini with Hot Pepper and Oil

Prep time: 5 minutes • Cook time: 15 minutes • Serves 4 to 6

1 lb. linguini

¼ cup olive oil

1 onion, chopped

3 tsp. chopped garlic

1 tsp. crushed red pepper flakes

Parmesan cheese

Salt and pepper

Boil water for pasta. While pasta is cooking, heat oil in a large skillet over low to medium heat, and sauté onion, garlic, and red pepper flakes. When pasta is done, drain. Turn up the heat under the skillet, and add the pasta to the oil and onion mixture. Serve immediately, topping with Parmesan cheese, salt, and pepper.

# Penne with Asparagus and Ham

Prep time: 5 minutes • Cook time: 15 minutes • Serves 4 to 6

1 lb. penne pasta

¼ cup olive oil

1 TB. chopped garlic

1 lb. fresh asparagus, stem ends removed, cut into 1-inch pieces

1 tsp. dried oregano

½ tsp dried sage

8 oz. ham, finely chopped

Parmesan cheese

Salt and pepper

Boil water for pasta. While pasta is cooking, heat oil in a large skillet over low to medium heat, and sauté garlic for three minutes. Add asparagus, oregano, and sage. Cook, stirring, for seven to nine minutes, or until asparagus reaches the desired level of softness (the more you cook it, the softer it will get). Stir in ham. When pasta is done, drain it, and put into a serving bowl. Pour asparagus mixture onto penne and stir to mix thoroughly. Serve immediately, topping with Parmesan cheese, salt, and pepper.

# Baby Spinach and Feta Penne

The dark green spinach adds color, flavor, and texture to this simple but delicious dish.

Prep time: 5 minutes   •   Cook time: 15 minutes   •   Serves 4 to 6

1 lb. penne

¼ cup olive oil

1 large onion, chopped

1 (8-oz.) pkg. feta cheese, crumbled

8 oz. baby spinach

Parmesan cheese

Salt and pepper

Boil water for pasta. While pasta is cooking, heat oil in a large skillet over low to medium heat, and sauté onion. When pasta is done, drain it, and return it to the pot. Add onion and oil, feta cheese, and baby spinach. Toss to mix thoroughly. Serve with Parmesan cheese, salt, and pepper.

# Chicken Chunk Pasta

Prep time: 5 minutes   •   Cook time: 15 minutes   •   Serves 4 to 6

1 lb. small pasta (your favorite shape)

1 batch 20-Minute Tomato Sauce (see Chapter 5)

1 tsp. dried thyme

8 oz. chopped cooked chicken pieces

Parmesan cheese

Salt and pepper

Boil water for pasta. While pasta is cooking, put sauce in a saucepan. Add thyme and chicken pieces and heat, stirring. When pasta is done, drain and distribute to serving plates and top with sauce. Serve with Parmesan cheese, salt, and pepper.

This is one of many recipes designed to take advantage of cooked meats. Cubed boneless chicken breasts could also be cooked at the same time to fit within the 20-minute time frame.

# Rotelle with Mushrooms and Spinach

The spinach in this recipe is cooked and simmered with the mushrooms and chicken broth for extra flavor.

Prep time: 5 minutes   •   Cook time: 15 minutes   •   Serves 4 to 6

| | |
|---|---|
| 1 lb. rotelle or other small pasta | 1 tsp. dried basil |
| ¼ cup olive oil | 1 tsp. dried oregano |
| 1 large onion, chopped | 1 (8-oz.) pkg. fresh baby spinach |
| 1 pint fresh mushrooms, sliced (or baby button mushrooms, whole) | Parmesan cheese |
| 1 cup chicken broth | Salt and pepper |

Boil water for pasta. While pasta is cooking, heat oil in a large skillet over low to medium heat and sauté onion. Add mushrooms and sauté for three minutes. Add chicken broth, basil, and oregano. Turn the heat to high and cook for seven minutes (broth will reduce in volume by about half). Add spinach, cook for one minute, cover the skillet, and remove from heat. When pasta is done, drain it, and return it to the pot. Pour in onion, mushroom, and spinach mixture, and toss to mix thoroughly. Serve with Parmesan cheese, salt, and pepper.

# Shrimp Shells

The rich taste of shrimp and garlic just might become your favorite.

Prep time: 5 minutes   •   Cook time: 15 minutes   •   Serves 4 to 6

| | |
|---|---|
| 1 lb. small-shell pasta | 1 lb. cooked small shrimp |
| ¼ cup olive oil | 1 (8-oz.) pkg. feta cheese, crumbled |
| 1 large onion, chopped | Parmesan cheese |
| 1½ TB. chopped garlic | Salt and pepper |

Boil water for shells. While pasta is cooking, heat oil in a large skillet over low to medium heat and sauté onion and garlic for five minutes. Add cooked shrimp and heat thoroughly. (Shelled raw shrimp can be used, add an additional three to five minutes, or enough time to cook them thoroughly.) When pasta is done, drain it, and add it to onion, garlic, and shrimp mixture in the skillet. Add feta cheese, and mix thoroughly so oil coats the pasta. Serve with Parmesan cheese, salt, and pepper.

Along with a salad, Italian bread, and a crisp white wine, this is a summer meal for the scrapbook.

# Pasta with Herbs

A light and flavorful pasta, just perfect with a glass of white wine.

Prep time: 5 minutes   •   Cook time: 15 minutes   •   Serves 4 to 6

| | |
|---|---|
| 1 lb. gemelli pasta (or your favorite) | 1 tsp. dried oregano |
| ¼ cup olive oil | 2 TB. dried parsley (or several sprigs fresh, chopped) |
| 1 bunch scallions, dark green parts removed, white and light green parts chopped | Parmesan cheese |
| 2 tsp. dried basil | Salt and pepper |

Boil water for pasta. While pasta is cooking, heat oil in a large skillet over low to medium heat, and sauté scallions, basil, and oregano. When pasta is done, drain it, and return it to the pot. Pour scallion mixture over, add parsley, and toss to coat. Serve with Parmesan cheese, salt, and pepper.

# Pizza, a Dream Food

If pasta is convenient, pizza is a dream food. All the same basics are there—flour, tomato sauce, and cheese (much more cheese, actually)—but manifested now as the ultimate portable feast. A traditional slice of pizza is pretty hard to spill. For kids, the sauce gets hidden under an acre of cheese, and who can object to cheese?

Like pasta, pizza is a vehicle for many ingredients, from flowers to flounder, so there's a slice with everyone's name on it. In addition to the common kid-friendly convenience of a pasta meal, pizza is …

- Finger food (limited cleanup compared to meals requiring cutlery).
- Neat (relative to pasta sauce!).
- Group-friendly.

**Cook to Cook**

Even homemade pizza is simple and quick to make, once you know the basic method. To many people's surprise, pizza can be as quick to prepare as pasta.

An Easy Timesaver, pizza dough takes five minutes to assemble in a bread machine, and the resulting dough makes three to four pies (depending on the size). When the mood strikes me, I'll make two or three batches of dough on a rainy weekend. As each batch is done, I separate it into four balls and freeze them in separate zipper-lock plastic bags. A time investment of 15 to 20 minutes total (spread through-out the day) yields enough dough for 10 to 12 10-inch pizzas and five to six meals, ready to go, stashed in the deep freeze.

# Basic Pizza Dough

Prep time: 5 minutes • Cook time: 60 minutes (unattended) • Makes 3 to 4 crusts, each serving 3 to 4 people

¼ cup olive oil

1½ cups water

1 tsp. salt

3 cups white flour

1½ tsp. instant yeast

Add oil, water, salt, flour, and yeast to bread machine in that order. Make a small hole in flour with a spoon for yeast. Set the machine to the dough cycle and press start.

### Cuisine Context

A fun way to prepare dough, like you see in pizza parlors, is to toss it, twirling, in the air, thereby using centrifugal force to spread the dough into a wide, thin, pizza-shape piece.

### Cook's Glossary

A **floured surface** is a counter or tabletop where flour has been spread to prevent dough from sticking.

When dough is ready, reserve the amount you want to save for later, take remaining pizza dough, and decide how you want to shape it. (One batch of dough will make three to four separate 10-inch crusts, so you might consider freezing two and using two.)

A fun way to prepare dough is to twirl it in the air. Some people find it more reliable to roll their pizza dough, on a *floured surface*, using a rolling pin, into a wide pizza-shape piece.

If the dough resists spreading, the words of my friend and pizza guru Lisa Cooper come to mind: "Treat stubborn pizza dough a lot like you would an uncooperative kid: Give it a five-minute time-out and then try again."

Once you've got the dough, pizza is so close you can taste it.

# 20-Minute Homemade Pizza

Prep time: 5 minutes   •   Cook time: 15 minutes   •   Serves 3 to 4

Cornmeal

1 ball pizza dough

1 TB. olive oil

⅔ cup 20-Minute Tomato Sauce

6 to 8 oz. mozzarella cheese, shredded

Preheat oven to 450°F. If you have a pizza stone or pizza brick, preheat that in the oven as well on the middle rack. Sprinkle cornmeal generously on a pizza paddle (or flat baking sheet with no edge) over an area the size of your crust. (This critical step keeps your pizza from sticking.) Lay out dough on the paddle, pulling it from the edge to remove any folds. Using a tablespoon measure, drizzle olive oil in a swirl over dough and spread it with the back of the spoon so it coats much of dough (painting every square inch is not necessary). Spoon sauce on-to dough, and spread with the back of the spoon so it evenly coats dough to within about ½ inch of the edge. Spread cheese by hand to cover sauce.

**Flare-Up**

When cleaning your pizza stone, use only water and a brush. Never use soap, because the porous surface of the pizza stone will absorb soap flavors. Pepperoni and Soap Pizza will probably not be on anyone's "favorites" list.

If you're using a pizza stone, open the oven and slide out the baking rack with baking stone. Lift the pizza paddle or baking tray and slide your pizza onto the stone. If the pizza doesn't want to slide, encourage it with a spatula around the edges.

If you're not using a pizza stone, assemble your pizza on a baking tray, and place the baking tray straight in the oven.

**Cook to Cook**

If you're a fan of super-crisp crust, consider cooking the dough for two to four minutes on the pizza stone, *then* adding the oil, sauce, cheese, and toppings.

Cook pizza in the preheated oven for 12 to 15 minutes until crust is crispy when you tap it with your finger, and cheese is bubbly.

Next is one of my favorite pizza crusts. Whole-wheat flour and cornmeal add a hearty crunch.

# Cornmeal Wheat Pizza Dough

Prep time: 5 minutes • Cook time: 60 (unattended) minutes • Makes 3 to 4 crusts, each serving 3 to 4 people

¼ cup olive oil

1½ cups water

1 tsp. salt

½ cup cornmeal

¾ cup whole-wheat flour

1¾ cups white flour

1½ tsp. instant yeast

Add oil, water, salt, cornmeal, whole-wheat flour, white flour, and yeast to bread machine in that order. Make a small hole in flour with a spoon for yeast. Set the machine to the dough cycle and press start.

# Favorite Pizza Recipes

For toppings for your pizza, there's really no limit. I mentioned flowers before, and I wasn't kidding; a pizza topped (as it comes out of the oven) with fresh edible marigold or nasturtium flowers is a sight to behold—and is delicious, too.

Here are three of my favorite pizza recipes.

# Feta and Black Olive Pizza

The creaminess of feta and the tang of olives make this a perennial favorite.

Prep time: 5 minutes • Cook time: 15 minutes • Serves 3 to 4

1 ball pizza dough

1 TB. olive oil

⅔ cup 20-Minute Tomato Sauce

6 to 8 oz. mozzarella cheese, shredded

4 oz. crumbled feta cheese

4 oz. sliced black olives

Follow the pizza preparation directions for 20-Minute Homemade Pizza, and spread feta cheese and then olives across pizza before sliding into preheated oven. Check at 12 minutes, but with the extra toppings this pie might take a few minutes longer.

# Shrimp and Basil Pizza

Prep time: 5 minutes   •   Cook time: 15 minutes   •   Serves 3 to 4

1 ball pizza dough

1 TB. olive oil

⅔ cup 20-Minute Tomato Sauce

6 to 8 oz. mozzarella cheese, shredded

5 oz. small precooked shrimp

1 tsp. dried basil

Pinch garlic powder

Follow preparation directions for 20-Minute Homemade Pizza and spread shrimp across pizza. Sprinkle with basil and dust with a pinch of garlic powder before sliding into the preheated oven. Check at 12 minutes.

Raw shelled shrimp can also be used but require a quick (three to five minutes or until done) cook in a skillet over medium heat with olive oil before topping your pizza.

# Roasted Red Pepper and Artichoke Pizza

Prep time: 5 minutes   •   Cook time: 15 minutes   •   Serves 3 to 4

1 ball pizza dough

1 TB. olive oil

⅔ cup 20-Minute Tomato Sauce

6 to 8 oz. mozzarella cheese, shredded

½ cup drained roasted red peppers, cut, if necessary, into bite-size pieces

½ cup drained artichoke hearts, cut into bite-size pieces

Pinch garlic powder

Follow preparation directions for 20-Minute Homemade Pizza. Spread red peppers and artichoke heart pieces across pizza. Dust with garlic powder before sliding into the preheated oven. Check at 12 minutes.

Roasted red peppers and artichoke hearts can be purchased in jars or cans at most grocery stores.

# Pasta and Pizza Easy Timesavers

Pasta and pizza are already extraordinarily quick dishes, so to take advantage of easy timesaving methods is to *really* move quickly.

Pasta's Easy Timesavers include fresh pasta (available in the deli section of the grocery store) and prepared sauces. Fresh pasta requires as little as six minutes in boiling water. When concurrently heated with a bottle of prepared sauce you've got a decent shot at a meal in 10 minutes (allowing time to boil water!). Myriad enhancers can add flavor and texture to your sauce, such as cubed ham from the deli, sliced mushrooms, and many other vegetables. A few minutes more, and you've got time to cook ground beef or sausage to add. Have some leftover grilled beef, chicken, or pork? Perfect to cube and add to the mix.

Prepared dough tops the list of Easy Timesavers for pizza, which is available at most grocery stores. For an even quicker start, precooked crusts can turn into a pizza in minutes. Pizza sauce and pasta sauce from the store also make tasty pizza. Try your favorite pasta sauce. One popular brand has a Florentine Spinach and Cheese Sauce that I think makes a great pie. Finally, packages of shredded mozzarella save minutes from shredding cheese yourself.

With all these ingredients ready to go, a pizza can be prepared in close to the same amount of time as pasta, and serving homemade pizza is impressive, not to mention a taste treat. Finally, make extra! I know this might bring back memories of pizza for breakfast, and I won't go that far, but homemade pizza will keep for several days in the fridge. Reheat on a preheated pizza stone and you've got a quick and tasty meal.

## The Least You Need to Know

- Pasta's convenience, kid appeal, and flexibility make it uniquely valuable to the 20-minute cook.
- Homemade pizza, contrary to popular understanding, can fit into the repertoire of the 20-minute cook.
- Pasta lends itself to advance preparation, enabling an Easy Timesaver for the second meal.
- Homemade pizza can easily beat store-bought pizza taste and provides a fun, easy meal for guests.

# Seafood

## In This Chapter

- The ideal 20-minute food
- Seafood seasoning chart
- Sure-fire seafood recipes
- Yes, you can microwave seafood

A fresh piece of fish is a delight for a busy cook. Seafood lends itself easily to 20-minute cuisine. Fish and shellfish (including clam, mussel, oyster, crab, shrimp, and lobster) bring delicate flavors and textures that can be preserved by quick cooking, so the featured methods of this book (frying and sautéing, grilling and broiling, steaming and boiling …) are a natural success story for seafood. Grilling is a natural success story for fish steaks, although care must be taken to avoid overcooking or overdrying small items. Even baking, a normally time-consuming method of cooking, works well with delicate and quick-cooking fish filets.

Always buy the freshest possible seafood from a vendor you trust. Fish should also be washed and patted dry with paper towels before cooking.

I've included some of my favorite seafood recipes in this chapter for a variety of ingredients, organized by cooking method. Each of these recipes serves four unless otherwise noted. (*Note:* In the rest of this book, I often provide recipes that can make enough for more than one meal. Seafood, however, is usually not a great leftover.)

# Seafood Seasoning

For perspective on cooking fish, you might find it useful to review the chart that follows. These categories are not necessarily exclusive: Soy sauce is, of course, both a source of moisture and a seasoning; poaching is both a cooking method and by default a source of moisture.

## Seafood Seasoning Guide

| Seafood | Seasoning | Coating | Cooking Method |
|---------|-----------|---------|----------------|
| Salmon | Dill | Soy sauce | Broiling |
| Swordfish | Ginger | Butter | Grilling |
| Halibut | Pepper | Olive oil | Frying |
| Shellfish | Tarragon | Lemon juice | Poaching |
| Bluefish | Basil | Mayonnaise | Baking |
| Light fish | Onion | Mustard | Boiling |
| | Marjoram | Broth | Microwave |
| | Cilantro | | Simmering |
| | Thyme | | Steaming |
| | Rosemary | | |
| | Garlic | | |
| | Chili powder | | |
| | Chives | | |
| | Coriander | | |
| | Fennel | | |
| | Red pepper | | |
| | Paprika | | |
| | Cumin | | |

This is not a "how-to" chart, but rather an at-a-glance guide to what works with fish; in a simplistic sense you can pick one ingredient from each column and have something that resembles a recipe. Each of these seasonings works in some seafood recipes, although some herbs and spices are better than others for specific dishes. Let's see, you could pick salmon, olive oil, garlic, and broil. That's pretty close to a good recipe (I added a bit of soy sauce, too).

**Cuisine Context**

Many of these recipes have common elements and methods. Once you're comfortable with those approaches to cooking seafood, you've got your license to start experimenting.

## Broiled Soy Salmon

Prep time: 5 minutes • Cook time: 8 minutes • Serves 4

2 TB. olive oil

1 TB. soy sauce

½ tsp. garlic powder

1½ lbs. salmon filets

Preheat the broiler. In a cup, mix olive oil, soy sauce, and garlic powder. Lay salmon filets in a baking dish and pour olive oil mixture over, turning once or twice to make sure they are coated on all sides. Broil for eight minutes, turning once, or until cooked through.

Serve with rice and steamed vegetables. Delicious!

As you review the recipes following, with the Seafood Seasoning Guide in mind, I hope you'll recognize the common theme with each of our main course chapters, that many of the recipes have common elements and methods.

**Cook to Cook**

Fatty acids in fish, especially salmon, are supposed to bring health benefits such as lower cholesterol. Eat up!

# Grilling and Broiling Recipes

If you're concerned about losing pieces of fish in the grill, consider using a fish basket. A fish basket is a grill top metal frame that holds your fish intact when turning. Foil can also be used, although wrapping a fish in foil tends to reduce grill flavors.

# Grilled Salmon Steaks

This family favorite appears on our grill-season table at least twice a month. Rich salmon meat holds up well to this spicy-crispy coating. My six-year-old asks for the skin first.

Prep time: 5 minutes   •   Cook time: 12 minutes   •   Serves 4

3 TB. olive oil

Juice of ½ lime

1½ lbs. salmon steaks

½ tsp. cumin

½ tsp. black pepper

½ tsp. chili powder

½ tsp. salt

Prepare grill. In a small bowl, combine olive oil and lime juice. Place salmon steaks in a large bowl. Pour olive oil and lime juice mixture over steaks. Turn to make sure all sides are coated. In a cup combine cumin, black pepper, chili powder, and salt. Sprinkle this mixture on all sides of fish steaks.

Move steaks to the grill, placing them over the coals, and cook for 12 minutes or until done, turning once. Drizzle with additional olive oil if necessary.

Serve with fresh sweet corn and bread for a summer feast. (Even if it's March, this meal will make you *feel* like it's summer.)

# Broiled Halibut Steaks

Prep time: 5 minutes   •   Cook time: 12 minutes   •   Serves 4

2 TB. olive oil

Juice of ½ lime

1½ lbs. halibut steaks

1 tsp. dried rosemary

½ tsp. dried tarragon

½ tsp. freshly ground black pepper

Fresh parsley (optional)

Preheat broiler. In a small bowl, combine olive oil and lime juice. Place fish steaks in a large bowl. Pour olive oil and lime juice mixture over steaks. Turn halibut to make sure all sides are coated. Sprinkle with rosemary, tarragon, and black pepper. Move steaks to baking pan and broil for 12 minutes or until done, turning once. Drizzle with additional olive oil, if necessary, and garnish with parsley.

Serve with fresh bread, salad with a light dressing (a heavy blue cheese dressing, for example, might overwhelm delicate fish flavors), and a glass of your favorite white wine.

**Flare-Up**

Choose your seafood meal's side dishes carefully. A heavy dressing on a salad can overwhelm delicate fish flavors.

# Sizzling Salmon

Prep time: 5 minutes  •  Cook time: 8 minutes  •  Serves 4

| | |
|---|---|
| ½ cup olive oil | ½ tsp. ginger |
| 1½ lbs. salmon filets | 1 onion, chopped |
| 1 TB. soy sauce | 2 sprigs fresh cilantro |

Preheat the broiler. In a small saucepan, heat olive oil over high heat while salmon is cooking. Put salmon filets in a baking dish. Drizzle filets with soy sauce. Sprinkle on ginger and onion pieces. Cook under the broiler for four minutes per side, or until cooked. When done, bring the baking pan out to the stovetop and sprinkle with cilantro leaves. Pour heated olive oil over salmon filets, taking care not to get too close to hot oil!

# Poaching, Boiling, Simmering, and Steaming Recipes

These recipes use water to preserve flavor and texture in delicate fish.

# Poached Black Pepper Cod

This simple dish brings a hint of pepper and the zing of lemon to delicate cod flavor.

Prep time: 4 minutes  •  Cook time: 8 minutes  •  Serves 4

| | |
|---|---|
| 1 cup white wine | 2 TB. butter |
| Juice of ½ lemon | ¼ tsp. freshly ground black pepper |
| 1 cup water | ½ tsp. salt |
| 1½ lbs. cod (or other white fish) filets | ¾ cup sour cream |

In a large saucepan or skillet mix wine, lemon juice, and water, and turn heat to medium. When wine mixture reaches a low boil, put in fish, and simmer for approximately eight minutes or until done. Meanwhile, heat a small skillet over medium heat. Add butter, stir until melted, and add pepper and salt. Heat, stirring, until bubbles appear. Turn off heat and stir in sour cream. Remove from heat and set aside. Remove fish, distribute to serving plates, pour pepper cream over each piece, and serve. Delicious with baked potatoes (20-Minute Microwave Baked Potatoes!) and buttered green beans.

# Gorgeous Seafood Stew

Prep time: 2 minutes   •   Cook time: 18 minutes   •   Serves 4 to 6

6 TB. extra virgin olive oil

2 tsp. chopped garlic

5 cups 20-Minute Tomato Sauce

2 TB. tomato paste

½ tsp. rosemary

1 tsp. dried parsley

1 tsp. dried basil

½ tsp. crushed red pepper

¾ cup red wine

1½ lbs. assorted calamari, scallops, shrimp, fish chunks

**Cook to Cook**

Don't feel the need to add lots of seasonings to seafood. Most fish and shellfish dishes succeed because they allow fresh seafood flavors to shine through.

In a large skillet, heat olive oil over medium heat. Add garlic and sauté for one minute. Add tomato sauce, tomato paste, rosemary, parsley, basil, and red pepper. Simmer for five minutes. Add red wine, return to simmer, and add calamari (if using). Cook for five minutes, then add scallops, shrimp, and fish. Cook until cooked through, seven to nine minutes. Serve with fresh Italian bread, a garden salad, and a white or light-bodied red wine. Don't forget to put candles on the table!

# Frying and Sautéing Recipes

Anyone who has enjoyed fish and chips, with that irresistible combination of crispy coating and moist, flaky interior, knows the appeal of fried fish. Frying and sautéing are methods appealing to the cook in a hurry; they are among the quickest possible cooking methods, and the rapid heating preserves flavor and moisture.

# Whisker-Licking Catfish

Prep time: 5 minutes  •  Cook time: 12 minutes  •  Serves 4

⅓ cup olive oil

½ cup cornmeal

½ cup whole-wheat flour

1 tsp. kosher salt

1 tsp. dried basil

1 tsp. coriander

3 catfish filets, about 1½ lbs. total

⅔ cup milk

Lemon wedges

Heat olive oil in a large skillet over medium-high heat. On a plate or wide shallow tray, mix cornmeal, flour, salt, basil, and coriander. Wash filets and pat dry. Put milk in another wide shallow bowl. Dip first filet in milk, being sure to coat both sides. Dredge filet through cornmeal mixture and place it in hot oil in the skillet. Repeat with other filets, making sure not to let the skillet get too crowded. Cook each filet for about six minutes, turning once, or until done.

Serve with lemon wedges. Crispy and delicate, and even my kids eat it.

# Brewpub Fried Fish

Prep time: 5 minutes  •  Cook time: 12 minutes  •  Serves 4

4 TB. olive oil

½ cup beer

1 egg

1 cup bread crumbs

1 tsp. rosemary

½ tsp. sage

1 tsp. salt

½ tsp. black pepper

1½ lbs. white fish filets, washed

Heat oil in a large skillet over medium-high heat. In a bowl, whisk together beer and egg. In a wide tray or bowl, mix bread crumbs, rosemary, sage, salt, and pepper. Dip filets in beer-and-egg mixture, then dredge through seasoned bread crumbs. Fry for approximately six minutes or until done, turning once. Serve with rice and salad for a quick, tasty, and healthy meal.

# Baking Recipes

Baking is a terrific way to cook seafood. Our challenge for this book is to identify those recipes that use this method yet fit within our 20-minute parameters. Here are some very tasty solutions.

## Baked Sole

A family tradition, this recipe is simple and delicious, with balancing flavors of fish and Parmesan. The secret to baking this within our 20-minute time frame is to use thin filets (such as scrod or catfish), a thin-walled baking pan (aluminum), and high heat.

Prep time: 3 minutes  •  Cook time: 17 minutes  •  Serves 4

| | |
|---|---|
| 4 TB. butter, sliced thin | ½ cup Parmesan cheese, shredded |
| 12 crumbled saltine crackers | ½ tsp. black pepper |
| 1½ lbs. fish filets (sole or other thin white fish), washed | Lemon wedges |

Preheat oven to 400°F. Arrange 2 tablespoons butter and six crumbled crackers across the bottom of a metal baking pan. Arrange filets in a single layer over crumbled crackers. Spread remaining crackers over fish, top with remaining butter, and sprinkle Parmesan cheese and pepper on top. Bake for 17 minutes or until done. Serve with lemon, sautéed snap beans, and fresh bread.

# Seafood Easy Timesavers

One cooking method we haven't reviewed yet, but which deserves a firm spot on the Easy Timesaver seafood list, is the microwave. Microwaving fish is incredibly quick, resulting in flavor and texture that resembles poaching. Following is one example.

# Microwave Poached Salmon

I've used salmon, but other fish can be substituted.

Prep time: 4 minutes  •  Cook time: 6 minutes  •  Serves 4

1½ lbs. salmon filets (Look for center cut pieces that will cook evenly; two ¾-lb. pieces are ideal.)

2 TB. olive oil

2 TB. white wine

Juice of ½ lemon

Lemon wedges to garnish

Salt and pepper to taste

Place salmon filets in a medium microwaveable casserole dish. Mix olive oil, wine, and lemon juice and pour on top of salmon. Cover and cook on high for four to six minutes or until done (cooking time will vary by oven). To serve, spoon poaching liquid on top of salmon and garnish with lemon wedges. Season, if desired, with salt and pepper.

Serve with white rice and steamed vegetables for a simple, tasty, lightning-fast meal.

**Cook to Cook**

One sure timesaving method for seafood is to choose a simple recipe that highlights the food rather than preparation.

Fresh seafood cooks so quickly that cutting even more time is a fun challenge. One sure success is to choose a simple recipe that highlights the food rather than the frame (seasonings). Here's just one example.

# Sole Meuniere

The slight brown crispness of the flour, the zing of lemon, the delicate flavor of the sole all combine to make this simple dish a delight.

Prep time: 4 minutes  •  Cook time: 6 minutes  •  Serves 4

2 TB. butter

Juice of ½ lemon

1 TB. flour

1½ lbs. sole filets

Lemon wedges for serving

In a skillet, melt butter over medium heat. Stir in lemon juice. Sprinkle flour on a clean countertop. Lightly press each side of each filet in flour and place in the heated skillet. Cook for approximately six minutes or until done, turning once.

Serve with lemon wedges, rice, steamed vegetables, and a glass of dry white wine. Ah.

Finally, don't forget frozen seafood mixes where at least part of the prep is done for you. Specialty food stores carry these mixes, ready to go from the freezer to the stovetop.

### Cuisine Context

Seafood stews echo the famous dishes of the Mediterranean and our own San Francisco: bouillabaisse and cioppino, dishes steeped in history as well as flavor.

# Quick Seafood Stew

Prep time: 5 minutes   •   Cook time: 15 minutes   •   Serves 4

2 TB. olive oil

1 large onion, chopped

1 large red pepper, seeded and chopped

2 tsp. chopped garlic

1 cup white wine

1 (1-lb.) pkg. seafood mix (such as scallops, shrimp, and calamari)

2 cups 20-Minute Tomato Sauce

2 TB. tomato paste

1 TB. dried basil

½ tsp. crushed red pepper

In a large skillet, heat oil over medium heat. Add onions, red pepper, and garlic and cook for five minutes. Add wine, bring to a boil, and add seafood mix. Reduce heat and simmer for 8 to 10 minutes or until seafood is done. Add tomato sauce, tomato paste, basil, and crushed red pepper. Heat two minutes, stirring, and serve either in bowls as a stew or over rice or pasta. *Mangia!*

## The Least You Need to Know

- The delicate flavors and textures of seafood are perfect for the quick-cooking methods of 20-minute cuisine.
- Simplicity of preparation and seasoning are added guarantees of delicious seafood.
- Master the basics and you have a license to explore and experiment.
- Pan-frying and microwave-cooking are perhaps the quickest seafood cooking methods.

# Chapter 10

# White Meats

## In This Chapter

- ◆ Grill, broil, fry, and sauté
- ◆ Pork and poultry seasonings
- ◆ Sure-fire white meat recipes
- ◆ Timesaving preparation

Almost by default, many busy cooks rely on pork and poultry (what I refer to here as "white meats") as the base for a large proportion of their meals. Reasons for this include the speed of preparation, affordability, ease of use, and the generally mild flavors and resulting flexibility with a wide variety of seasonings and methods.

Every type of cuisine, from east to west, from mild to spicy, use these versatile meats. In this chapter, I've also included veal, because of its similarly mild characteristics (though not inexpensive). Veal is meat from a calf, generally characterized by mild flavor and tenderness. Certain cuts of veal, such as cutlets and scaloppini, are well suited to quick cooking. In addition, I have avoided larger cuts of meat in this chapter. Although delicious, they generally take much longer to cook than 20 minutes.

# White Meat Seasoning

With 20-minute cuisine in mind, the cut of meat is very important. Thin cuts of pork—chops, ribs, and tenderloin medallions—and of *poultry*—boneless breasts, legs, wings, thighs, and drumsticks (both components of a chicken leg)—are the pieces most amenable to quick cooking. Larger pieces I'll avoid (some are possible within this timeframe if cooking is accelerated with the microwave).

To give you a sense of how flexible these meats are, with many of these recipes, you could actually swap between chicken and pork, and even veal, and do just fine. (I prefer, though, to give slightly more special treatment to veal because of its expense.)

**Cook's Glossary**

**Poultry,** for the purposes of this book, refers to chicken and turkey.

I've focused on grilling, broiling, frying, and sautéing as the 20-minute methods of choice for both speed and flavor. Ground turkey and ground chicken, because of their close similarity in preparation techniques with ground beef, are considered in the next chapter with ground beef–based recipes.

## White Meat Seasoning Guide

| Ingredient | Seasoning | Moisture | Cooking Method |
|---|---|---|---|
| Pork | Cumin | Olive oil | Grilling |
| Chicken | Thyme | Butter | Frying |
| Turkey | Garlic | Lemon juice | Broiling |
| Ham | Tarragon | Lime juice | Microwave |
| Veal | Basil | Mustard | |
| | Onion | Soy sauce | |
| | Oregano | Mayonnaise | |
| | Cilantro | Egg | |
| | Ginger | Chicken broth | |
| | Rosemary | | |
| | Black pepper | | |
| | Chili powder | | |
| | Chives | | |
| | Coriander | | |
| | Fennel | | |
| | Red pepper | | |

| Ingredient | Seasoning | Moisture | Cooking Method |
|---|---|---|---|
| | Paprika | | |
| | Dill | | |
| | Marjoram | | |
| | Salt | | |

As in the previous chapter, this table is intended to help show what goes with what, and once again picking one representative from each column should resemble a recipe. (It's not quite that simple, but you get the idea.) Let's see, we could pick pork, cumin, olive oil, and grill. That's pretty close to one of my favorites.

# Grilled Pork with Cumin and Lime

Spicy and juicy grilled pork chops are just the right thing for a summer night with friends or family.

Prep time: 5 minutes • Cook time: 10 minutes • Serves 4

2 TB. olive oil

Juice of ½ lime

1 tsp. ground cumin

2 tsp. salt

1½ lbs. center cut pork chops

Preheat the grill. In a cup, mix olive oil, lime juice, cumin, and salt. Place chops in a dish, and pour olive oil mixture over, turning once or twice to make sure it is coated on all sides. Poke chops with a fork to tenderize and allow marinade to penetrate meat. Place chops on the grill. Grill over medium-high heat for 10 minutes, turning once, or until cooked through.

Serve with rice and Sautéed Summer Squash.

**Cook to Cook**

Many "white meats" are also "light"; in other words, low in fat. Because of this, it is often important to add moisture (oil, butter, and so on), as well as to watch these meats closely as they cook to prevent drying.

As you read through these recipes, look once again for common elements and methods. Master the method, and it's like learning to ride a bike … you never forget!

# Grilling and Broiling Recipes

Grilling and broiling are not only terrific quick-cooking methods, they also bring appealing smoky grill flavors. There's something appealing and satisfying about food prepared in this manner.

> **Cook to Cook**
>
> Pork tenderloin is one of the most delicious cuts of pork available. It generally is a two- to three-pound piece. For quick cooking, I like to slice it into medallions about one-inch thick. This Rosemary and Garlic Tenderloin recipe will work with broiling as well as grilling, although I find that grilling is faster and provides more flavor.

# Rosemary and Garlic Tenderloin

Prep time: 5 minutes  •  Cook time: 10 minutes  •  Serves 4

3 TB. olive oil

1 TB. chopped garlic

1 tsp. dried rosemary

Juice of ½ lime

½ tsp. cracked pepper

1½ lbs. pork tenderloin medallions

> **Cook to Cook**
>
> How do you know when it's done? To check for doneness, pierce the center of the piece of pork with a sharp knife. When liquid runs slightly pink (for rare) or clear (well done), the meat is cooked. If liquid is red, keep cooking!

Heat the grill or broiler. Mix together olive oil, garlic, rosemary, lime juice, and cracked pepper. Place medallions in a bowl, pour olive oil mixture over, and turn to coat.

Place medallions on the heated grill and cook over medium-high heat for 10 minutes or until done, turning once. When turning, drizzle with remaining olive oil mixture.

Serve with white rice, salad, and chilled sauvignon blanc. A great meal.

# Veal Scallopini

This simple classic highlights the delicate flavor of veal.

Prep time: 5 minutes  •  Cook time: 8 minutes  •  Serves 4

3 TB. butter

1½ lbs. veal scallopini (A very thin cut of veal, available at the butcher and many grocery stores.)

Salt and pepper

¼ cup flour

1 tsp. capers

Juice of ½ lemon

Melt butter over medium heat in a large skillet. Season veal with salt and pepper and dredge through flour. Add veal to the skillet and sauté for six to eight minutes, turning once, or until cooked through. Add capers and lemon juice during the last minute of cooking, stirring to ensure contact with veal on all sides.

Distribute veal to serving plates and drizzle with remaining pan juices. Serve with fresh bread and a salad.

**Cuisine Context**

Because of its light flavor and similarities in qualities with poultry and pork, veal can also be considered a "white meat."

# Quick Home-Style Barbecued Chicken

Microwave precooking accelerates this meal. Homemade (and quick!) barbecue sauce makes this a real treat. To save a few minutes, do a barbecue sauce tune-up.

Prep time: 3 minutes  •  Cook time: 15 minutes  •  Serves 4 to 6

3 lbs. chicken legs, cut into parts for quicker cooking

1 batch Grampy's Barbecue Sauce (recipe follows)

Preheat the grill. Place chicken legs in a large, microwave-safe bowl and microwave for 10 minutes, turning to assure even cooking. Move hot, partially cooked chicken carefully to the grill and brush generously with barbecue sauce. Grill about five minutes until done and skin is crispy.

Serve with bread and salad for a quick, flavorful summer-theme meal.

**Flare-Up**

If you like to use barbecue sauce for dipping, be sure to keep it separate from the sauce used for brushing the chicken to avoid contamination from raw meat.

# Grampy's Barbecue Sauce

A sweet-spicy sauce that will keep you coming back.

Prep time: 8 minutes • Serves 8

1 cup ketchup

2 TB. cider vinegar

3 TB. molasses

1 TB. ground mustard

½ tsp. cumin

½ tsp. ginger

¼ tsp. dried sage

¼ tsp. ground red pepper

¼ tsp. ground black pepper

Mix ketchup, vinegar, molasses, mustard, cumin, ginger, sage, red pepper, and black pepper thoroughly.

# Chicken Kebabs

Prep time: 5 minutes • Cook time: 8 minutes • Serves 4

Kebab skewers (available in most grocery stores)

1½ lbs. boneless, skinless chicken breast, cut into 1-inch cubes

1 pint grape tomatoes, halved

½ sweet onion, cut into 1-inch pieces

3 TB. olive oil

Juice of ½ lemon

1 TB. chopped garlic

½ tsp. cumin

Salt and pepper

Preheat the grill.

On grill skewers, assemble kebabs, alternating pieces of chicken, tomato, and onion. Arrange kebabs on a plate. Mix olive oil, lemon juice, and garlic in a small bowl and drizzle the mixture over kebabs. Sprinkle kebabs with cumin, salt, and pepper.

Grill for eight minutes or until done, turning to ensure even cooking. Serve with rice.

# Recipes for Frying and Sautéing

Frying is a time-honored cooking tradition across the country. From north to south, east to west, everybody has favorite methods and seasonings. These recipes pick up on several of these tasty regional themes.

# Derek's Buffalo Wings

Prep time: 8 minutes  •  Cook time: 10 minutes  •  Serves 4 to 6

| | |
|---|---|
| 4 lbs. chicken wings | ¼ cup butter |
| Salt and pepper | 2 to 5 TB. Tabasco sauce |
| 4 cups oil for deep-frying | 1 TB. white wine vinegar |

Remove and discard tips. Cut each wing in two pieces and trim fat. Rinse wings and pat dry. Sprinkle with salt and pepper. Heat oil in deep fryer. Add about half the wings. Deep-fry for 10 minutes or until golden brown. Stir occasionally. Drain and place on a warm platter. Melt butter. Add Tabasco sauce and vinegar and mix well. Drizzle over wings.

The Tabasco acts as the heat throttle. The more you add, the hotter it gets. If you are hesitant about spicy foods, start with 2 tablespoons and go from there.

# Drumroll Chicken

Prep time: 8 minutes  •  Cook time: 9 minutes  •  Serves 4

| | |
|---|---|
| ¾ cup canola oil | 1 tsp. dried sage |
| 1 egg | ¼ tsp. ground red pepper |
| ½ cup milk | ¼ tsp. ground black pepper |
| ½ cup cornmeal | 2 lbs. chicken drumsticks |

Heat oil in a medium-size saucepan over high heat. Whisk egg and milk in a glass measuring cup. Mix cornmeal, sage, red pepper, and black pepper in a bowl.

Dip each drumstick in egg and milk mixture, roll meat end in cornmeal mixture, and place in hot oil. Cook for nine minutes or until done.

Serve with Cheddar Broccoli and Scalloped Potatoes.

Crispy and fun food for kids and adults alike. For an adult table, ramp up the red pepper. For a kid table, tone it down.

**Cook to Cook**

For a barbecue sauce tune-up, mix 2 tablespoons soy sauce and 2 tablespoons canola oil into a cup of standard barbecue sauce. If you like this, also try adding a little vinegar, mustard, or Worcestershire sauce.

# The Magic Chicken Breast

Here are a few examples of the many manifestations of the chicken breast. They are quick-cooking, low in fat, and high in nutrition. Next to the egg, the chicken breast might be called another ideal food … especially for the 20-minute cook.

## U. B.'s Salsa Chicken

Prep time: 5 minutes   •   Cook time: 11 minutes   •   Serves 4

2 TB. olive oil

¼ cup flour

4 skinless, boneless chicken breast halves

Salt and pepper

1 cup salsa (your favorite)

1 can chopped tomatoes, drained (or 2 small tomatoes, chopped)

¼ cup sliced black olives (Kalamata have the best flavor.)

¼ cup white wine

Heat oil in a large skillet over medium heat. Put flour on a plate or shallow bowl. Season chicken breasts with salt and pepper, dredge through flour, and cook in skillet for six to eight minutes or until done, turning once. Remove to warm plate, cover with foil.

In a bowl, combine salsa, tomatoes, and black olives.

Add wine to skillet and stir in salsa mixture. Heat through, about three minutes. Distribute chicken pieces to four plates and pour salsa mixture in even portions over each piece of chicken. *Olé!*

## Aunt Jean's Dijon Chicken

Prep time: 5 minutes   •   Cook time: 12 minutes   •   Serves 4

⅓ cup bread crumbs

1 TB. grated Parmesan cheese

½ tsp. dried basil

½ tsp. dried oregano

½ tsp. dried thyme

¼ tsp. salt

¼ tsp. pepper

2 TB. Dijon-style mustard

4 skinless, boneless chicken breast halves

2 TB. olive oil

Combine bread crumbs, Parmesan cheese, basil, oregano, thyme, salt, and pepper in a shallow bowl. Brush mustard on both sides of chicken and and dredge chicken pieces through bread crumb mixture.

Heat oil in large skillet over medium heat cook chicken for 12 minutes or until done, turning once. Serve with rice and snow peas.

# "Tarragarlic" Chicken

Prep time: 5 minutes  •  Cook time: 13 minutes  •  Serves 4

| | |
|---|---|
| 2 TB. olive oil | ¼ cup sour cream |
| 2 tsp. chopped garlic | Juice of ½ lemon |
| 4 skinless, boneless chicken breast halves | 1 tsp. dried tarragon |
| Salt and pepper | ½ tsp. salt |
| ¼ cup white wine | |

Heat oil over medium heat in a large skillet. Cook garlic for three minutes in oil. Season chicken breasts with salt and pepper and cook in skillet, still over medium heat, for seven to eight minutes or until done, turning once.

While breasts are cooking, combine white wine, sour cream, lemon juice, tarragon, and salt in a bowl.

Distribute chicken pieces to four plates, pour sauce into skillet, heat for two minutes, and pour even portions over each piece of chicken. Ah.

# Chicken Marsala

This classic chicken recipe, described with a twist or two, is a real crowd pleaser.

Prep time: 5 minutes  •  Cook time: 15 minutes  •  Serves 4

| | |
|---|---|
| 2 TB. butter | 2 TB. olive oil |
| ¼ cup flour | 1 cup chicken broth |
| ½ tsp. dried marjoram | ½ cup marsala wine |
| ½ tsp. black pepper | 1 cup sliced mushrooms |
| ½ tsp. salt | Juice of ½ lemon |
| 4 boneless, skinless chicken breast halves | |

Heat butter in a large skillet. Mix flour with marjoram, pepper, and salt. Dredge chicken breasts in flour mixture and put them in the skillet. Cook for eight minutes, or until done, turning once. When done, remove breasts to a warm plate and cover with foil to keep warm. Turn the heat up under the skillet, and add olive oil, broth, wine, mushrooms, and lemon juice. Cook, stirring, for seven minutes or until liquid is reduced in volume by half. Distribute chicken breasts to serving plates and pour sauce over chicken breasts.

# Chive Chicken

This piquant recipe makes the most of the onion family for a dish just bursting with flavor.

Prep time: 5 minutes  •  Cook time: 15 minutes  •  Serves 4

| | |
|---|---|
| 2 TB. olive oil | 1 cup chicken broth |
| 4 boneless, skinless chicken breast halves | ½ tsp. salt |
| Salt and pepper | 1 tsp. dried thyme |
| ¼ cup flour | ⅓ cup sour cream |
| 1 onion, chopped | ⅓ cup fresh chives, chopped |
| 2 tsp. chopped garlic | |

Heat olive oil in a large skillet over medium heat. Season chicken breasts with salt and pepper, dredge through flour in a shallow bowl, and cook for eight minutes or until done, turning once. Remove to a warm plate and cover with foil.

Add onion and garlic to the skillet and sauté for two minutes, until onion becomes translucent and tender. Turn the heat to high, add chicken broth, salt, and thyme and cook, stirring, for five minutes. Add sour cream and cook for one minute more. Distribute chicken to serving plates and pour sauce over each piece. Sprinkle chives over each piece.

Serve with rice and steamed broccoli.

# White Meat Easy Timesavers

There are many ways to save time with preparation of poultry and pork. One of these ways is to take advantage of partially (or completely) prepared ingredients. The other is to prepare the meats for even quicker cooking than normal.

Most grocery stores offer partially prepared poultry and pork. For example, I like pre-marinated lemon-pepper chicken breasts. Several similar products are likely to be available at your local grocer. Marinated and shrink-wrapped, they are ready to cook immediately and can be on the table in minutes. I've also tried several versions of marinated pork tenderloin, with seasoning such as teriyaki or cracked pepper. Sliced into medallions and grilled, they are delicious. Finally, we couldn't talk about marinated meats without nodding to the wealth of products in

**Cook to Cook**

For quick preparation, most of the recipes in this chapter, particularly those featuring chicken breasts, could easily be considered Easy Timesavers themselves. Chicken breasts, after all, are a partially prepared meat. However, there are ways to speed up even the speediest recipe by accelerating cooking and minimizing prep time.

the barbecue-sauce and marinated-meat section of the store. At my local grocery store I can choose between several brands, all offering quick flavor on the dinner table in way under 20 minutes.

Here are a few examples.

# Grilled Sweet and Spicy Pork

This recipe is proof that terrific flavor is quick and easy.

Prep time: 4 minutes  •  Cook time: 10 minutes  •  Serves 4

1½ lbs. pork chops

2 TB. canola oil

2 TB. honey

1 tsp. paprika

1 tsp. cumin

Preheat grill. Put pork chops in a bowl. Mix oil, honey, paprika, and cumin in a glass measuring cup and pour over chops, turning to coat. Place pork chops on the grill and cook 10 minutes or until done, turning once.

# Brigitte's Speedy Chicken

This recipe takes advantage of quick cooking made possible by skinny slices of chicken breast.

Prep time: 4 minutes  •  Cook time: 10 minutes  •  Serves 4

2 TB. canola oil

4 boneless, skinless chicken breasts, cut lengthwise into ¼-inch strips

2 onions, sliced

1 tsp. salt

Place oil, chicken, onions, and salt in a skillet over high heat. Cook for two minutes, turn breasts, cover, and cook for eight minutes or until done.

Serve with peas and couscous or rice.

*Variation:* Sprinkle in 1 teaspoon Indian spice such as curry powder or garam masala at the beginning.

## The Least You Need to Know

◆ The humble chicken breast has almost unlimited flexibility and can host a wide variety of seasonings and cooking methods.

◆ When it comes to pork and poultry, grilling, broiling, frying, and sautéing are fail-safe 20-minute methods of choice for both speed and flavor.

◆ Master the basics and then you have a license to explore and experiment.

◆ Microwave-cooking is one way to accelerate cooking of larger cuts of meat to fit within our 20-minute range.

# 11

# Richer Meats

## In This Chapter

- ◆ Twenty-minute flavor explosion
- ◆ Beef and lamb seasoning chart
- ◆ Sure-fire beef and lamb meat recipes
- ◆ Premake, season, and ground for time

If many cooks turn to pork and poultry for speed, many others would prefer beef and lamb (what I refer to here as "richer meats") for terrific flavor. Some have a misperception that richer meats somehow inherently require longer to cook, and thus are unsuited for 20-minute cuisine. Perhaps this is because of images of vast holiday roasts that need a week in the oven. In the hope of changing that perception, this chapter is in large part devoted to giving examples of 20-minute cuisine featuring beef and lamb. Many richer meat cuts and methods of preparation are well suited to quick cooking.

## Richer Meat Seasoning

Richer meats bring flavors that stand out in beef and lamb recipes, flavors that feature more prominently than in a similar recipe made with lighter meats. A steak is flavor all by itself, while a chicken breast is more likely to serve as a vehicle for other flavors.

The cut of meat is very important for 20-minute preparation of beef and lamb. Consistent with the last chapter, thin cuts, such as filets, steaks, chops, tips, and strips are in; larger ones, such as roasts and legs, are out. My objective here is to pick the easiest pieces to work with and then give the most enjoyable, straightforward ways to treat those pieces. Other rich meats, such as venison and other game, certainly fall into the "rich" category but they also tend to be special occasion fare, and thus perhaps less likely to be the focus of people interested in quick preparation. No offense, deer.

This seasoning table, like in other chapters, is intended to provide a sense of what goes with what. I've included some of my favorites, but as you can see, there are a huge number of possible ingredient combinations, just waiting for you to explore … in 20 minutes.

### Cuisine Context

Although there are many methods of cooking beef and lamb, in this chapter I focus on frying/sautéing and grilling/broiling as the methods of choice for the cook in a hurry. I've also included preparation examples for ground poultry and pork because of the common characteristics they have with ground beef preparation.

## Richer Meat Seasoning Guide

| Ingredient | Seasoning | Moisture | Cooking Method |
|---|---|---|---|
| Beef | Onion | Egg | Frying |
| Lamb | Cumin | Olive oil | Grilling |
| Ground beef | Thyme | Butter | Microwave |
| (or poultry) | Garlic | Lemon juice | Broiling |
| | Tarragon | Lime juice | Baking |
| | Basil | Mustard | Poaching |
| | Onion | Soy sauce | Steaming |
| | Oregano | Mayonnaise | |
| | Cilantro | Beef broth | |
| | Ginger | | |
| | Rosemary | | |
| | Black pepper | | |
| | Chili powder | | |
| | Chives | | |
| | Coriander | | |
| | Fennel | | |

| Ingredient | Seasoning | Moisture | Cooking Method |
|---|---|---|---|
| | Red pepper | | |
| | Paprika | | |
| | Dill | | |
| | Marjoram | | |
| | Salt | | |

For our "what goes with what" exercise, we could pick ground beef, onion, egg, and fry. That inspires another favorite that I learned from a German friend (well, his mother, actually).

**Flare-Up**

Smaller pieces of meat will cook much faster. If you're in a hurry, consider grilling steak strips rather than one big thick piece. Keep a close eye on them to avoid overcooking! If the grill has a "hot spot," rotate pieces of meat from that spot to cooler areas of the grill so all pieces will be done at the same time.

# Fleisch Kuchle (Austrian Meat Cakes)

Hearty and quick, with the comfort food attributes of meatloaf or a good burger.

Prep time: 5 minutes  •  Cook time: 14 minutes  •  Serves 4

4 TB. canola oil

1 lb. ground beef

2 slices bread, crusts removed, torn into pieces

2 eggs

1 onion, finely chopped

1 cup dry bread crumbs

½ cup milk

½ cup sour cream

1 tsp. salt

Heat oil in a skillet over medium heat. Mix ground beef, bread, eggs, and onion into patties, roll in bread crumbs, and fry each cake in oil for 10 minutes or until done, turning once. Remove meat cakes from skillet to serving plates. To remaining oil and pan drippings add milk, sour cream, and salt. Mix thoroughly, scraping up any bits attached to the bottom of the pan. Reduce heat to low, heat for four minutes, and pour over the cakes.

Serve with boiled new potatoes, dill, and salt.

# Grilling and Broiling Recipes

Rich meats and grilling go together like Mom and apple pie. The rich flavor of a steak, for example, stands up beautifully to the smoky char of the grill. Hearty and flavorful, grilled and broiled rich meats are year-round favorites and can be prepared in a wide variety of recipes.

## Quick Cajun Kebabs

Prep time: 10 minutes  •  Cook time: 10 minutes  •  Serves 4 to 6

4 to 8 kebab skewers (available at most grocery stores)

1 lb. steak tips, cut into 1-inch pieces

1 Vidalia onion, cut into 1-inch pieces

1 large green pepper, cored and seeded, and cut into 1-inch pieces

1 pint button mushrooms

2 TB. olive oil

2 tsp. Cajun seasoning (available at most grocery stores)

Preheat the grill. On each skewer, slide alternating pieces of steak, onion, green pepper, and mushroom. Repeat until the skewer is full to within two inches of the end. Place skewer on a large plate. Repeat with other skewers until ingredients are used up. Mix olive oil and Cajun seasoning and drizzle generously over each skewer. Place each skewer, one parallel to the next, on grill over flame. Cook for 10 minutes or until meat is cooked, turning frequently. If the grill has a "hot spot," when turning your kebabs rotate the less done ones to the hot spot and the more done ones out to cooler areas of the grill so all the kebabs will be done at about the same time.

**Cook to Cook**

If you don't have Cajun seasoning, use instead 1 teaspoon salt, ½ teaspoon crushed red pepper, ¼ teaspoon black pepper, ½ teaspoon garlic pow-

Other ingredient possibilities: cherry tomatoes (use firm tomatoes so they will not slide off your skewer), hot peppers, zucchini or summer squash, or precooked eggplant.

"Cajun" and "kebab" in the same dish paint an interesting cross-cultural image, but they sure are good. I use Vidalia onions because of their sweet, mild onion flavor.

Kebabs include their own vegetable, so all you need with this recipe is rice or bread and a glass of light red wine and you're set for a pleasant meal.

# Frying and Sautéing

Stovetop cooking is another quick-cooking method well suited to richer meats.

## Beef Wrap

Inspired by Mediterranean ingredients, with balanced cool and spicy flavors.

Prep time: 8 minutes   •   Cook time: 6 minutes   •   Serves 4

| | |
|---|---|
| 1 tsp. olive oil | ½ cucumber, peeled and finely chopped |
| 1 lb. sirloin, cut into thin strips | ½ tsp. ground pepper |
| ¼ tsp. ground cumin | 2 tsp. lemon juice |
| Salt and pepper | 1 pkg. (8 pieces) small pita bread |
| 1 cup plain yogurt | ¼ head green cabbage, cut into thin strips |
| 1 TB. crushed garlic | |

Heat oil over medium heat in a large skillet. Season beef strips with cumin, salt, and pepper, and sauté until done, about six minutes.

Mix yogurt, garlic, chopped cucumber, pepper, and lemon juice.

Slice an opening in each piece of pita. Insert beef strips in each piece, arranging them lengthwise. Top beef with cabbage strips, and top with the seasoned yogurt mixture. Ready to go!

> **Cook to Cook**
>
> Many beef- and lamb-based mixtures, including chili and stews, are not only delicious immediately but also improve as the seasonings have time to meld. Talk about a reason to look forward to leftovers!

# Wonder Burgers

Burgers don't have to be made with beef. Ground poultry, pork, and lamb also make delicious burgers that can be prepared with almost identical method but result in "new and different" flavors … and add a new and different twist to an old friend.

The seasonings are flexible for ground meats, although based on your taste you might find some work better than others with a particular ingredient. Here are some of my preferences:

- For lamb, rosemary is a natural.
- For poultry, I like basil.
- For pork, I use garlic, rosemary, and oregano.
- For ground beef, onions, black pepper, and cumin.

# Burgers with a Twist

I usually make these burgers with ground lamb, but the basic concept is the same with ground poultry, pork, or beef.

Prep time: 10 minutes • Cook time: 10 minutes • Serves 4

| | |
|---|---|
| 1 lb. ground lamb | 1 egg |
| 1 small onion, finely chopped | 2 tsp. olive oil |
| 1 tsp. dried rosemary | |

In a bowl, thoroughly mix lamb, onion, rosemary, and egg. (If you're not squeamish, the best way to do this is with your hands!) Shape into round, flat patties approximately 2½ inches in diameter. If mixture is too moist, add ¼ cup dry bread crumbs. Heat olive oil in a large skillet over medium heat. Cook burgers in the skillet, adding as many as can easily fit without touching each other. Cook for 10 minutes or until done, turning once.

These burgers are terrific served on a bun with cheese, sliced sweet onion, fresh tomato slices, crispy lettuce, and ketchup. They are also great just topped with ketchup and served with bread and salad for a quick and flavorful meal.

# Sandra's Easy Meatballs

Prep time: 10 minutes • Cook time: 8 minutes • Serves 4

| | |
|---|---|
| 1 lb. ground beef | ½ tsp. sugar |
| 1 TB. crushed garlic | ¼ cup olive oil |
| 6 oz. sun-dried tomato spread | 1 tsp. dried basil |

Mix beef, garlic, tomato spread, and sugar by hand (once again!) and shape into balls between the size of a large grape and a golf ball. Heat oil in a large skillet over medium heat and stir in basil. Cook meatballs in oil-basil mixture for eight minutes or until done, turning frequently.

With spaghetti? In a submarine sandwich? Eaten alone? It's up to you. Fast, flexible, and tasty. Yes, they can also be made with lamb, pork, or poultry.

**Cuisine Context**

People have different ideas about eating meatballs. For some, meatballs come with spaghetti. For others, meatballs must come in a grinder (a large submarine sandwich) with provolone. For others, meatballs are eaten plain, bite by tasty bite. My preference? I'll take all three, thanks very much.

# Unbelievably Good Chili

My brother once said, "This is unbelievably good." How can I resist that name? One secret is the consistency, thick and rich, thanks to refried beans. With prep time, this takes a couple minutes more than 20, but it will provide at least two, possibly three meals (a make-ahead Easy Timesaver).

Prep time: 5 minutes • Cook time: 20 minutes • Serves 4, two or three times

3 TB. olive oil

1 large onion, coarsely chopped

1 lb. ground beef

1 (16-oz.) can cut corn, drained

1 (28-oz.) can plum tomatoes, with juice

1 (16-oz.) can red kidney beans

1 (16-oz.) can *refried beans*

2 cups 20-Minute Tomato Sauce

2 TB. chili powder

2 tsp. ground cumin

1 tsp. salt

½ tsp. ground black pepper

Heat olive oil in a large skillet, add onion and ground beef, and cook until beef is done, about eight minutes. Add corn, tomatoes with juice, kidney beans, refried beans, tomato sauce, chili powder, cumin, salt, and pepper. Stir to mix thoroughly and simmer for 12 minutes.

**Cook's Glossary**

**Refried beans** are cooked pinto beans softened into a thick paste, and often seasoned with peppers and spices. Refried beans are a side dish in their own right, but also a terrific way to thicken chili. For a vegetarian recipe, be sure to look for refried beans that do not contain lard.

I enjoy this chili both by itself, topped with sour cream and salsa, and served over rice. With corn bread, this is a meal that will satisfy the biggest hunger. Chili tastes even better the next day.

# Richer Meat Easy Timesavers

The grocery store and butcher shop offer a wealth of Easy Timesavers featuring beef and lamb. To get started in a flash, look for items where some of the work has been done for you, such as the following:

- Premade kebabs. They come shrink-wrapped complete with beef (or fish, or other meat) and vegetables. All they need are quick seasoning and they're ready to cook. Some are seasoned or marinated already. Don't have time to even heat the grill? Broil that kebab instead.

- Seasoned and marinated meats, such as steak tips marinated in teriyaki or other seasoning blends.

- Never forget humble ground meats. Preshaped ground meat patties can be cooked and ready in 10 minutes. Most grocery stores also sell frozen packages of burgers, some with interesting meats such as buffalo. (How's that for an Easy Timesaver? Serve someone a buffalo burger! It's fast, and it's a bonus new taste experience.)

## The Least You Need to Know

- Contrary to some perceptions, richer meats can be very appropriate for the quick-cooking methods of 20-minute cuisine.

- Smaller pieces of meat cook more quickly. (The ultimate example of this observation is ground beef, but beef strips follow the same logic.)

- The flavors of richer meats feature more prominently in recipes than lighter meats.

- Pan-frying and grilling are the beef and lamb cooking methods of choice for 20-minute cuisine.

# Chapter 12

# Vegetarian

## In This Chapter

- ◆ Vegetarian cuisine: a 20-minute natural
- ◆ Seasoning vegetarian dishes
- ◆ Vegetarian recipes as a way of life
- ◆ The need for speed

In the past, there has been a popular misunderstanding that vegetarian food meant brown rice and tofu, with implicit banishment to bland taste-bud purgatory. Nothing could be farther from the truth. Like any quality ingredient-based cooking, a focus on vegetarian ingredients presents an opportunity to let unique flavors and seasonings shine through in ways just not possible with meat-based dishes. In addition, vegetarian cuisine tends to be lower in fat and calories and is considered to be part of an extremely healthy diet.

There are several levels of vegetarianism, ranging from a diet that includes dairy products to a strict interpretation allowing no animal products whatsoever. For the purposes of this chapter, I use a definition that includes no meat of any kind, but does include animal products (eggs, milk, cheese, and so on).

# How Good Is Vegetarian Food?

Our family is not vegetarian, but when we took stock of recipes we love, and the day-by-day ingredients we choose, we were surprised by the number of vegetarian main course dishes that made our favorites list. Just as food for thought (sorry about the pun), here's the list:

- Fresh vegetable pasta
- Tortilla wraps
- Pizza (all kinds, such as sautéed onion and feta)
- Ratatouille
- Quick nachos
- Vegetable chili

There are many others that I've included in this chapter, but I found the number of meatless dishes we'll actively choose to be interesting. And although a number of recipes on this list could be considered "meatless alternatives," an equal number are just plain better because they use vegetables, fruits, and grains alone.

**Cook to Cook**

Many vegetarian recipes are perfect for 20-minute cuisine. Vegetables and herbs require shorter cooking times than meats and are much more flexible in their range of acceptable "doneness." Some people prefer their broccoli raw and crunchy, whereas others prefer it well cooked and soft; *the same range doesn't apply to chicken.*

The ingredients at the disposal of the vegetarian cook are different from those building blocks in the nonvegetarian kitchen. One fundamental requirement of a balanced vegetarian diet is that the ingredients provide the nutrients, such as protein, that come from meat, but of course also come from other sources (such as beans, brown rice and tofu!). Another goal, of course, is flavor and pleasure. In the absence of meat, vegetarian dishes taste different than meat dishes do because herbs and spices manifest themselves in different ways.

# Vegetarian Recipe Seasoning

The chart that follows suggests combinations based on their main ingredients: grains, tofu, beans, vegetables, dairy products, and eggs. Because many vegetarian dishes are flavorful mixtures, the purpose of this chart is to invite thought into the seasonings, moisture, and cooking method that will together build an appealing recipe and best spotlight these ingredients.

## Vegetarian Recipe Seasoning Guide

| Ingredient | Seasoning | Coating | Cooking Method |
|---|---|---|---|
| Grain dishes | Onion | Soy sauce | Steaming |
| Bean dishes | Cumin | Oil | Broiling |
| Cheese dishes | Chili powder | Butter | Microwave |
| Egg dishes | Garlic | Lemon juice | Grilling |
| Vegetable | Paprika | Lime juice | Baking |
| Tofu | Basil | Mustard | Frying |
| | Red pepper | Mayonnaise | |
| | Oregano | Egg | |
| | Cilantro | *Vegetable broth* | |
| | Ginger | | |
| | Rosemary | | |
| | Black pepper | | |
| | Marjoram | | |
| | Chives | | |
| | Coriander | | |
| | Fennel | | |
| | Tarragon | | |
| | Thyme | | |
| | Dill | | |

**Cook's Glossary**

**Vegetable broth** is a liquid that adds body and flavor to many dishes and serves as an alternative to chicken or beef broth in many recipes.

Let's see; for the columns to inspire a recipe, we could choose rice and beans, onion and red pepper, oil, and fry. Did somebody say New Orleans?

# Red Beans and Rice

Prep time: 5 minutes  •  Cook time: 13 minutes  •  Serves 4

| | |
|---|---|
| 2 TB. canola oil | 1 tsp. black pepper |
| 1 onion, chopped | 1 tsp. salt |
| 1½ tsp. Cajun seasoning or crushed red pepper | 3 cups prepared white rice |
| 1 TB. chopped garlic | Juice of ½ lemon |
| 1 cup vegetable broth | 8 oz. crumbled feta cheese |
| 1 (14.5-oz.) can red kidney beans | |

Heat oil in a large skillet over medium heat, and sauté onions and Cajun seasoning (or crushed red pepper) for five minutes. Add garlic and cook for one minute. Turn up the heat to medium high. Add broth, kidney beans, black pepper, and salt. Cook, stirring, for eight minutes. In the meantime, reheat rice (if it's left over). Turn off the heat below the skillet, stir in lemon juice and feta cheese, and pour red bean mixture over rice on serving plates.

### Cook to Cook

Many vegetarian dishes are naturally low in fat, a wonderful health benefit. For added flavor and texture, however, most recipes will call for moisture of some form to be added.

Red beans and rice, a classic dish from the South, is flavorful, rich, and a meal unto itself. Though not strictly authentic, I like to add crumbled creamy salty feta cheese to this savory mix. I'll leave that part up to you.

I suggest you review these recipes for common elements and methods. Same as before—once you know the tune, you can start making culinary music of your own.

# Sure-Fire Vegetarian Recipes

I've included here a range of recipes from soups to enchiladas. I hope you'll find them all both interesting and inspirational; vegetarian recipes can be found from all styles of cuisine.

# Rosemary's Quick Enchiladas

Colorful and tasty. This recipe can be doubled easily.

Prep time: 5 minutes    •    Cook time: 15 minutes    •    Serves 4 to 6

| | |
|---|---|
| 1 (16-oz.) can black beans (drained) | ½ tsp. cumin |
| 1 cup corn kernels (fresh, frozen, or canned) | ⅔ cup + ⅓ cup salsa |
| 4 oz. light cream cheese | 4 large flour tortillas |
| 8 oz. Monterey jack or cheddar cheese, shredded | |

Preheat oven to 400°F. Combine drained beans, corn, cream cheese, 4 ounces cheese, cumin, and ⅔ cup salsa in large pan. Heat until cheese is melted and ingredients are combined.

Place ¼ heated mixture in a tortilla and roll it up. Repeat until mixture is used up. Should make four medium or three large filled enchiladas. Place them close together in a baking pan. Spoon remaining ⅓ cup salsa over tightly spaced enchiladas. Sprinkle with remaining cheese. Bake 10 minutes, or until top is golden brown and bubbly.

# Butternut Squash Soup

This soup is the definition of richness and the antidote for a cold winter's day.

Prep time: 5 minutes    •    Cook time: 15 minutes    •    Serves 4

| | |
|---|---|
| 1 butternut squash | 1 cup sour cream |
| ¼ cup water | 2 egg yolks |
| 1 (16-oz.) can vegetable broth | Salt and pepper |

Slice squash in two lengthwise. Scrape out seeds and threads with a spoon. Place squash face down in a microwave-safe baking dish, add ¼ cup water, cover with plastic wrap (poke some steam holes on top), and microwave on high for 8 to 10 minutes. When squash has cooked and is soft, spoon squash flesh out of skin and into your food processor or blender, add some broth, and purée. Pour squash into a large saucepan with the rest of broth, and heat over high heat until it boils. Reduce heat.

In a small bowl, whisk together sour cream and egg yolks, and pour mixture into the saucepan, stirring. Cook for one minute over medium heat, season with salt and pepper, pour into soup bowls, and season with a dollop of sour cream, fresh chives or scallions, and a few toasted seeds.

# Make-Ahead Vegetable Lasagna

This is a vegetable-only version of my favorite, using rich portobello mushrooms in place of ground beef. Once again, I rationalize including this because it will last for several meals, becoming a make-ahead Easy Timesaver.

Prep time: 15 minutes  •  Cook time: 65 minutes (most unattended)  •  Serves 10 to 12

| | |
|---|---|
| 3 TB. olive oil | 1 lb. lasagna noodles |
| 2 medium onions, chopped | 6 cups 20-Minute Tomato Sauce (or your favorite pasta sauce) |
| 1 lb. portobello mushrooms, sliced | |
| 1 tsp. salt | 1 (2-lb.) container ricotta cheese |
| ½ tsp. ground black pepper | 2 (10-oz.) pkgs. frozen spinach, thawed and drained of excess water |
| 1 tsp. dried oregano | 1 lb. mozzarella, shredded |
| ½ tsp. crushed red pepper | ⅓ cup Parmesan cheese |

Preheat the oven to 350°F and boil water for lasagna noodles. In a large saucepan, heat olive oil over medium heat. Add onions and sauté for five minutes. Add sliced mushrooms, salt, pepper, oregano, and red pepper. Cook, stirring, for about six minutes, until browned and cooked through.

While mushrooms are cooking, cook lasagna noodles to al dente (still slightly firm), remove from water, and rinse with cold water to stop softening.

In a large casserole or baking dish, layer as follows:

Enough sauce to cover bottom

1 layer noodles

Half mushroom mixture

Half ricotta

All spinach

Half mozzarella

Half remaining sauce

Repeat, starting with pasta (omit spinach). Top with a layer of noodles and sauce. Reserve ½ cup mozzarella to put on top.

Top with Parmesan and remaining mozzarella cheeses. Bake for 45 to 55 minutes, until top is bubbly and any protruding noodles are crispy. Remove and let rest for 10 minutes. Then eat, refrigerate, cut for the freezer, or all the above.

# Potato and Leek Soup

This hearty soup will last for several meals and is a prime candidate for serving as a make-ahead Easy Timesaver.

Prep time: 5 minutes  •  Cook time: 15 minutes  •  Serves 6 to 8

5 (14.5-oz.) cans vegetable broth

4 TB. butter

White parts from 1 bunch of leeks, sliced thin and rinsed (Leeks have little notches at the base of exterior leaves that can hide soil.)

4 medium-size all-purpose potatoes, peeled and chopped

¼ cup sour cream

½ tsp. cumin

1 (4-oz.) pkg. fresh baby spinach

Salt and pepper

Heat broth to boiling in a large saucepan. While broth is heating, melt butter in a large skillet over high heat, and cook leeks for five minutes. Add leeks and potatoes to boiling broth and cook for 10 minutes until potato is soft. Add sour cream and cumin and cook for five minutes. Mix in the baby spinach, season with salt and pepper, and serve.

Delicious with fresh bread and cold, dry white wine.

**Cook to Cook**

For dishes that call for vegetable broth, you can also use Vegetarian Vegetable Bouillon, available in most grocery stores.

# Around the World with Flavor

In many parts of the world, vegetarian cuisine is a way of life. Vegetarian recipes, as a result, often come with a taste-bud tour of the world. Here are just a few delicious examples.

# Minestrone Pasta

Hearty and flavorful, this pasta dish inspires visions of our table on that romantic hillside in Tuscany. Again. This large recipe is good for two meals.

Prep time: 5 minutes • Cook time: 13 minutes • Serves 8

| | |
|---|---|
| 1 lb. gemelli or other small pasta | 2 zucchini, striped and chopped |
| 3 TB. olive oil | 1 TB. dried basil |
| 2 onions, chopped | 1 (15.5-oz.) can cannellini beans, drained |
| 1 tsp. chopped garlic | 2 cups 20-Minute Tomato Sauce |
| 1 (14.5-oz.) can vegetable broth | Salt and pepper |
| 2 carrots, scraped and chopped | Parmesan cheese |

Cook pasta. While pasta is cooking, heat oil in a large skillet over medium heat and sauté onions and garlic for five minutes. Add vegetable broth and carrots, bring to a boil, and cook for three minutes. Add zucchini, basil, cannellini beans, and tomato sauce. Heat to boiling, and cook for five minutes. When pasta is done, drain, and return to cooking pot. Add vegetable mixture, toss to thoroughly mix, and serve seasoned with salt, pepper, and Parmesan.

# Rice Palao

Prep time: 5 minutes • Cook time: 15 minutes • Serves 4

| | |
|---|---|
| 1 TB. butter | 1 tsp. salt |
| 1 TB. canola oil | 2 TB. golden raisins |
| 2 cups quick-cooking white rice | 8 cashews, sliced lengthwise |
| 1 tsp. ground cardamom | 10 almonds, sliced lengthwise |
| 1 bay leaf | ¼ tsp. ground cloves |
| 3½ cups water | ½ tsp. coriander |

Heat butter and oil in a large skillet over medium heat. Add rice, cardamom, and bay leaf. Cook, stirring, over medium heat until rice starts to stick. Add water and salt. When rice and water boils, add raisins, cashews, almonds, cloves, and coriander. Cover and cook 10 minutes or until done.

# Sautéed Greek Mushrooms

Prep time: 4 minutes   •   Cook time: 16 minutes   •   Serves 4

⅔ cups olive oil

1 TB. chopped garlic

2 tomatoes, chopped

1 cup dry white wine

½ cup water

½ tsp. coriander

½ tsp. dried oregano

¼ tsp. black pepper

1 bay leaf

1 lb. mushrooms, quartered if they are large, whole if they are small

Lemon wedges to season.

Salt

Heat oil in a large skillet over high heat. Add garlic and cook for one minute. Add the tomatoes, wine, water, coriander, oregano, black pepper, and bay leaf. Cook for seven minutes. Add mushrooms and cook for five minutes. Using a slotted spoon, remove mushrooms to a serving dish but continue to cook sauce for three to four minutes to reduce it. Pour sauce over mushrooms and pass the serving dish around the table with lemon wedges and salt to season.

# Spiced Vegetable Kebabs

Prep time: 10 minutes   •   Cook time: 10 minutes   •   Serves 4

Kebab skewers (available at most grocery stores)

1 large eggplant, peeled and cubed into 1-inch pieces

1 large red pepper, cored, seeded, and cut into 1-inch pieces

1 Vidalia onion, cut into 1-inch pieces

1 pint button mushrooms

2 TB. olive oil

2 tsp. spice seasoning blend featuring red pepper, pepper, paprika, and salt, such as Cajun, Italian, or even curry

Preheat the grill to medium-high. On each skewer, slide alternating pieces of eggplant, pepper, onion, and mushroom until the skewer is full. Repeat with other skewers. Mix olive oil and seasoning and drizzle generously over each skewer. Place skewers on grill over flame. Cook for 10 minutes, turning frequently.

**Cook to Cook**

This chapter is not the only place to find delicious, quick vegetarian recipes. Also check out Chapters 13, 14, and 18!

# Unbelievably Good Vegetarian Chili

This recipe will last for two meals or more.

Prep time: 5 minutes • Cook time: 20 minutes • Serves 8

3 TB. olive oil

1 large onion, coarsely chopped

1 (15.5-oz.) can cut corn, drained

1 (28-oz.) can plum tomatoes, with juice

1 (15.5-oz.) can red kidney beans

1 (15.5-oz.) can refried beans

2 cups 20-Minute Tomato Sauce

2 TB. chili powder

2 tsp. ground cumin

1 tsp. salt

½ tsp. ground black pepper

Heat olive oil in a large skillet over medium heat, add onion, and cook for eight minutes. Add corn, tomatoes with juice, kidney beans, refried beans, tomato sauce, chili powder, cumin, salt, and pepper. Stir to mix thoroughly, and simmer for 12 minutes.

With the rich mixture of spices and seasonings, this chili is a keeper with beef or without.

# Vegetarian Easy Timesavers

With vegetarian cuisine, many recipes that need speed also often use fresh ingredients and, as a result, are very appealing. Here are a few samples.

**Cook to Cook** _____

Every time you make a batch of pasta or rice, double it and store the extra in the fridge. This ready base is a huge assist when you need a meal on the fly.

# Bill's Arugula Pasta

Sour spicy arugula, sweet tomatoes, and rich Parmesan make this pasta something special. If you use pasta left over from last night, this can be a five-minute menu.

Prep time: 15 minutes    •    Serves 4 to 6

1-lb. box penne or other tube-shaped or ridged pasta

1 large bunch fresh arugula, well washed and drained

2 to 3 TB. olive oil

1 clove garlic (or to taste), chopped

8 to 9 plum tomatoes

Salt and pepper

8 oz. shredded mozzarella cheese

Parmesan cheese

Bring water for pasta to a boil. Add pasta and cook according to directions. Drain when finished and return to cooking pot. Turn off burner.

While pasta is cooking, wash and drain arugula. Chop roughly. Set aside. Combine oil and chopped garlic in mixing bowl. Chop tomatoes into eighths. Put in bowl with oil and garlic. Add salt and pepper to taste. Cover with plastic wrap and set aside.

Add tomato mixture to drained pasta and toss. Add mozzarella cheese and mix. Add arugula and toss together. Serve immediately. Finish with grated Parmesan cheese.

# Rice Medley

Prep time: 4 minutes    •    Cook time: 10 minutes    •    Serves 4

3 TB. olive oil

1 medium onion, chopped

1 tsp. crushed red pepper

8 oz. oil-packed sun-dried tomatoes, drained and chopped

3 cups cooked rice

½ cup sliced black olives

8 oz. feta cheese, crumbled

Salt and pepper

Heat olive oil in a large skillet over medium heat and sauté onion, red pepper, and sun-dried tomatoes for six minutes. Add rice and olives to skillet and heat, stirring, for four minutes. Stir in feta cheese and serve, passing the salt and pepper.

# Greek Cucumber Dip (Tsatsiki)

This dip is refreshing and delicious.

Prep time: 5 minutes  •  Serves 4

1 cup plain yogurt

½ cucumber, peeled and finely chopped

1 TB. chopped garlic

½ tsp. ground pepper

2 tsp. lemon juice

1 TB. olive oil

½ tsp. salt

Combine yogurt, cucumber, garlic, pepper, lemon juice, olive oil, and salt in a bowl and serve with pita bread.

**Cuisine Context** _____

Each ingredient brings its own image. This recipe, with feta and olives, evokes Greek food. Substitute chickpeas and cumin, and perhaps we're on the other side of the Mediterranean.

## The Least You Need to Know

◆ Cooking vegetarian presents an opportunity for unique flavors and seasonings to shine through in ways just not possible with meat-based dishes.

◆ In many parts of the world, vegetarian cuisine is a way of life. Vegetarian recipes, as a result, often come with a taste-bud tour of the world.

◆ Make-ahead bases, such as pasta, rice, and beans, are simple to make in large batches and are extremely useful to jump-start a quick meal.

◆ With vegetarian cuisine, many recipes that need extra speed often use extra fresh ingredients—a double bonus.

# Part 3

# Make the Meal Complete

I've included in this part all the elements that truly make a meal complete; starchy side dishes, vegetable dishes, breads, and of course desserts.

Side dishes, such as rice, pasta, and potatoes, balance a meat-based main course. Vegetable dishes are both important for nutritional balance (they take up a lot of real estate on the food pyramid), and a natural for 20-minute cuisine. Fresh vegetables are tasty and naturally quick cooking. Here you'll find some terrific, quick methods and recipes.

Breads form a comforting, essential part of many of our meals. We face a conundrum here, because most yeast breads take hours to cook. How do we solve this problem? Read on …

NO, A HEALTHY TWENTY-MINUTE MEAL *ISN'T* TWENTY BAGS OF MINUTE RICE.

# Chapter 13

# Show Your Good Side (on the Plate)

## In This Chapter

- ◆ White, instant, and brown rice
- ◆ New and "old" types of potatoes
- ◆ Save time with microwave potatoes and pasta

In Part 2, we reviewed the "main dish" part of our meal. We're most of the way through our meal, but as a painting looks better with a good frame, a main dish tastes better with a good side or two.

Your side dish brings balance. If the main dish features meat, it now needs a starch and a vegetable to attain nutritional completeness (remember the food pyramid from Chapter 1). With the exception of one-pot meals, which bring a range of ingredients, sides bring that balance. Sides also offer taste variety and interest—the ability to, for example, offset spiced meats with a soothing starch, like rice. In this chapter, we'll look at some terrific starchy sides and in the next at vegetable dishes.

# Magical Side Dishes

Part of the 20-minute challenge of sides, of course, is that they just can't take any extra time. For that reason, I've included many recipes where the main dish, like kebabs, include vegetables and rice. A meal complete as is!

**Cuisine Context**

Every culture has at least one staple ingredient, one that is served with every meal and often *is* the meal. A rich source of carbohydrates, these staples, including rice, pasta, and potatoes, are often considered "side dishes" in the United States.

This chapter reviews the basics for side-dish ingredients and preparation. We focus here on what I call the "magic ingredients" from Chapter 6: standards that work with almost any meal and can be made in double batches to lurk in the fridge to give you a head start the next night:

- Rice
- Potatoes
- Pasta

We've already devoted a lot of attention to pasta in Chapter 8, so here I focus mostly on rice and potatoes. Then, following the basics, I'll list recipes for my favorite side dishes that build on these basics.

# Rice: White, Instant, and Brown

Rice is grown throughout the world, from the United States to the Far East and is a staple for the peoples of many countries. For the purposes of this book, there are two types of rice: various types of white rice that can be prepared within 20 minutes, and brown rice and wild rices that take longer than 20 minutes to prepare.

**Flare-Up**

Overcooked rice can still be eaten, but it turns unappetizingly soggy. Test your rice after it has cooked for 15 minutes by scooping out some with a spoon and tasting it. It should still feel slightly firm against your teeth.

White rice is convenient, quick, and tasty. It is simultaneously quicker to prepare and lighter in color because it has had its outer parts, the bran and germ layers, removed. A drawback is that unless it has been fortified, white rice generally has a lower nutritional value than brown rice.

Instant rice is white rice that has been precooked to enable really quick heating, often 10 minutes or less. The trade-off for speed, however, is often texture and flavor. Cooking directions differ for each brand.

Brown rice offers a rich, nutty flavor and terrific nutritional value, and because of this should not be dismissed because of its long prep time. I prepare large batches and then use brown rice in recipes throughout the week. Cooking brown rice, or wild rice (which only resembles rice but is actually a different type of grain), takes 30 to 40 minutes.

# Boiled Rice (Both White and Brown)

Prep time: 2 minutes  •  Cook time: 15 minutes  •  Serves 8 to 10

| | |
|---|---|
| 6 cups water | 2 TB. butter |
| ½ tsp. salt | 3 cups white or brown rice |

Add water, salt, butter, and rice to a large saucepan. Bring to a boil and then simmer over low heat, covered. Check white rice after 15 minutes. When it's softened to your taste, remove from heat. Check brown rice after 30 minutes; when it's softened to your taste, remove from heat. Cooked brown rice is less soft than cooked white rice.

Serve as part of many main dishes, with butter, or with other ingredients such as herbs, vegetables, and cheese, for a more dressed-up side dish.

Enough for two to three meals. The butter is not critical but helps keep rice from sticking. This recipe is for a big batch, but as long as you maintain the 2:1 ratio of water to rice, you can vary the size of your batch.

**Cook to Cook**

Another way to add flavor and interest to rice is to use a flavorful broth instead of water as the cooking medium. Chicken, beef, and vegetable broth all work very well. I've also used the savory liquid left over from sautéing or steaming vegetables, and even the broth from poaching fish (as long as the fish is your main dish, and you don't mind carrying the seafood flavor theme over to your side dish!).

# You Say Potato, I Say ...

Originating in South America, potatoes have crossed oceans to become staples in many countries, from the United States to Europe. Satisfying, flavorful, and nutritious, the potato is extremely flexible. It can be fried, baked, microwaved, and boiled, and many potato-based dishes can be prepared in 20 minutes.

## New and Baking Potatoes

Even though there are many kinds of potatoes, for our purposes here we'll mash them into two types: "new" and "baking." New potatoes are generally small, thin-skinned potatoes that are sweeter (less starchy) than older potatoes, and are great for boiling and salads. Baking potatoes (you can also use "all-purpose" potatoes) are usually larger, thick-skinned, starchier potatoes great for baking, frying, mashing, and other uses.

# Boiled New Potatoes

A quick, easy, fail-safe way to cook new potatoes.

Prep time: 3 minutes • Cook time: 15 minutes • Serves 4

| | |
|---|---|
| 1½ lbs. new potatoes | 1 tsp. salt |
| Water to cover | |

Scrub potatoes with a vegetable brush. (I don't recommend peeling new potatoes, because much of the nutrition and taste is in the tender, thin skin.) Place potatoes in a large saucepan, cover with cold water, sprinkle with salt, and heat over high heat to boiling. Boil for about 15 minutes, or until tender enough for a fork to easily penetrate.

Distribute to serving plates, top with butter and salt and pepper for a simple, satisfying side. Other options include sprinkling with dill or chives or spreading with sour cream.

Make extra, then use the extras for Jen's Potato Salad.

❧

# Jen's Potato Salad

A delicious way to dress up cooked new potatoes

Prep time: 5 minutes • Serves 8

| | |
|---|---|
| 1½ lbs. new potatoes | 3 TB. prepared mustard |
| 3 TB. white vinegar | ½ tsp. dried dill |
| ⅓ cup mayonnaise | Salt and pepper to taste |

Prepare potatoes according to the instructions for Boiled New Potatoes. While they are still warm, place them in a large bowl, splash them with vinegar, then slice them into ⅓-inch-thick medallions. In a separate small bowl, mix mayonnaise, mustard, and dill, pour over potatoes, and toss to coat. Season with salt and pepper.

*Optional:* Add 3 tablespoons sweet relish or 1 small sweet onion, finely chopped.

❧

## Microwave Potatoes

The microwave and potatoes are natural partners for the cook in a hurry.

# Emergency Microwave Baked Potato

Prep time: 1 minute   •   Cook time: 8 minutes   •   Serves 4

4 potatoes (This is the shortest recipe in this book!)

Scrub baking or all-purpose potatoes, poke several holes in each with a fork, put them on a plate, and microwave on high for eight minutes or until soft, turning the plate once.

Serve with butter, salt and pepper, and sour cream.

**Flare-Up** _____

Put holes in potatoes before cooking them to allow the steam a place to escape. Otherwise, pressure builds, with possibility of creating the Amazing Exploding Side Dish.

# Microwave Sliced Potatoes

Prep time: 3 minutes   •   Cook time: 8 minutes   •   Serves 4 to 6

1½ lbs. baking potatoes                    ½ tsp. salt

1 cup water

Peel and slice potatoes crosswise in sections about ½ inch thick. Arrange slices in a microwave-safe baking dish with a lid, pour water over, and sprinkle with salt. Cover and microwave on high for eight minutes or until soft, turning dish once. Drain and serve with butter, salt, and pepper.

**Cook to Cook** _____

Microwave cooking times will vary according to the power of the oven. I've seen models that range from 600 to 1,200 watts. If you own one of the more powerful microwaves, test your dishes beforehand!

# Fast and Easy Scalloped Potatoes

This is a quick variation of the dish I ate all the time growing up.

Prep time: 4 minutes  •  Cook time: 16 minutes  •  Serves 4 to 6

1½ lbs. baking potatoes

1 cup milk

½ tsp. salt

3 TB. butter

1 large onion, sliced thin

Peel and slice potatoes. Follow the procedure for Microwave Sliced Potatoes, except use milk in place of water: Arrange slices (about ½ inch thick) in a microwave-safe baking dish with a lid, pour milk over, and sprinkle with salt. Cover and microwave on high for 8 minutes or until soft, turning dish 180 degrees once.

### Cook to Cook

Milk adds richness, and I also prefer butter over oil for the flavor, although olive oil will work fine.

While potatoes are cooking, heat butter in a large skillet over medium heat and cook onions during the whole time the potatoes are cooking. They will turn soft, translucent, and sweet.

When potatoes are done, add them to the skillet with milk, turn heat to high, and cook for eight minutes.

Serve with salt and pepper, and, if you like, a sprinkling of Parmesan cheese. Add chopped ham when adding potatoes to the skillet for a quick, hearty main course.

# Skillet Potatoes

These potatoes are given a head start in the microwave, then finished in the frying pan. Crisp outside, tender inside—this method is a kid favorite. They'll want ketchup.

Prep time: 5 minutes  •  Cook time: 15 minutes  •  Serves 4 to 6

4 large baking potatoes

2 TB. canola oil

**For skillet:**

½ cup canola oil

1 tsp. salt

Scrub potatoes and slice lengthwise into sections that resemble dill pickle spears. Place spears in a large microwave-safe bowl, drizzle with the 2 tablespoons canola oil (to prevent sticking) and microwave on high for 5 minutes.

While potatoes are cooking in the microwave, heat ½ cup oil in a large skillet. With a fork, transfer potato spears to the heated frying pan, arranging them in a single layer. Sprinkle with salt. Cook for 10 minutes over medium heat, turning to ensure that all sides are cooked. Re-move when done to drain on a plate with paper towels.

## Easy Mashed Potatoes

There is a comfort-food bell somewhere that rings every time this dish is served. This recipe uses the microwave to accelerate the process.

Prep time: 7 minutes  •  Cook time: 13 minutes  •  Serves 4

4 large potatoes, peeled and cut into 1-inch cubes

Salt

½ cup milk

4 TB. butter

Arrange cubes in a microwave-safe baking dish and sprinkle with salt. Cover and microwave on high for 12 minutes or until soft. Then, heat milk for 1 minute in the microwave, adding butter to milk for the last 30 seconds (butter will not totally melt, but it will soften).

Pour butter-and-milk mixture over potatoes. Mash with a fork or a mashing tool to get rid of the big lumps. Blend with a whisk or hand beater to make potatoes lighter and creamier. Don't mash too much; some lumps are okay.

One classic variation on mashed potatoes is *garlic* mashed potatoes. While the potatoes are cooking, boil 5 cloves of garlic in a small saucepan for about 15 minutes, until the cloves are soft. Then, with a food processor or a blender, thoroughly mix garlic with butter-and-milk mixture before whipping it into the potatoes.

# Side Dish Easy Timesavers

Here are a few more favorite pasta recipes, perfect for side dishes.

## Brendan's Penne Pasta Salad

Much too simple to be this good.

Prep time: 8 minutes  •  Serves 6 to 8

1 (1-lb. pkg.) penne pasta, cooked

1 bag spinach, washed and coarsely chopped

1 large sweet onion, such as Vidalia, finely chopped

1 (6.5-oz.) can sliced olives, drained

1 lb. feta, crumbled

1 (8-oz.) bottle Caesar dressing

Mix pasta, spinach, onion, olives, and feta. Pour dressing over and toss to coat ingredients. Serve, sit back, and watch it disappear.

# Carol Ann's Tortellini Salad

Prep time: 8 minutes • Serves 6 to 8

1 lb. tortellini (your favorite variety)

1 lb. frozen Italian vegetables

½ cup bottled Italian dressing

¼ cup shredded Parmesan cheese

¼ tsp. garlic powder

½ tsp. dried basil

Salt and pepper to taste

Cook tortellini according to directions. Put vegetables in colander in sink. Drain tortellini over colander to rapidly heat vegetables. Rinse with cold water. Put tortellini-vegetable mixture in a large bowl and mix with dressing, cheese, garlic powder, and basil. Salt and pepper to taste and serve.

## The Least You Need to Know

- ◆ Rice, potatoes, and pasta help bring nutritional and taste balance to a meal.
- ◆ White rice is quick to prepare, but brown rice is higher in nutrition.
- ◆ The potato is simple and quick to prepare in the microwave … or at least with the help of the microwave.

# Savor the Season: Quick Vegetable Dishes

## In This Chapter

- ◆ Salads 101
- ◆ Take advantage of fresh flavors
- ◆ Quick-cooked vegetable recipes

Almost more than any other ingredient, vegetables are perfect for 20-minute cuisine. They often require either no cooking or a bare minimum. Most of the flavor is already there, bursting from the fresh peppers, onions, tomatoes, greens, and herbs you'll be using; to subject them to extensive heating and preparation is to risk losing the taste and nutrition that's already there. If your potato, rice, or pasta brings balance and heartiness, vegetables bring taste and freshness. This chapter focuses on fresh and offers several ways to prepare, serve, and enjoy delicious vegetable dishes.

## Salads 101

The first, the easiest, and one of my favorite vegetable dishes is a garden salad. Because a salad requires no cooking and can be as simple or as elegant as you want to make it, it's an easy finishing touch that helps move a meal from fuel to pleasure. And without the need for cooking, the time needed for preparation is measured in single-digit minutes.

To give a sense of the potential of a salad, Janet's Salad Grid (that follows) lists some of the many ingredients that can be used. If your image of a salad is lettuce and dressing, this might show just how far you can go—and these are only the most common ingredients!

A sure winner will always have a vegetable and a source of moisture, most often an acid and an oil such as vinegar and olive oil. Adding ingredients from other columns adds variety and interest.

## Janet's Salad Grid

| Vegetables | Moisture | Seasoning | Fruit | Meat/Cheese | Nuts |
|---|---|---|---|---|---|
| Lettuce | Olive oil | Parsley | Cherries | Ham | Almonds |
| Mesclun | Canola oil | Dill | Cranberries | Chicken | Peanuts |
| Spinach | Lemon juice | Basil | Grapes | Shrimp | Walnuts |
| Tomatoes | Wine vinegar | Cilantro | Apples | Steak | Soy |
| Cucumbers | Cider vinegar | Chives | Pears | Mozzarella | Pine |
| Carrots | Balsamic vinegar | Garlic | Olives | Blue cheese | |
| Onions | Mayonnaise | Tarragon | Others | Cheddar | |
| Avocados | Dressings | Fennel | | Parmesan | |
| Celery | Others | Sugar | | Feta | |
| Others | | Others | | Others | |

## Salad Dressings

Salad dressings, of course, come in a huge range of flavors and prices. Ready right out of the bottle, they are an essential for the weeknight salad. Different types of dressings are appropriate for different meals. Popular varieties include the following:

- Oil dressings, including vinegar and oil, Italian, and others

- Rich dressings, including ranch, thousand island, Russian, and others

- Cheese dressings, with names like blue cheese, Parmesan, cracked pepper, and so on

Think about the dressing you choose in the context of your main dish. If you're serving a light fish dish, for example, consider a salad with oil dressing rather than potentially overwhelming blue cheese.

**Flare-Up**

Consider using tomatoes in your salad only when they are in season, or when you are willing to splurge on hothouse fruit. February tomatoes, shipped over long distances, usually just won't have the flavor and texture that makes them pleasant to eat.

## Salad Favorites

The following are some of my favorite salads, starting with the basics. I then move on to some salad variations that bring an ordinary salad to new heights of flavor and interest.

# Tossed Salad

As per Janet's Salad Grid, variations are almost infinite, but a natural enhancement is to top this salad, after you have dressed it, with croutons.

Prep time: 5 minutes   •   Serves 4 to 6

2 medium heads romaine lettuce (or your favorite)

⅓ Vidalia onion, thinly sliced

1 large fresh tomato, sliced thin and then each slice quartered

1 carrot, scraped, sliced lengthwise, and cross-cut into ¼-inch pieces

Wash lettuce, break into bite-size pieces, and dry. (This is where your salad spinner comes in handy.) Place lettuce in a large serving bowl. Top with onion, tomato, and carrot and serve tossed with your favorite dressing.

**Cook to Cook**

To make a quick dinner salad, add ½ pound chopped ham and ½ pound cubed or shredded cheddar cheese and serve with bread.

# Jean's Oriental Cabbage Salad

Prep time: 5 minutes • Serves 4 to 6

6 TB. wine vinegar

½ cup canola oil

6 TB. sugar

Spice packet from 1 (3-oz.) package ramen noodle soup mix (oriental flavor)

Noodles from soup mix

6 cups shredded cabbage

1 cup peanuts

6 TB. sesame seeds

Mix vinegar, oil, sugar, and spice packet in a small bowl and set aside. Crumble dry noodles and mix into cabbage. Add peanuts. Pour dressing over salad, add sesame seeds, toss salad thoroughly, and serve.

# Pear and Walnut Salad

An exotic, delicious salad.

Prep time: 10 minutes • Cook time: 10 minutes (concurrent with prep time) • Serves 4

½ cup walnuts

6 TB. walnut oil

2 TB. sherry vinegar

1 tsp. Dijon mustard

1 TB. sherry

2 tsp. runny honey (heat in microwave)

Black pepper

1 pkg. mesclun salad

½ cup crumbled blue cheese

1 pear, cored and sliced thinly

Preheat oven to 350°F and toast walnuts on a baking tray for 10 minutes. While walnuts are toasting, mix walnut oil, vinegar, mustard, sherry, honey, and pepper. Put mesclun in a serving bowl. Pour dressing over salad and toss well, add blue cheese, arrange pear slices, and top with toasted walnuts.

**Cook to Cook**

In a hurry? Many fresh vegetables can be served with a minimum of preparation. Carrots and cucumbers need only to be scraped, sliced, and served with salt and pepper, vinegar, or salad dressing to be a tasty, nutritious snack or side dish. Broccoli, cauliflower, and even beans can be washed, cut, and served with a dip or dressing as well.

## Spinach Salad

This salad could also easily serve as a light meal.

Prep time: 8 minutes  •  Cook time: 8 minutes (concurrent with prep time)  •  Serves 4 to 6

¼ lb. bacon

1 (10-oz.) pkg. baby spinach

2 hard-boiled eggs, sliced

¼ lb. fresh mushrooms, sliced

Oil-based dressing

1 cup croutons (your favorite flavor)

Cook bacon until crispy; dry on paper towels and crumble into ½-inch pieces. In a large bowl, combine spinach, eggs, mushrooms, and bacon. Dress and toss to coat salad. Top with croutons and serve.

# Cooked Vegetable Dishes

Many vegetables are extremely appealing with a minimum of preparation and seasoning. Their fresh flavors shine through all the more because of your light touch. This is a sample of some of my quick favorites.

## Sautéed Green Beans and Scallions

Olive oil will work, but the butter flavor is just terrific.

Prep time: 4 minutes  •  Cook time: 14 minutes  •  Serves 4 to 6

3 TB. butter

1 bunch (6 to 8) scallions, washed, with roots and dark green parts cut off, white and light green part cut into ¼-inch sections

1 lb. green beans, trimmed

1 TB. balsamic vinegar

Salt and pepper

Melt butter in a large skillet over medium heat. Sauté scallions for eight minutes or until soft. Add beans and sauté, stirring, for an additional six minutes or until beans reach the tenderness you like. Remove from heat, drizzle with balsamic vinegar, and serve with salt and pepper.

**Flare-Up**

Be careful not to overcook vegetables. They become soggy and lose their flavor. The more snap, the more flavor you'll get, and the quicker you'll be ready to eat.

# Pepper Medley

Prep time: 5 minutes   •   Cook time: 10 minutes   •   Serves 4 to 6

3 TB. olive oil

1 small onion, chopped

2 tsp. chopped garlic

1 large red pepper, seeded and sliced crosswise into rings

1 large yellow pepper, seeded and sliced crosswise into rings

1 large green pepper, seeded and sliced crosswise into rings

Salt and pepper

Heat oil in a large skillet over medium heat. Sauté onion and garlic for five minutes. Add red, yellow, and green peppers and cook, stirring, for five minutes. Serve with salt and pepper.

**Cook to Cook**

For an Easy Timesaver, look in your grocer's frozen foods section for one-pound packages of frozen red, yellow, and green peppers. Ready to go!

# Quick Chinese Cabbage Stir-Fry

Prep time: 5 minutes   •   Cook time: 12 minutes   •   Serves 4 to 6

2 TB. oil (If you've got sesame oil, use 1 TB. canola and 1 TB. sesame oil; otherwise use 2 TB. canola oil.)

1 small onion, sliced thin

½ head *bok choy* or *Chinese cabbage*, sliced into bite-size pieces, keeping the thick stalk ends separate from the leaves

1 TB. soy sauce

Salt and pepper

Heat oil in a wok or large skillet over medium heat and cook onion for five minutes. Add bok choy or cabbage stalks and cook for four minutes. Add leaves and soy sauce, cook for two to three minutes or until leaves have wilted, and serve with salt and pepper.

**Cook's Glossary**

**Bok choy** and **Chinese cabbage** are both members of the cabbage family, with thick stems, crisp texture, and fresh flavor. They are just perfect for stir-frying.

# Bacon and Cabbage

Prep time: 5 minutes    •    Cook time: 15 minutes    •    Serves 4 to 6

| | |
|---|---|
| ½ head cabbage, sliced into ribbons about 3 inches long | ½ tsp. thyme |
| | ½ tsp. sage |
| 1 lb. bacon | Salt and pepper |

Steam cabbage in a vegetable steamer for 15 minutes or until done. While cabbage is steaming, fry bacon in a large skillet over medium heat until crispy. Remove bacon to paper towels. Add cooked cabbage to rendered bacon fat in the skillet. Sprinkle with thyme and sage. Cook one minute, stirring. Crumble bacon into cabbage, stir to mix, and serve with salt and pepper.

Add 3 cups cooked rice to the skillet during the last few minutes of cooking to create a quick, hearty main dish.

# Corn and Red Pepper Mélange

Savory and delicious, you'll have people asking for seconds.

Prep time: 5 minutes    •    Cook time: 15 minutes    •    Serves 4 to 6

| | |
|---|---|
| 2 TB. olive oil | 2 large sweet red peppers, chopped |
| 1 large onion, chopped | 1 tsp. crushed red pepper |
| 2 tsp. chopped garlic | 1 tsp. paprika |
| 1 (1-lb.) pkg. frozen corn or 2 (15.5-oz.) cans corn kernels, drained | 8 oz. crumbled feta cheese |
| | Salt and pepper |

Heat oil in a large skillet over medium heat. Cook onion and garlic for five minutes. Add corn, red pepper, crushed red pepper, and paprika and cook for four minutes. If corn is frozen, add it to the skillet first, cook for two minutes; then add red pepper, crushed red pepper, and paprika and cook for four minutes. Add feta cheese, cover, and cook for one minute.

Serve with salt and pepper. Serve mixed with 1 pound cooked lamb pieces to make a tempting one-dish meal.

**Cook's Glossary**

**Mélange** is French for "a mixture" or "a blend." I have a lot more fun calling something I'm cooking a "mélange" rather than a "mix."

# Cheesy Broccoli

I haven't met anyone yet who objects to cheese sauce!

**Prep time: 3 minutes  •  Cook time: 15 minutes  •  Serves 4 to 6**

| | |
|---|---|
| 1 head broccoli, washed and cut into florets | 1 TB. Madeira wine (or cooking sherry) |
| **Sauce:** | 3 TB. flour |
| 2 TB. butter | ½ cup shredded Swiss cheese |
| 1 cup milk | Salt and pepper |

Steam broccoli in a vegetable steamer or saucepan with one inch water over medium-high heat for 15 minutes or until cooked to desired softness.

While broccoli is steaming, melt butter in a skillet. Heat milk in a microwave-safe measuring cup in the microwave on high for one minute.

Add Madeira and flour to the skillet, stirring, until mixture thickens and bubbles. Add milk to the skillet, stirring. The sauce will thicken. Then slowly add cheese, stirring until cheese melts.

Season sauce with salt and pepper to taste. Distribute the broccoli to serving plates and pour melted cheese over each helping.

# Sautéed Mushrooms, Olives, and Sun-Dried Tomato Penne

**Prep time: 5 minutes  •  Cook time: 15 minutes  •  Serves 4 to 6**

| | |
|---|---|
| 1 lb. penne pasta | ⅓ cup chicken broth |
| ⅓ cup olive oil | 1 lb. button mushrooms, cut in half |
| 2 tsp. chopped garlic | 1 cup Kalamata olives |
| 1 tsp. oregano, dried | ½ cup oil-packed sun-dried tomatoes, drained and chopped |
| 1 tsp. basil, dried | 1 TB. lime juice |
| ½ tsp. salt | |
| 1 bay leaf | |

Cook pasta. While pasta is cooking, in a large saucepan combine oil, garlic, oregano, basil, salt, and bay leaf. Stir for three minutes over medium heat. Add broth and cook over medium-high heat for five minutes. Add mushrooms, reduce heat to low, and cook for five minutes, covered. Add olives and sun-dried tomatoes, cook for one minute more, remove from heat, and drizzle with lime juice. Distribute pasta to serving plates top with mushroom mixture, and serve.

# Onion Rings

A classic that's always popular, using whole-wheat flour for added flavor and maybe a bit of nutrition.

Prep time: 5 minutes  •  Cook time: 12 minutes  •  Serves 4

¾ cup canola oil

1 egg

¼ cup milk

1 large Vidalia or other sweet onion, sliced crosswise and rings separated

1 cup whole-wheat flour

Salt to taste

Heat oil in a small skillet over medium-high heat (oil should be at least ⅓ inch deep). In a bowl, whisk egg and milk. In a separate bowl, spread flour. Dip onion rings in egg-milk mixture; then dredge through flour to thoroughly coat. Cook several pieces at once in oil for four minutes per piece or until browned and crispy, turning once. Drain on paper towels and serve.

**Cuisine Context** _____

Several vegetables get along quite well with the microwave. Cooked in a loosely covered microwave-safe dish with a little water, the effect is quite like steaming. This method works with peas, beans, summer squash, sliced carrots, and corn, to name just a few.

## The Least You Need to Know

♦ For a healthy side dish with minimum prep time, use raw vegetables, from salad to cut carrots.

♦ For reliable and instant weeknight salad, get acquainted with the packaged salad section of your grocery store. Convenience never tasted so good.

♦ Fresh flavors of good vegetables respond well to quick cooking and a minimum of seasoning, both attributes that make vegetables a natural part of 20-minute cuisine.

♦ Many cooked vegetable dishes can become one-pot meals by serving with rice or pasta, and adding cheese, or even cooked meat.

# Chapter 15

# Breads

## In This Chapter

- The wonder food
- Quick breads
- Bread machine magic
- Bread recipes

No discussion of any meal, whether it takes 20 minutes or a week, is complete without some discussion of bread. From the simplest slice to the heartiest loaf, bread brings with it connotations of warmth, richness, and comfort.

In this chapter we discuss how bread can be a realistic part of 20-minute cuisine. We face a conundrum here, because yeast-risen bread takes hours to prepare, yet I don't think you or I are willing to give it up. I suggest several solutions to the challenge of good bread in a hurry:

- **Quick breads and muffins.** These take 20 minutes or less to prepare.
- **Bread machine breads.** These take two hours or more in the machine, but only five minutes of *your time* to measure and load the ingredients. A loaf of bread machine bread will last for a dinner and then breakfast the next morning—not bad for a five-minute investment. I like to make

a couple loaves on the weekend, and then use them during the early part of the work week. I enthusiastically believe that the bread machine, and the hours of work it does for us, is a critical tool for 20-minute cuisine.

♦ **Easy Timesavers:** buying ready-made bread from the grocery store or your favorite bakery.

# Quick Breads

These breads rely on a chemical agent such as baking powder or baking soda to create the little bubbles of carbon dioxide that raise bread and make it light. Yeast breads rely on the yeast to do the same thing.

## Scones

Less sweet than scones you might find at the bakery, these are hearty and rich and just perfect with butter and jelly.

Prep time: 5 minutes • Cook time: 15 minutes • Serves 4 to 6

1¾ cups flour

¼ cup wheat germ

2 tsp. baking powder

1 tsp. sugar

½ tsp. salt

4 TB. butter

¾ cup sour cream

2 eggs, beaten

½ cup currants (optional)

Preheat oven to 425°F. In a bowl, mix flour, wheat germ, baking powder, sugar, and salt. Add this mixture to a food processor and, with the cutting blades, blend in butter until mixture is fine and crumbly. Mix in sour cream and eggs. Add currants, if using. Turn dough onto a floured counter, knead for a minute, then flatten with your hands to about ¾ inch thick. Cut into wedges, place in a greased baking pan or cookie sheet, and bake for 15 minutes or until done.

**Cook to Cook**

If you would like sweeter scones, use 1 tablespoon sugar in the dough, and, before putting scones in the oven, brush them with melted butter and sprinkle them with more sugar. That brushed butter is also what gives scones that great glazed look.

# Skillet-Baked Cornbread

Prep time: 3 minutes   •   Cook time: 17 minutes   •   Serves 4 to 6

| | |
|---|---|
| 1 cup flour | 1 egg |
| 1 tsp. salt | 1 TB. honey |
| 2 tsp. baking powder | ¾ cup milk |
| 1 cup cornmeal | ¼ cup sour cream |
| ¼ cup sugar | ¼ cup canola oil |

Preheat oven to 425°F. In a large bowl mix flour, salt, baking powder, cornmeal, and sugar. In a small bowl, whisk egg, honey, milk, and sour cream, pour into large bowl, and mix into dry ingredients. Heat oil in a medium (12-inch) cast-iron or oven-safe skillet. Pour oil onto dough and stir to mix. Scrape dough into hot skillet, place in oven, and cook for 17 minutes or until top browns.

# Buttermilk Biscuits

Nicely browned on the outside, moist and chewy on the inside.

Prep time: 5 minutes   •   Cook time: 15 minutes   •   Serves 4 to 6

| | |
|---|---|
| 1¾ cups flour | 5 TB. butter (if using salted butter, omit ½ tsp. salt), cut into pieces |
| ¼ cup buttermilk powder | |
| 2 tsp. sugar | ⅔ cup water (if you have fresh buttermilk, use ⅔ cup buttermilk instead of water and 2 cups flour) |
| 1 TB. baking powder | |
| ½ tsp. salt | |

Preheat oven to 450°F. In a bowl, mix flour, buttermilk powder, sugar, baking powder, and salt. Add to a food processor and, using the cutting blades, blend in butter until mixture is fine and crumbly. Remove to a mixing bowl and stir in water until it is absorbed and dough becomes uniform.

Turn dough onto a floured counter, knead for a minute, then flatten with your hands to about ¾ inch thick. Cut into wedges (or shapes if you have a cookie cutter), place in a greased baking pan or cookie pan, and bake for 15 minutes or until browned and crusty.

# Yeast Breads

A lot of people have a bread machine they received as a gift, hiding in the closet or cabinet. It sits there, ominous … and unused. Dust off that machine and give it a whirl. Fresh bread is wholesome, nutritious, and a pleasure to eat. Even if you don't already own a bread machine, consider the investment. Less than five minutes in the morning is enough to add ingredients and set the timer on a typical machine.

> **Cuisine Context**
>
> With the price of bread machines coming down, and their capabilities increasing, a fresh loaf of bread is within reach for dinner tonight.

When you get home from work, the kitchen is filled with warm, yeasty baking smells, and a fresh, hot loaf of bread is waiting for you. *Now that's a "welcome home" smell!*

I've recounted here a couple basic recipes and some other favorites that offer wholesome ingredients and rich flavor. I've assumed you're using a bread machine that makes a 1½-pound loaf. Ingredients can be scaled to make a larger loaf.

> **Cuisine Context**
>
> A teaspoon of yeast contains many millions of tiny fungi that react with water, sugar, flour, and heat to release carbon dioxide bubbles. These bubbles raise your bread. The yeast also provides that wonderful warm, rich smell and flavor.

# Basic White Bread

Prep time: 5 minutes  •  Cook time: about 150 minutes, depending on the machine (unattended)  •  Serves 4 for two meals

| | |
|---|---|
| 1½ cups water | 3 cups white flour |
| 2 TB. honey | 2½ tsp. yeast |
| 1½ tsp. salt | |

Add water, honey, salt, and flour to machine. Make an indentation in flour and add yeast. Bake per machine instructions.

### Cuisine Context

For most bread machines, follow this procedure:

- ◆ Add liquid (water, milk, etc.) to bread machine pan.
- ◆ Add dry ingredients, salt first.
- ◆ Add yeast last, pouring into a small indentation in the top of flour.

# Buttermilk Oat Bread

This bread is delicious toasted.

Prep time: 5 minutes  •  Cook time: about 150 minutes, depending on the machine (unattended)  •  Serves 4 for two meals

| | |
|---|---|
| 1½ cups buttermilk (or 1½ cups water and ⅓ cup buttermilk powder added with dry ingredients) | 1 cup oatmeal |
| | 1½ cups bread flour |
| | ½ cup whole-wheat flour |
| 2 TB. honey | 2½ tsp. yeast |
| 1 tsp. salt | |

Add buttermilk, honey, salt, oatmeal, bread flour, and whole-wheat flour to machine. Make an indentation in flour and add yeast. Bake per machine instructions.

# Healthy White Bread

I've added just a touch of wheat germ and whole-wheat flour for nutrition and nutty flavor.

Prep time: 5 minutes   •   Cook time: about 150 minutes, depending on the machine (unattended)   •   Serves 4 for two meals

| | |
|---|---|
| 1½ cups water | ¼ cup wheat germ |
| 2 TB. honey (optional) | ½ cup whole-wheat flour |
| 1½ tsp. salt | ½ tsp. yeast |
| 2¼ cups white flour | |

Add water, honey (if using), salt, white flour, wheat germ, and whole-wheat flour to machine. Make an indentation in flour and add yeast. Bake per machine instructions.

> **Flare-Up**
>
> Good bread dough should form a soft ball. The first time you try a specific bread recipe, watch the machine get to work during the first few minutes to ensure the dough is not too dry or too moist. If it's too dry and crumbly, add liquid a tablespoon at a time. If it's too wet and spongy, add flour a tablespoon at a time.

# Rich Breakfast Bread

Prep time: 5 minutes   •   Cook time: about 150 minutes, depending on the machine (unattended)   •   Serves 4 for two meals

| | |
|---|---|
| 1½ cups milk | 2½ cups white flour |
| 1 egg, beaten | ⅔ cup whole-wheat flour |
| 1½ TB. honey | ¼ cup buckwheat flour |
| 1 tsp. salt | 2½ tsp. yeast |

Add milk, eggs, honey, salt, white flour, whole-wheat flour, and buckwheat flour to machine. Make an indentation in flour and add yeast. Bake per machine instructions.

> **Cook to Cook**
>
> Bread flour and all-purpose flour will both work in recipes calling for white flour, although bread flour works slightly better.

# Delicious Whole Wheat

This recipe calls for a special King Arthur brand "100% white whole-wheat" flour. Regular whole-wheat flour can be substituted.

Prep time: 5 minutes   •   Cook time: about 150 minutes, depending on the machine (unattended)   •   Serves 4 for two meals

| | |
|---|---|
| 1½ cups warm water | ⅔ cup eight-grain flour |
| 3 TB. canola oil | 2 cups 100% white whole-wheat flour |
| 3 TB. honey | 2 TB. gluten |
| 1½ tsp. salt | 3 tsp. yeast |
| ½ cup white flour | |

Add water, oil, honey, salt, white flour, eight-grain flour, whole-wheat flour, and gluten to machine. Make an indentation in flour and add yeast. Bake per machine instructions.

≈

# Wheatena Bread

The popular hot cereal brings a nutty crunch to this bread.

Prep time: 5 minutes   •   Cook time: about 150 minutes, depending on the machine (unattended)   •   Serves 4 for two meals

| | |
|---|---|
| 1⅓ cups water (or 1¼ cup buttermilk) | ⅓ cup buttermilk powder |
| 2½ TB. honey | ½ cup whole-wheat flour |
| 1½ tsp. salt | ⅓ cup Wheatena |
| 2 cups white flour | 2½ tsp. yeast |

Add water, honey, salt, white flour, buttermilk powder, whole-wheat flour, and Wheatena to machine. Make an indentation in dry ingredients and add yeast. Bake per machine instructions.

≈

# Banana-Oatmeal Breakfast Bread

Toasted with jelly, this is a slice of the perfect breakfast.

Prep time: 5 minutes • Cook time: about 150 minutes, depending on the machine (unattended) • Serves 4 for two meals

1 overripe banana, mashed with a fork in a 2-cup measuring cup

Milk poured over the banana to reach the 1¼ cup line

2½ TB. canola oil

⅓ cup molasses

1 egg

1½ tsp. salt

1 tsp. *baking spice* (or cinnamon)

2½ cups white flour

1 cup oatmeal

½ cup whole-wheat flour

2½ tsp. yeast

Add banana-milk mixture, oil, molasses, egg, salt, baking spice, white flour, oatmeal, and whole-wheat flour. Make an indentation in flour and add yeast. Bake per machine instructions.

### Cook's Glossary

**Baking spice** is a rich mixture of seasonings associated with dessert, usually including cinnamon, nutmeg, cloves, and allspice. It is very similar to apple pie spice, which can also be used.

# Bread Easy Timesavers

I've ignored up until now the 600-pound gorilla in the grocery store: the entire aisle devoted to nothing but prepared bread. Now that I hope you've seen that making bread is actually quite simple and quick, I'll admit that that aisle exists.

*We don't always have even five minutes ahead of time to make something.*

### Cook to Cook

Although making bread is fun, buying it is often more convenient and a great way to try something new and then experiment with making it in the bread machine.

I always keep a loaf of whole-wheat sliced bread from the grocers in my freezer, ready to go in seconds for sandwiches or to serve with dinner. Even better, I've plotted the bakeries close to my house.

If I'm in a hurry but still want good bread, the kind only a baker can provide, I know where to go, and a ready-made, flavorful loaf of bread on the side is only a few dollars away.

# Recipes Where Bread Is the Star

Several recipes in this book explicitly call for bread, including the following: French Toast, and just plain *toast* (see Chapter 7) and Fondue (see Chapter 21).

This is in addition, of course, to all the recipes throughout that simply say "Serve with bread." Here are a few of my other bread-intensive favorites.

## Bruschetta

The perfect destiny for Italian bread.

Prep time: 5 minutes  •  Cook time: 5 minutes  •  Serves 6 to 8

| | |
|---|---|
| 1 loaf Italian bread | 2 tomatoes, chopped |
| 1 TB. garlic | 2 tsp. dried basil |
| 2 TB. olive oil | 1 tsp. kosher salt |

Slice bread into ½-inch slices, and toast or broil each side to a light brown. Mix garlic and 1 tablespoon olive oil in a cup and brush each side of each piece of bread with some of the mixture. In another bowl, mix tomatoes, basil, remaining olive oil, and salt. Top each piece of bread with a portion of tomatoes and serve.

**Flare-Up**

Although the broiler is a terrific tool for quick cooking, be sure to watch bread closely. The difference between lightly toasted and burnt offering is a matter of seconds.

# Jamie's Welsh Rarebit

This version, from friends in Scotland (just a bit closer to Wales), is quicker than stateside rarebit and is perfect for thick slices of homemade bread.

Prep time: 3 minutes • Cook time: 5 minutes • Serves 4

4 thick slices bread

8 oz. sharp cheddar cheese, grated

1 TB. mayonnaise

1 tsp. mustard

Toast bread in a toaster or under the broiler (turn it once) until browned and slightly crisp on both sides. Mix cheese, mayonnaise, and mustard in a bowl. Spread over toast, and then place under the broiler for three minutes or until hot and bubbling. Serve immediately.

# Sun-Dried Tomato Canapés

A quick *hors d'oeuvre* with thinly sliced bread as the vehicle of choice.

Prep time: 5 minutes • Cook time: 8 minutes • Serves 4

1 baguette or long loaf of bread, sliced into ½-inch thick pieces

2 tsp. crushed garlic

½ cup olive oil

¾ tsp. salt

1 (8-oz.) jar oil-packed sun-dried tomatoes, drained and chopped

1 cup shredded mozzarella cheese

Preheat your broiler. Arrange bread slices in a single layer side by side on a baking tray. Mix garlic, olive oil, and salt in a small bowl, and brush some of mixture on each piece of bread. Broil for two minutes, or until just barely beginning to brown. Turn the pieces over. Brush again with olive oil mixture, then broil again until just turning light brown.

Remove tray from oven, distribute tomato pieces among slices of bread, then top each piece of bread with a pinch of mozzarella.

Broil again for one minute, or until cheese is melted. Serve warm canapés to guests, and receive warm appreciation.

Ingredients for *canapés* are limited only by imagination. Popular ingredients include the following:

◆ Cream cheese

◆ Parmesan cheese

◆ Roasted peppers

◆ Sliced black olives

◆ Asparagus tips

**Cook's Glossary**

**Hors d'oeuvres** are appetizers. **Canapés** are hors d'oeuvres made up of small toasts topped with your favorite ingredients (commonly cheese, vegetables, and herbs).

What else can you think of? Use your imagination!

## The Least You Need to Know

◆ Quick breads offer a 20-minute, tasty bread to serve with your meal.

◆ Although yeast breads require two or three hours to cook, they ironically only take a few minutes of your time to set in motion. A few minutes work, then forget about it—that's 20-minute cuisine in my book.

◆ Commercial breads are a source of both convenience and inspiration for types to try in the bread machine.

◆ Bread-based hors d'oeuvres and side dishes are fast and convenient.

# Chapter 16

# Dessert Time!

## In This Chapter

- Pies, fruit, and cookies, *oh my!*
- Ice cream
- Favorite dessert recipes
- Easy Timesavers

Adults recognize the need for a balanced diet. We obligingly chomp our broccoli, slice our steak, and munch our bread. But turn the inquisitor's light on our soul, and many of us would confess to really be biding time until dessert. For my kids, there's no secret. The point of a meal is to get to dessert—as quickly as possible.

For the 20-minute cook, our attention must focus on a subset of the universe of desserts out there. Many sweet endings take an awfully long time to prepare, not just in cooking but in assembling ingredients. That said, there are several areas in this chapter that are wide open for us to explore:

- Pie … and just plain filling!
- Ice cream
- Fruits and cheeses
- Cookies

# It's Not the Pie; It's the Filling

Pies, tarts, and crumbles all take advantage of two key elements: a rich, usually sweet filling; and a flour- or grain-based shell or topping. The combination of these two elements is sweet poetry, and there are a number of ways to accelerate the process. Here are some of my favorite quick recipes.

## Grampa Phil's Pudding Pie

Prep time: 5 minutes • Cook time: 20 minutes • Serves 8

2½ cups milk

¾ cup sugar

2 oz. unsweetened solid baking chocolate

½ tsp. salt

2 TB. flour

3 TB. cornstarch

2 eggs, beaten, in a bowl or measuring cup

1½ tsp. vanilla

1 tsp. butter

In the top part of a *double boiler* (if you've got one), heat 2 cups milk, sugar, chocolate, and salt (all over the bottom part, which contains a few inches of boiling water). A saucepan can be used instead, but stir constantly. Heat until just simmering. Place remaining ½ cup milk in a small bowl or measuring cup, and with a fork mix in flour and cornstarch until thoroughly combined. Slowly pour milk-and-flour mixture into milk-and-chocolate mixture on the stove, stirring constantly.

Add a spoonful of chocolate mixture to beaten eggs, stirring. Add two more spoonfuls, stirring. Then pour egg mixture into pudding, stirring.

Cook for one minute, add vanilla and butter, cook for one minute longer, then serve. As pudding, I love it warm; as pie, I love it chilled.

Without the pie shell, it's pudding. With the pie shell, it's chocolate pie. Top pie with whipped cream; it's a slice of pure pleasure.

To dress it up even more, sprinkle whipped cream with chocolate shavings or dust with powdered chocolate (like from instant cocoa).

**Cook's Glossary**

A **double boiler** is a set of two pots designed to nest together, one inside the other. The bottom one holds water (not quite touching the bottom of the top pot), the top one holds the ingredient you are trying to heat. A double boiler provides consistent heat for things that need delicate treatment.

**Cook to Cook**

Rather than simply dumping eggs into a hot mixture, we add spoonfuls of that mixture to the eggs first to start warming them so they don't cook and

# Grammalane's Lemon Pie

Not too sweet. Too delicious.

Prep time: 2 minutes • Cook time: 18 minutes • Serves 6 generously

1 cup sugar

1 cup + ⅓ cup water

Juice of 2 lemons

4 TB. + 2 tsp. corn starch

3 egg yolks, beaten, in a small bowl or measuring cup

1 TB. butter

In the top part of a double boiler (if you've got one), heat sugar and 1 cup water. Add lemon juice. Put remaining ⅓ cup water in a bowl or measuring cup, and whisk in corn starch until blended and smooth. Slowly add to the double boiler, stirring. It will thicken.

Add a spoonful lemon mixture to the beaten egg yolks, stirring (this is to start warming up the yolks). Add two more spoonfuls, stirring. Repeat one more time. Then pour egg mixture into double boiler, stirring, along with butter.

Pour mixture into a pre-baked pie shell and put it into the fridge to *set*.

Top with whipped cream for a quick topping or meringue (see next recipe) for a complete lemon cream or lemon meringue pie.

**Cook's Glossary**

To **set** is to harden or firm up—a critical characteristic of a pie that you don't want to be liquid!

# Meringue

Use egg whites left over from the lemon pie!

Prep time: 5 minutes • Cook time: 5 minutes • Serves 6 as topping for lemon pie

Whites from 3 eggs

½ tsp. salt

⅛ tsp. cream of tartar

4 TB. sugar

Preheat the broiler. Allow egg whites to reach room temperature. (If you use whites from making a lemon pie, all you need to do is leave them out while you finish the pie.) Add salt and cream of tartar and beat rapidly until mixture expands and forms stiff peaks when you lift the beaters. Add sugar slowly, gently folding it into stiff egg whites so as not to deflate them. The meringue will firm up. Spread over pie; place under the broiler for four minutes or until meringue begins to brown.

# Dad's Baked Fruit

This is a right-brain recipe, which means it can use many different fruits, depending on your mood and the season. This is one delicious example. The microwave is used to move things along at a brisk pace.

Prep time: 5 minutes • Cook time: 9 minutes • Serves 4 to 6

1 (1-lb.) pkg. frozen mixed berries (Approximately 1 cup each blueberries, blackberries, and raspberries. Fresh fruit is even better; I've listed frozen for the convenience.)

3 TB. granulated sugar

2 TB. flour

Juice of ½ lemon

**Topping:**

¼ cup brown sugar

¾ cup oatmeal

¼ cup flour

½ tsp. baking spice or ½ tsp. cinnamon

4 TB. butter, chilled, cut into small pieces

Place berries in an 8 × 8 microwave-safe pie pan or baking pan. Add sugar, flour, and lemon juice and toss together.

In a separate bowl, mix brown sugar, oatmeal, flour, and spice. Add butter by pinching together with your fingers until it's incorporated and a crumble texture. Sprinkle evenly over top of fruit and cover dish with plastic wrap.

Place in microwave and cook on high for seven minutes. Turn once or twice if your microwave does not have a carousel tray.

Preheat the broiler. Remove plastic wrap and place under the broiler (not too close), and broil for two minutes or until top begins to crisp.

# Sara's Instant Chocolate Mousse

A luscious, thick crowd-pleaser—and boy is it quick.

Prep time: 10 minutes  •  Serves 4

| | |
|---|---|
| 1 pint whipping cream | ½ cup sugar |
| 4 TB. instant hot chocolate powder | 2 tsp. vanilla |

Whip cream. Slowly add hot chocolate powder, sugar, and vanilla as you whip. When your mousse doubles in size and has soft waves standing, you're ready to serve.

For added visual appeal, pour mousse into a large zipper-seal food storage bag. With a scissors, snip off ½ inch of one corner of the bag, and squeeze the mousse in swirls into serving bowls. This trick can also be used to create a parfait of dark and light layers, using one bag with mousse and the other with regular whipped cream.

### Cuisine Context

To make whipped cream, pour whipping cream into a chilled bowl (whipping your cream in a chilled bowl accelerates the whipping process, although a bowl at room temperature will work). Using a wire whisk, hand beater, or electric beater, rapidly beat the cream. The faster you beat the cream, the more rapidly it expands. With an electric beater, cream will double in size and produce soft waves (the desired result) in about two minutes. Using a wire whisk or hand beater will give you a workout and require patience, but will work if you're persistent.

Whipping cream with an electric beater is quick and easy, but watch the process carefully. As soon as your cream reaches the light, fluffy whipped cream consistency, stop beating … otherwise you'll suddenly make butter!

# Fruits

Fresh fruits do half the work for you, because half the flavor is already there. A dessert with fresh fruit should be simple, to spotlight that flavor.

# Strawberries and Thick Cream

This simple dish evokes a warm summer evening, a wide front porch, quiet conversation—and appreciative lip-smacking.

Prep time: 10 minutes  •  Serves 6

1 quart strawberries, washed, caps removed, and sliced

2 TB. + ¼ cup sugar

½ cup light cream

1 cup sour cream

Prepare strawberries, sprinkle with 2 tablespoons sugar, and set aside in a covered bowl to *macerate*. Wait at least five minutes.

In a bowl, mix light cream, sour cream, and ¼ cup sugar. Distribute strawberries to small bowls and top with cream.

**Cook's Glossary** _____

Mixing sugar or another sweetener with fruit initiates a process called **maceration**; the fruit softens and a delicious juice is released.

# Poached Pears

An aura of sophistication surrounds this dish. Be sure to serve it in your grand dining room (the one with the table that seats 36). You'll need to multiply the dish if that table is full.

Prep time: 8 minutes • Cook time: 12 minutes • Serves 4

½ cup brown sugar

1½ cups cooking sherry or red wine

½ cup water

1 tsp. baking spice or 1 tsp. cinnamon

1 tsp. lemon juice

4 pears, peeled, sliced in half lengthwise, and *cored*

Confectioner's sugar as garnish

Combine brown sugar, sherry, water, baking spice, and lemon juice in a saucepan and heat to a simmer. Add pears and simmer for 12 minutes or until pears are tender. Turn off the heat and allow fruit to cool in its juices. Place two pear halves on each plate, spoon a bit of sauce over, and sprinkle with confectioner's sugar. (If you really like juice, serve in bowls and distribute liquid with pears.)

### Cook's Glossary

To **core** a piece of fruit is to remove the unappetizing middle membranes and seeds. With pear halves, this is done with a paring knife or other small, sharp knife, cutting out the center part of the fruit.

# Warm Apples

Comfort food as dessert.

Prep time: 5 minutes • Cook time: 8 minutes • Serves 6

4 TB. butter

¼ cup raisins

4 apples (your favorite), peeled, cored, and sliced

¼ cup honey

½ tsp. baking spice (or apple pie spice) or ½ tsp. cinnamon

Melt butter in a large skillet over medium heat. Add raisins and sauté for two minutes. Add apples and sauté for two minutes. Add honey and baking spice. Cook, stirring, for four minutes, then serve.

Serving ideas: Top with whipped cream or serve over vanilla ice cream.

### Cuisine Context

Each variety of apple has a distinct texture and tartness that will show through when you use it to make a dessert. For some dishes, the type of apple is very important. For warm apples, you can use your favorite. I use Granny Smith, because I like the firm texture and tart flavor, even as a dessert. Another variety, such as a golden delicious, will translate as a sweeter, softer dish.

# Cookies

Some desserts are portable, sweet, and irresistible. Even though Mom insists on "no cookies in the living room," they are a cherished part of the dessert menu.

# Oatmeal Chocolate-Chip Cookies

I can't resist the whole wheat in cookies. I pretend that eating one extra cookie is good for me.

Prep time: 10 minutes  •  Cook time: 10 minutes  •  Serves 8

| | |
|---|---|
| ½ cup shortening | ½ tsp. baking powder |
| 1 cup brown sugar | ½ tsp. salt |
| ½ cup white flour | 2 eggs |
| ½ cup whole-wheat flour | 1 tsp. vanilla |
| 1 cup oatmeal | 1 cup semi-sweet chocolate chips |

Preheat the oven to 375°F. Thoroughly mix shortening and brown sugar in a large bowl. Whisk together white flour, whole-wheat flour, oatmeal, baking powder, and salt, and stir into shortening-sugar mixture in the bowl. Add eggs and vanilla and mix into dough. Add chocolate chips and mix again.

Scoop spoonfuls of cookie dough onto a greased baking pan or cookie sheet and bake for 10 minutes or until done. Slightly less cooking results in moist, chewy cookies. Slightly more results in crisp, crunchy cookies. Each version has avid fans.

If we're using more than one cookie sheet, my wife insists on rotating trays from bottom to top oven shelves after five minutes to ensure uniform cooking.

# Joe Frankenfield's Brickle

I include this traditional Pennsylvania treat, even though it requires time in the fridge to cool, because it takes as little as 15 minutes to prepare, and people just rave about the results. This is not health food, but it is irresistible.

Prep time: 5 minutes • Cook time: 10 minutes • Cooling time: 2 hours (unattended) • Serves 8

| | |
|---|---|
| Enough saltine crackers to cover a large cookie sheet in a single layer (about 40) | 1 cup brown sugar |
| | 1 (12-oz.) bag chocolate chips |
| 1 cup butter (two sticks; don't use margarine) | 1 cup finely chopped almonds |

Line cookie sheet, including the sides, with aluminum foil. Line sheet with a single layer of saltines, face up and touching.

Preheat oven to 400°F. Heat saucepan with butter over medium heat. When butter is melted, stir in brown sugar and heat mixture to a boil. Boil three minutes, stirring, and pour immediately over saltines, distributing mixture evenly with the back of a spoon. Bake for five minutes.

Sprinkle tray with chocolate chips. In two minutes, use the back of a spoon to level melted chocolate across the sheet. Then sprinkle almonds over mixture.

Refrigerate two hours. Brickle will harden and become brittle. Lift out of the foil and break brickle into pieces (cutting is not a good idea; breaking is better). Store in fridge in a sealable container (if there are any leftovers, which is doubtful—you'll see).

# Dessert Easy Timesavers

Your grocery store has a wealth of desserts just ready to go, from ice cream that's ready instantly, to cookie mixes easily ready in 20 minutes. Some more interesting options include prepared desserts with a hint of the unusual. One specialty store I frequent, for example, sells frozen orange, lemon, and coconut halves, each filled with orange sherbet, lemon sherbet, and coconut ice, respectively. No work involved, but people love them (especially little people).

There are also a wide variety of treats to assemble and enjoy in minutes. Here are some of my sweet favorites.

**Cook to Cook**

If you don't have a cookie cutter for cutting dough into shapes, use the rim of a 2½-inch- or 3-inch-round glass.

# Lightning Strawberry Shortcake

Fresh sweet fruit makes this recipe a quick favorite.

Prep time: 5 minutes • Cook time: 8 minutes • Serves 6

1 pint strawberries, washed, caps removed, and cut into quarters

3 TB. sugar

2¼ cups baking mix (the kind that only requires addition of milk)

¾ cup milk

Whipped cream

Prepare strawberries, sprinkle with sugar, and set aside in a covered bowl to macerate.

Preheat oven to 450°F. Pour baking mix into a large bowl and stir in milk to create dough. Turn dough onto a floured counter and knead for 30 seconds. Flatten dough with your hands to about ½ inch thick. Cut into your favorite shape (circles if you have a cookie cutter, squares, triangles … have some fun!), place on an ungreased baking pan or cookie sheet, and bake for eight minutes or until browned and crusty.

When done, cool to handling temperature and slice horizontally so you have two flat pieces. Distribute bottom pieces to serving plates, top each with a large spoonful of strawberries and juice. Place top of each biscuit on strawberries, and top each with the remaining strawberry and juice mixture. Top with whipped cream.

**Flare-Up**

Don't assemble short-cakes and other juice-and-cake desserts too far in advance. If you do, you'll end up with a soggy dessert.

**Cook to Cook**

For an even quicker strawberry dish (although this time it would be called Strawberry Sponge Cake), use store-bought sponge cakes from the bakery section instead of baking shortcake.

# Maple Sundae

In a bit of a sundae twist, the syrup goes on top of the whipped cream.

Prep time: 4 minutes (at same time as walnuts are cooking)  •  Cook time: 10 minutes  •
Serves 4

| | |
|---|---|
| 1 cup toasted walnut pieces | 4 cups vanilla ice cream |
| ⅔ cup maple syrup, warmed | Instant whipped cream |

Preheat oven to 425°F. Spread walnut pieces on a baking tray, and toast in the oven for 10 minutes.

When walnuts are almost done, heat maple syrup in a microwave-safe cup for 30 seconds. Scoop ice cream into four separate bowls, top with whipped cream, and drizzle warm maple syrup over each serving. Top with warm toasted walnuts. Wow.

# Charles River Mud Pie

Decadent and rich. I've included my favorite flavors, but of course feel free to experiment.

Prep time: 5 minutes  •  Serves 4

| | |
|---|---|
| 2 cups coffee ice cream | 1 cup fudge sauce (available at grocery stores), heated |
| 2 cups chocolate ice cream | |
| ½ cup chopped walnuts | 1 store-bought graham-cracker or chocolate-cookie-crumb crust |
| ½ cup semi-sweet chocolate chips | 1½ cups whipped cream |

Combine coffee ice cream and chocolate ice cream in a large bowl. Stir in walnuts, chocolate chips, and fudge sauce. Scrape into graham-cracker crust, and press to smooth. Top with whipped cream and serve. Yum.

If you've got a few extra minutes, put pie in the freezer to firm up before spreading on whipped cream.

# Sabra's Meringue Kisses

This is a make-ahead Easy Timesaver. I couldn't resist adding these because they are so easy … just minutes of prep. The catch is the finishing time in the oven, but that happens while you sleep!

Prep time: 7minutes • Cook time: 3 to 8 hours (unattended) • Serves 8

| | |
|---|---|
| 2 egg whites | 1 tsp. vanilla |
| ⅔ cup sugar | 1 cup chocolate chips |
| Pinch salt | ½ cup chopped nuts (optional) |

Preheat oven to 375°F. Beat egg whites until stiff. Beat in sugar, salt, and vanilla. Then mix in chips and nuts.

Drop on greased cookie sheet by heaping teaspoonfuls. Place sheet in preheated oven and immediately turn off the oven. Come back to the oven later, or even the following morning, and the kisses will be ready.

## The Least You Need to Know

- ◆ Just because something is homemade and delicious does not mean it has to take a long time to make.
- ◆ Whipped and thick creams are luxuriant, delicious, and speedy ways to dress up a quick dessert.
- ◆ Fresh fruit is a sure success, made quickly because the flavors are there already.
- ◆ Store-bought desserts, such as ice cream, can form the basis for quick and delicious desserts.

# Part 4

# Theme Cuisine

If variety is the spice of life, variety also adds interest to cooking. I've assembled an eclectic mix of food themes and recipes in this part to add interest to the everyday meal. There's a world of food out there. We take a quick tour of recipes, and seasoning inspiration, from culinary traditions around the globe. Then, we'll whip up a shortlist of delicious dishes specifically chosen because they offer high nutrition (and are often low fat).

Finally, you might not think that the words "entertain" and "20 minutes" belong in the same sentence, much less the same chapter. Here we'll dispel the doubt and provide some tasty and impressive dishes for guests.

# Chapter 17

# Easy Timesavers

## In This Chapter

- ◆ Tortilla surprise
- ◆ Breads that make magic

We're all busy. The pace of life, particularly during the week, means that we often don't have 20 minutes to prepare a meal. We can face a time crunch, be done with time to spare, and not have to resort to tv dinners. The secret is in the ingredients and in the preparation.

Throughout this book I've listed "Easy Timesaver" recipes, dishes that can be cooked (or not cooked, as the case may be) in *less* than 20 minutes. As you've seen, Easy Timesavers are possible with every main ingredient, from pasta and seafood (especially seafood!), to white meats, richer meats, and vegetarian dishes. Sides can even be quicker, and vegetables, as we've discussed, are offended if you cook them too long.

To finish the discussion, this chapter focuses on reliable, quick Easy Timesavers that can be made with easy-to-find ingredients.

# Tortillas

For a tasty, entertaining variation on bread, go south of the border to Tortillaville. Made from wheat, corn, and occasionally other grains, tortillas serve as a vehicle for many a quick, delicious meal.

Basic forms of tortillas, ready to go, include the following varieties:

♦ **Soft tortillas.** Two round sizes are widely available, roughly 8 inches and 12 inches in diameter.

♦ **Taco shells.** Ready to fill.

♦ **Tortilla chips.** Crispy and irresistible (who can eat only one?).

> **Cook to Cook**
>
> Easy Timesavers rely on quick-cooking, healthful ingredients, simple preparation, and interesting seasoning.

> **Cuisine Context**
>
> You'll notice that most recipes in this chapter feature a grain-based ingredient (such as tortillas and bread) cheese of various kinds, and often a vegetable. This combination, with infinite variety, is nutritionally balanced, and forms the basis of quick meals across the globe. As with other parts of this book, my hope is that you'll see the underlying combinations, and then feel free to experiment on your own.

The following is a list of appropriate partners with tortillas:

♦ Jack cheese (or other cheeses)

♦ Guacamole

♦ Salsa

♦ Fresh cilantro

♦ Corn

♦ Fresh tomato

♦ Sliced black olives

♦ Lime

♦ Seafood (all kinds!)

♦ Refried beans

♦ Ground beef (or other meats)

♦ A whole range of seasonings, including chili powder, cilantro, cumin, oregano, basil, paprika, crushed red pepper, and more

These ingredients are only some of the more common, conventional ones that are easily available. As you'll see, we'll expand on this theme a bit with some of the recipes you find in this chapter.

# Bacon and Swiss Tortilla Melt

This combination is a bit unconventional, I'll admit, but nevertheless delicious … and ready in minutes.

Prep time: 5 minutes  •  Cook time: 8 minutes  •  Serves 4

6 pieces bacon

2 large soft flour tortillas

1 (8-oz.) pkg. shredded Swiss cheese

Preheat the broiler. Heat a large skillet over medium heat, and cook bacon until crispy, about five minutes, turning once. Remove bacon strips to a paper plate covered with paper towels to drain.

Meanwhile, place each tortilla on a baking sheet, and toast under the broiler for three minutes, turning once, until tortillas begin to brown and turn crispy.

Carefully remove the tortillas on their baking sheets and rest on a heatproof surface. Sprinkle each tortilla with half the Swiss cheese. Crumble three bacon strips over each tortilla.

Slide the baking sheet with tortilla back under the broiler for two to three minutes, until cheese is melted and starting to bubble. Slice on a cutting board and serve pizza-style.

**Flare-Up**

Watch any food that's broiling closely, remove it just when done, and enjoy the benefits of this quick-cooking method.

# Joaquin's Tortilla and Scallion Pizza

A touch of sour cream makes this a magical bite.

Prep time: 3 minutes  •  Cook time: 6 minutes  •  Serves 4

2 large soft flour tortillas

8 oz. shredded Monterey Jack cheese

4 scallions, washed, dark green parts and roots removed, white and light green parts thinly sliced

1 tsp. chili powder

Preheat the broiler. Place each tortilla on a baking sheet, and toast under the broiler for three minutes, turning once, until tortillas begin to brown and turn crispy.

Carefully remove tortillas on their baking sheets from the oven, and sprinkle each with half the cheese. Distribute scallions and sprinkle ½ teaspoon chili powder over each tortilla.

Slide the baking sheet and tortilla back under the broiler for two to three minutes, until cheese is melted and starting to bubble.

# Tortilla Roma

Okay, okay, so this is mixing cultural influences … try it, you'll like it. This recipe calls for less cheese than others because of Romano's richness. Even so, you'll find this a flavor explosion.

Prep time: 3 minutes  •  Cook time: 9 minutes  •  Serves 4

2 large soft flour tortillas

1 TB. olive oil

1 tsp. chopped garlic

6 oz. Romano cheese

1½ cups roasted red pepper, chopped into ½-inch pieces

1½ cups cooked chicken, chopped into ½-inch pieces

Salt and pepper to taste

Preheat the broiler. Place each tortilla on a baking sheet and toast under the broiler for three minutes, turning once, until tortillas begin to brown and turn crispy. Meanwhile, mix olive oil and garlic in a cup.

Carefully remove tortillas on their baking sheets and rest on a heatproof surface. Spoon oil-and-garlic mixture over each tortilla, and spread with the back of a spoon. Sprinkle each tortilla with Romano cheese. Slide the baking sheet and tortilla back under the broiler for two to three minutes, until cheese begins to melt. Then arrange red pepper and chicken pieces over each tortilla, and broil for three additional minutes, watching closely to prevent burning.

Salt and pepper to taste, slice on a cutting board, and serve pizza-style.

≈~

# Quick Guacamole

Fresh guacamole is a taste treat, whether as an appetizer by itself or as part of a recipe.

Prep time: 8 minutes  •  Serves 6 as an appetizer

2 large ripe avocados

2 TB. lemon juice

¼ cup sour cream

2 TB. sweet onion (such as Vidalia), finely chopped

Dash hot pepper sauce

Salt and pepper to taste

Peel avocados, place flesh in a bowl and mash with a fork (as coarsely or finely as you like). Add lemon juice, sour cream, onion, pepper sauce, salt, and pepper, mix thoroughly with a fork, and serve.

≈~

# Nachos

Nachos are one of those dishes whose definition changes not only from country to country, but also house to house. The two reliable ingredients are melted cheese and crispy tortilla chips. Here's my favorite version, hearty enough to be a meal by itself, and simple enough to be prepared in less than 10 minutes. Have a favorite topping? Add it!

Prep time: 3 minutes • Cook time: 11 minutes • Serves 4

1 (16-oz.) can nonfat refried beans

1 bag salted white corn tortilla chips (not flavored)

2 (16-oz.) bags shredded Mexican-style cheese (available at most grocery stores)

Pinch chili powder

Salsa and sour cream for topping

Place refried beans in a microwave-safe bowl and heat for three minutes or until hot; stir to loosen beans. If necessary, add a little canola oil to enable beans to be easily spread.

While beans are heating, arrange chips in a double, loose layer on four plates. Spoon refried beans across the chips. Sprinkle cheese over refried beans, and microwave each plate for two minutes or until cheese is melted. Sprinkle a bit of chili powder over each plate, and top nachos to taste with salsa and sour cream.

# Quick Tacos

Spice from the seasoned ground beef and guacamole balances deliciously with the coolness of the tomato and sour cream.

Prep time: 5 minutes • Cook time: 12 minutes • Serves 4 to 6

1 lb. ground beef

¼ cup water

1 tsp. chopped garlic

2 tsp. chili powder

½ tsp. salt

10 taco shells

1 large tomato, diced

1 cup guacamole (store-bought or homemade)

1 cup shredded Monterey Jack cheese

1 cup sour cream (optional)

In a large skillet, brown ground beef over medium heat for seven minutes or until cooked. Drain fat from the skillet, and add water, garlic, chili powder, and salt. Stir and cook for five minutes.

Distribute seasoned meat between taco shells. Spoon tomatoes over ground beef, add guacamole, and top with shredded cheese.

For added flavor, top with sour cream.

# Quick Enchiladas

Hearty and quick. This version is vegetarian, although meat can be added for even more heft.

Prep time: 5 minutes • Cook time: 6 minutes • Serves 4

1 (16-oz.) can fat-free refried beans

4 large flour tortillas

1 large tomato, finely chopped

1 tsp. chili powder

8 oz. shredded cheddar cheese

Preheat the broiler. Scoop refried beans into a microwave-safe bowl and heat on high for three minutes or until hot. Stir beans to loosen. Place a large tortilla on a plate, scoop ¼ of beans onto each tortilla in a roughly straight line across center. Top with ¼ chopped tomato and a pinch of chili powder. Roll tortilla around filling and place in a baking tray, leaving room for the other three. Repeat with remaining tortillas, placing them next to each other in the baking tray. Sprinkle cheddar cheese over the top of enchiladas, and sprinkle remaining chili powder over cheese.

Broil for three minutes or until cheese is melted.

Serve, topping with guacamole, sour cream, and salsa, if desired.

**Cook's Glossary**

An **enchilada** is a dish made by wrapping a tortilla around a savory filling, often served with a sauce or topping.

# Breads

Bread is much more than a vehicle for butter; it's a platform for a quick meal. I'm not only talking sandwiches, although that's a good place to start. Imagine these items together, calling your name …

- ◆ Whole-wheat bread
- ◆ Cheddar (or other) cheese
- ◆ Tomato slices
- ◆ Cooked meats
- ◆ Sliced sweet onion
- ◆ Lettuce

Just listing these ingredients, don't you start to taste the possibilities? Of course there are more possibilities; use your imagination!

These recipes feature some that may be quite familiar (variations on the sand-wich), as well as one or two that might just be new to you. As you might sense from the ingredients and seasonings, our source of influence now shifts toward Europe.

# Crostini

Crostini is grilled or toasted bread, usually used in this country as a platform for other ingredients as part of an appetizer, as in the recipe that follows.

Use your imagination with crostini. These superfast appetizers can feature a variety of ingredients, including the following:

- Artichoke hearts
- Sun-dried tomatoes (Drained oil-packed ones are best; regular dried are tough.)
- Sliced olives
- Fresh basil and tomato
- Fresh mozzarella slices

## Crostini with Roasted Red Pepper

Glistening red peppers topped with rich Romano cheese make these appetizers irresistible.

Prep time: 5 minutes • Cook time: 5 minutes • Serves 4

1 loaf slender bread, such as a baguette

1 TB. garlic

2 TB. olive oil

2 cups roasted red peppers (available in jars in the canned vegetable section of grocery stores), chopped into ½-inch pieces

⅓ cup shredded or grated Romano cheese

1 tsp. kosher salt

Preheat the broiler. Slice the bread into ½-inch-thick pieces and arrange on a baking sheet. Mix garlic and olive oil in a cup and brush tops of bread pieces with some of the mixture. Broil with topping side up one or two minutes until toasted to a light brown. Flip each piece, brush with garlic-and-oil mixture, broil for another minute, and remove tray from the broiler (leave broiler on). Top each piece of bread with pieces of red pepper, a sprinkling of cheese, and a tiny pinch of salt. Broil for two minutes or until cheese begins to melt. Serve on a large platter.

## Cook's Glossary

An **open-faced** sandwich means that the top is not "closed" by a second piece of bread. The ingredients are open to the sky. To **render** is to melt fat, as from bacon.

## Hot, Open-Faced Sandwiches

There's something magical about a hot sandwich. The heat melds the ingredients, toasts (or grills) the bread, and brings flavor to new levels.

Growing up, my mom would frequently serve *open-faced* sandwiches. As kids, we loved the melted cheese. I now realize, as a parent, that I also love the quick convenience. Here are two samples, but again, use these as a guide, not a rigid rule.

# Mom's Open-Faced Bacon and Tomato Sandwich

Bacon and tomato, a heavenly combination to begin with, is perhaps made just a bit better when added to melted cheese. I cook the bacon halfway before adding it to the sandwich to lessen the fat.

Prep time: 5 minutes • Cook time: 10 minutes • Serves 4

4 thick bacon slices

4 slices whole-wheat bread

4 slices cheddar cheese (or your favorite)

4½-inch fresh tomato slices

## Cook to Cook

With open-faced sandwiches, the challenge is to reach that balance between crispness and moisture, which is why these recipes call for toasting each side of a piece of bread before adding the feature ingredients.

Preheat the broiler. In a large skillet, cook bacon for four minutes or until it begins to crisp and some of the fat is *rendered*. Turn off heat under skillet.

While bacon is cooking, arrange bread on a baking sheet. Broil one side for two minutes, flip pieces, and broil other side for two minutes, until bread begins to brown. Top each piece of bread with cheese and broil for two minutes until cheese begins to melt. Then top each piece of bread with a slice of tomato and a piece of bacon (the bacon will need to be folded into a V shape). Broil for four minutes, or until the bacon is crisp and cheese around the edge of tomato begins to bubble.

# Italian Turkey and Sprout Sandwich

In college, this delicious, quick dish was a regular feature in our tiny kitchen.

Prep time: 4 minutes   •   Cook time: 8 minutes   •   Serves 4

4 slices whole-wheat bread

4 slices deli turkey

1½ cups alfalfa sprouts

4 slices cheddar cheese (or your favorite)

Arrange bread on a baking sheet and broil one side for two minutes, flip pieces, and broil other side for two minutes, until bread begins to turn a light brown. Top each piece of toasted bread with a turkey slice, ¼ sprouts, and a slice of cheese. Broil for four minutes or until the cheese melts and begins to bubble.

∽

## Super Sandwiches

A sandwich is more than PB&J; it's an opportunity to showcase your favorite ingredients. Pick healthy, tasty fresh bread to give yourself a head start. I often choose whole wheat for the rich, nutty taste and high nutrition.

**Flare-Up**

Eat sandwiches with moist ingredients immediately, so that, for example, water from a juicy tomato slice doesn't soak the bread.

# Tomato and Fresh Mozzarella

This sandwich is simple, juicy, and flavorful. It also sings a summer song.

Prep time: 8 minutes   •   Serves 4

8 slices fresh whole-wheat bread

¼ cup shredded or grated Parmesan cheese

4 large tomato slices, ¼ inch thick

½ lb. fresh mozzarella cheese, thinly (¼ inch) sliced

Salt and pepper

Assemble each sandwich as follows: a slice of bread, 1 tablespoon Parmesan spread evenly across bread, a tomato slice, a layer of mozzarella, and a sprinkling of salt and pepper. Cover with a slice of bread.

Serve with a glass of white wine on your vine-covered terrace.

∽

# Grilled Chicken and Sweet Onion

This sandwich is a compelling reason to make extras when grilling. This next-night dish is practically instant ... and also disappears practically instantly.

Prep time: 8 minutes   •   Serves 4

4 TB. mayonnaise

8 slices fresh whole-wheat bread

1½ cups thinly (¼ inch) sliced cooked chicken

Salt and pepper

4 very thin slices (⅛ inch) sweet onion, such as Vidalia

4 pieces crisp lettuce

Spread 1 tablespoon mayonnaise on four pieces of bread. Distribute chicken between pieces, and sprinkle with salt and pepper, add a slice of onion and a piece of lettuce. Finish with a slice of bread. Devour.

# Lion Eggs

This quick recipe, perfected to an art at the Roaring Lion bed and breakfast in Waldoboro, Maine, makes the most of two quick ingredients: fresh bread and fresh eggs. Scale as needed.

Prep time: 5 minutes   •   Cook time: 3 minutes   •   Serves 4

1 TB. oil or bacon fat

4 bread slices (Sourdough tastes great.)

2 TB. butter or margarine

4 eggs

Salt and pepper

Heat oil in a large skillet over medium heat. Toast bread, spread butter or margarine on both sides, and, with a sharp knife, cut a round piece, about 2½ inches in diameter, in the center of each piece of toast. Remove the round piece but keep it.

Place toast in the heated skillet, and crack an egg into the hole. Cook for three minutes, turning bread and egg once, or to your preferred doneness level. Slide toast and egg onto a plate, and replace round piece as a "lid" over the egg. Season with salt and pepper.

Serve with bacon, a slice of cantaloupe, juice, and coffee, and you've got another candidate for the perfect breakfast.

## The Least You Need to Know

◆ If you're in a hurry, even 20 minutes might be too long to take to prepare a meal. This chapter provides inspiration for dishes that take *less than* 20 minutes.

◆ Super-quick recipes, requiring only 5 to 10 minutes, are easy when you pick your ingredients and cooking methods carefully.

◆ Tortilla and bread-based recipes are prime Easy Timesaver candidates.

◆ Broiling is a terrific super-quick cooking method.

Chapter **18**

# Comfort Foods

## In This Chapter

- ◆ Appetizers to comfort you
- ◆ Soups to feel good about
- ◆ "Looking back" on pasta and vegetables

Although comfort food means something slightly different to each of us, there tend to be several common characteristics. Comfort food reminds us of a place where we feel relaxed, and it typically uses familiar ingredients. In this country, at least, comfort food tends to be warm and filling—think of meat loaf, roasts, or casseroles.

The problem with the idea of comfort food, in the context of 20-minute cuisine, is that much of it involves slow cooking (so to the earlier examples, add slow-cooked stews). There are many dishes, however, that fit firmly into both the comfort and the 20-minute cuisine categories. Through this book you've already seen a number of these recipes. In this chapter, we set our sights firmly on even more comfort. Kick back, relax, and pick your favorite.

# Appetizers

Here are two easy appetizers that easily fall into the "comfort" category.

## "Uncle" Marcia's Cheese Puffs

Prep time: 5 minutes   •   Cook time: 15 minutes   •   Serves 4 as an appetizer

1 cup grated cheese (mixture of sharp cheddar and Swiss is recommended)

½ cup flour

2 TB. butter, softened

Water

2 TB. grated or minced fresh onion

Dash cayenne pepper

With your fingertips, mix cheese, flour, butter, and just enough water to make a *stiff dough*. Add onion and cayenne pepper and mix. Roll dough into 1-inch balls, place on greased cookie sheet, and bake 15 minutes at 400°F. Serve hot.

**Cook's Glossary** _____

A **stiff dough** is a dough that is solid and holds its shape (as opposed to a dough with a lot of liquid that, if you left it on the counter, would spread).

## Hot Artichoke Dip

This is the definition of rich and provides an elegant appetizer for when company comes.

Prep time: 5 minutes   •   Cook time: 15 minutes   •   Serves 4

1 large can artichoke hearts in water, drained, cut into quarters

½ cup Parmesan cheese

½ cup grated cheddar cheese

1 cup mayonnaise

Dash cayenne pepper

Mix artichoke hearts, Parmesan cheese, cheddar cheese, mayonnaise, and cayenne pepper together and place in shallow baking dish. Bake at 375°F for 20 minutes, until hot and melted. Serve with crackers or baguette slices.

# Comfort in a Bowl

There's something homey and comfortable about all soups, but for many people, chicken soup is where those feelings start. Our legendary mom would have made it, it's supposed to ward off everything from colds to evil spirits, and it appeals to our practical sensibilities; most ingredients, from the broth to the rice and chicken, can be from leftovers.

## Chicken, Spinach, and Rice Soup

This version is simple but hearty—a meal in a bowl. A big bowl.

Prep time: 10 minutes   •   Cook time: 10 minutes   •   Serves 4 to 6

| | |
|---|---|
| 2 TB. olive oil | ½ tsp. crushed red pepper |
| 1 onion, chopped | ½ tsp. oregano |
| 1 (10-oz.) pkg. frozen chopped spinach | ½ tsp. salt |
| 1 cup cooked chicken, chopped into ½-inch pieces | ¼ tsp. black pepper |
| 1½ cups cooked rice | 6 cups chicken broth (3 cans) |

Heat oil in a large skillet over medium heat and sauté onion for five minutes.

Meanwhile, thaw spinach in the microwave by heating on defrost for five minutes or until thawed (defrost times vary depending on the power of your microwave).

When onion has cooked, add spinach, chicken pieces, rice, red pepper, oregano, salt, and black pepper to the skillet, stirring, and cook for one minute. Add chicken broth and heat to a low boil; simmer for 10 minutes.

Serve with crusty bread for a "comfort food 101" meal.

# Nostalgia Menu

These bring back memories for me; how about you?

### Cuisine Context

I recently asked a group of people whether they had eaten tuna melts as a kid. Everyone remembered a version of this dish. And no wonder. The combination of nutrition and speed (good for parents), and *melted cheese* (appealing to kids) make this a honored member of the quick comfort food chapter.

## Tuna Melts

For a big group, this recipe can easily be increased in size.

Prep time: 8 minutes   •   Cook time: 8 minutes   •   Serves 4

1 (6-oz.) can solid white, water packed tuna, drained

¼ cup mayonnaise

½ cup finely chopped celery

¼ tsp. dried dill

Dash Tabasco or other hot sauce (optional)

Pinch salt

Pinch black pepper

4 slices bread, toasted

4 thick slices cheddar cheese

Preheat the broiler. Combine tuna, mayonnaise, celery, dill, hot sauce (if using), salt, and black pepper in a bowl. Toast bread and arrange pieces on a baking sheet. Distribute tuna mixture between toast pieces, spreading across the middle of toast. Top each piece of toast with a slice of cheese. Broil for three minutes or until cheese is melted.

# Grilled Ham and Swiss

Prep time: 5 minutes  •  Cook time: 8 minutes  •  Serves 4

1 TB. margarine or butter

8 slices whole-wheat bread

½ tsp. garlic powder

8 slices Swiss cheese

8 sandwich-size slices honey ham

Heat a large skillet over medium heat. Spread margarine (or butter) on four slices of bread, and dust margarine side with a pinch of garlic powder. Place, margarine side down, in skillet. (Depending on the size of your skillet, you may need to do this in two batches.)

Place a slice of cheese on bread in the skillet, followed by a slice of ham. Spread other pieces of bread with margarine, dust with garlic powder, and place bread on sandwich in skillet, margarine side up. Cook for four minutes, or until cheese begins to melt. Using a spatula to tip up a corner of a sandwich shows that the bread is nicely browned. Flip sandwich carefully, and cook for four additional minutes.

**Cook to Cook**

Although I generically refer to some sandwiches as "grilled," they are actually sautéed.

Serve with Dijon-style mustard or with Quick Grilled Cheese Dipping Sauce (recipe follows).

# Quick Grilled Cheese Dipping Sauce

Prep time: 4 minutes  •  Serves 4 for a couple meals as a dipping sauce

¼ cup ketchup

¼ cup mayonnaise

¼ cup sweet relish

2 TB. Dijon-style mustard

Dash hot pepper sauce (optional)

Mix ketchup, mayonnaise, relish, mustard, and pepper sauce, if using, in a bowl. Extras can be stored, covered, in the fridge for several weeks.

# Grilled Cheddar Chicken Sandwich

This sandwich is a great destination for leftover sliced Tuscan Chicken (see Chapter 6).

Prep time: 5 minutes  •  Cook time: 8 minutes  •  Serves 4

| | |
|---|---|
| 1 TB. margarine or butter | 8 slices cheddar cheese |
| 8 slices whole-wheat bread | 1½ cups thinly (¼ inch) sliced cooked chicken |
| ½ tsp. dried oregano | |

Heat a large skillet over medium heat. Spread margarine (or butter) on four slices of bread, and dust bread with a pinch of oregano. Place, margarine side down, in skillet. (Depending on the size of your skillet, you may need to do this in two batches.)

Place a slice of cheese on bread in the skillet, followed by several pieces of chicken. Spread other pieces of bread with margarine, dust with oregano, and place bread on sandwich in skillet, margarine side up. Cook for four minutes, or until cheese begins to melt and bread is browned. Flip sandwich carefully, and cook for four additional minutes.

# Grilled Brie and Mushroom Sandwich

Is it possible for grilled cheese to be elegant? It all depends, I suppose, on the ingredients. Baguette slices are small, hence the larger number of sandwiches.

Prep time: 5 minutes  •  Cook time: 6 minutes  •  Serves 4

| | |
|---|---|
| 1 TB. margarine or butter | 16 (¼-inch) slices brie, enough to fill 8 sandwiches (Depending on your taste, you may choose to remove the rind.) |
| 16 baguette slices, ½ inch thick | |
| ½ tsp. dried oregano | 1 cup thinly sliced (¼ inch) white mushrooms |

Heat a large skillet over medium heat. Spread margarine (or butter) on four slices of bread, and dust bread with a pinch of oregano. Place, margarine side down, in skillet. (Depending on the size of your skillet, you may need to do this in two batches.)

**Flare-Up**

Brie melts quickly, so watch closely to remove the sandwich before the cheese "runs" away.

Arrange brie on bread in the skillet, followed by mushroom slices. Spread other pieces of bread with margarine, dust with oregano, and place bread on sandwich in skillet, margarine side up. Cook for three minutes, or until cheese begins to melt and bread is browned. Flip sandwich carefully, and cook for three additional minutes.

## Pasta

A reliable theme throughout this book, pasta might just be the most comforting food of all. Here are some favorites.

# Penne à la Vodka

Prep time: 5 minutes   •   Cook time: 15 minutes   •   Serves 6 to 8

¼ cup olive oil

1 TB. chopped garlic

1 (28- or 35-oz.) can Italian peeled plum tomatoes, broken in can with knife

1 tsp. dried parsley

½ tsp. crushed hot pepper

1 lb. penne pasta

⅓ cup vodka

½ cup heavy cream

Parmesan cheese, freshly grated

Salt and pepper

Put water on for pasta. Heat oil in a large pot over medium heat, add garlic and cook for a minute, then add tomatoes, parsley, and hot pepper. Cook for about 10 minutes. Meanwhile, cook pasta for five minutes and drain.

Mix vodka and cream into tomato mixture, then add partially cooked, drained pasta. Continue cooking until pasta is cooked, about five minutes. Serve with Parmesan cheese and salt and pepper (and fresh minced parsley if you like).

### Cook to Cook

I thought I'd never meet someone who did not have a favorite recipe. On a vacation trip to the Mountainview Grand in New Hampshire, however, my belief was put to the test. Our bartender told us he never cooked, and walked away. For five minutes, I thought I'd been proven wrong. But then he came back, and said "well, there is one dish I do make all the time, but it's nothing fancy." That recipe follows … I *still* haven't met someone without a favorite recipe.

# John Q's Mac and Cheese (with Slight Variation)

Prep time: 5 minutes • Cook time: 10 minutes • Serves 4

2 boxes macaroni and cheese mix

1 lb. ground beef

1 tsp. salt

1 (16-oz.) can chopped tomatoes

Pinch crushed red pepper

Prepare macaroni and cheese according to box instructions. Meanwhile, cook ground beef in a large skillet with salt over medium-high heat until done, and drain. When macaroni and cheese is complete, stir in ground beef, chopped tomatoes, and crushed red pepper.

## Fried Vegetables

What is it about fried foods? Somehow they evoke a warm kitchen and family all around. Years ago, recipes such as these would have used animal fat for cooking, and thus would taste great but be just too high in fat for me to recommend. Using olive oil, however, reduces the saturated fat and preserves much of that delicious flavor.

# Fried Red Peppers

A succulent vegetable dish that even people who "don't like vegetables" will find tough to resist.

Prep time: 5 minutes • Cook time: 8 minutes • Serves 4

⅓ cup olive oil

2 cups roasted red peppers in large pieces

2 egg whites

⅓ cup skim milk

1 tsp. salt

1 cup dried bread crumbs

Heat oil in a large skillet over medium heat. Place pepper pieces in a large bowl. Whisk egg whites and milk in a small bowl. Pour mixture over pepper pieces, turning to coat. Mix salt with bread crumbs and pour crumbs onto a plate. Roll pepper pieces one by one in bread crumbs and place in the skillet. Fry for four minutes, or until bread crumbs begin to crisp, turning once.

### Cook to Cook

When cooking breaded items in oil, be sure to leave enough room so that the pieces in the skillet do not touch. This way they will turn crispy all around, and will not clump together.

# Roasted Vegetables

Prep time: 5 minutes  •  Cook time: 15 minutes  •  Serves 4

1½ lb. broccoli, cauliflower, or asparagus

¼ cup olive oil

Salt and pepper

Preheat oven to 425°F, and cover a cooking sheet with aluminum foil. Clean broccoli or cauliflower by cutting into small florets, trimming the stems to your liking. If using asparagus, trim hard ends, cutting approximately 1½ inches off the bottom. Place cleaned vegetables in a mixing bowl. Add olive oil, salt, and pepper to taste, mixing with your hands until vegetables are uniformly coated.

Pour vegetables out onto the cooking sheet, spreading them out until they are in one loose layer. Place in the oven for 10 to 15 minutes, depending on how brown you desire. Remove and serve.

# Fried Tomatoes

I came across this method when looking for a way to use up extra ripe and unripe tomatoes at the end of the season. Whether you like 'em fried green (like the movie), or fried red, this is another unusual vegetable dish that will have people asking for seconds.

Prep time: 5 minutes  •  Cook time: 10 minutes  •  Serves 4

⅓ cup + 2 TB. olive oil

2 large red or green tomatoes, sliced in ½-inch pieces

1 tsp. salt

Pinch ground red pepper

1 cup dried bread crumbs

¼ cup Parmesan cheese

Heat ⅓ cup olive oil in a large skillet over medium heat. Place tomato pieces in a large bowl. Drizzle tomato slices with 2 tablespoons olive oil, turning to coat. Mix salt and red pepper (if using) with bread crumbs and pour crumbs onto a plate. Coat tomato slices one by one in bread crumbs and place in the skillet. Fry three minutes for red tomato slices, five for green, or until coating begins to crisp, turning once. Distribute pieces to serving plates, sprinkling each piece with Parmesan cheese. Ah.

**Flare-Up**

When frying tomatoes, be sure to both use firm fruit (if red—green tomatoes will be firm), and to watch them closely to avoid overcooking. Otherwise, you'll find yourself picking up pieces.

## The Least You Need to Know

- ◆ Comfort food does not need to take a long time to prepare.
- ◆ Comfort foods include meat-based, as well as vegetable-based dishes.
- ◆ Comfort foods tend to be warm, hearty dishes.
- ◆ Comfort food can be low in fat, such as Chicken, Spinach, and Rice Soup, and the vegetable dishes in this chapter.

# Chapter 19

# Ethnic Magic

## In This Chapter

- New—and different—seasoning combinations
- A nutty 20-minute world tour
- Favorite recipes and timesavers

Until I experimented with different world styles of cooking, I would have never thought of including peanuts in a dinner meal, or mint with yogurt, or garlic with yogurt for that matter. Exploring the world through food is to open yourself to new ideas, and through taste to glimpse a facet of another culture.

In this chapter, we indulge in a tour of quick cooking around the world. The topic is a fascinating one, because it presents an opportunity to experiment with new combinations and new ingredients, seasonings, and methods.

## Expand Your ... Spice Rack

Playing with new seasonings expands our culinary horizon. I now use ingredients I would never have thought of a few years ago, and because of the increased variety of ingredients, I've created a few really fun dishes.

**Cook's Glossary**

**Fusion** cuisine is a method or style that marries two or more styles of cooking, such as Chinese and French. The concept has been quite trendy at some restaurants.

Because of the huge diversity covered in the examples here, I won't attempt to provide a seasoning chart that brings it all together. That's an attempt at *fusion* I'll leave to you.

These recipes for the most part are dinnertime fare, although that also is up to your taste. Highland Eggs, for example, is one dish that I would be happy to wake up to, have for lunch, or enjoy for dinner.

# Highland Eggs

Prep time: 5 minutes • Cook time: 10 minutes • Serves 4

2 TB. olive oil

1 onion, diced

6 eggs

½ cup milk

½ lb. smoked salmon, diced

1 TB. capers

½ tsp. dill

Salt and pepper

Heat oil in a large skillet over medium heat, and sauté onion for five minutes, until soft and translucent. Turn the heat under the skillet to low. Meanwhile, in a separate bowl, whisk eggs and milk.

**Cook to Cook**

Our Scottish friends raved about this egg dish (Scottish Eggs) from one of Scotland's most famous hotels: Slainté.

Add eggs to the skillet and cook, stirring slowly, for three minutes. Eggs should still be runny but be starting to thicken. Add salmon pieces, capers, and dill, and continue cooking for two minutes, or to desired consistency.

Serve with crisp wheat toast. If this is breakfast, you're done. If it's dinner, a salad goes well with Highland Eggs.

# Chicken and Shrimp Paella

This quick version brings to life some of that magic taste.

Prep time: 8 minutes • Cook time: 12 minutes • Serves 4 to 6

3 bags boil-in-bag rice

3 TB. olive oil

2 tsp. paprika

¾ lb. boneless, skinless chicken breasts, sliced crosswise into ¼-inch thick pieces

Salt and pepper

3 TB. butter

1 onion, chopped

1 TB. crushed garlic

1 (16-oz.) can chopped tomatoes, with juice

1 cup baby peas (available fresh or frozen at your grocery store)

Pinch saffron (about ⅛ tsp.)

3 TB. sherry or cooking wine

½ tsp. crushed red pepper

¾ lb. cooked jumbo shrimp

Juice of ½ lemon

Salt and pepper

Cook rice per package instructions (usually 10 minutes). When done, set aside, ready for adding later.

Meanwhile, heat olive oil in a large skillet over medium-high heat. Sprinkle paprika over all sides of sliced chicken, season with salt and pepper, and cook chicken strips in oil, turning, for five minutes or until done. Remove chicken strips to a plate.

Melt butter in the skillet and add onion. Cook onion for five minutes, add garlic, and cook for one minute. Add chopped tomatoes, peas, saffron, sherry, and crushed red pepper, and cook for four minutes. Stir in shrimp and cooked rice, and heat for three minutes. (If you're using frozen shrimp, defrost before using by running under cold water in a colander.)

Serve from the skillet or from a serving platter, drizzling first with lemon juice. Season with salt and pepper.

## Cook's Glossary

**Paella,** a feast for the eyes as well as the stomach, is a grand Spanish mélange of rice, shellfish, onion, meats, rich broth, and herbs. You will note that many of the recipes that evoke the cuisine of the world feature rice as a key ingredient. After all, rice is a staple upon which much of the world relies.

# Lightning Chicken Curry

This is a brief glimpse into Indian cooking, a rich and diverse cuisine that one could spend a lifetime exploring.

Prep time: 5 minutes • Cook time: 15 minutes • Serves 4 to 6

2 TB. olive oil

1 lb. boneless, skinless chicken breasts, cut into 1-inch cubes

3 TB. butter

1 onion, finely chopped

1½ tsp. curry powder (available at most grocery stores)

3 TB. flour

¾ tsp. salt

¾ tsp. sugar

⅛ tsp. ground ginger

1 cup chicken broth (or 1 chicken bouillon cube dissolved in 1 cup hot water)

1 cup milk

1 tsp. lemon juice

4 cups cooked rice

Heat oil in a medium-size skillet over medium heat and cook chicken, stirring, for eight minutes or until cooked through. Turn off heat.

Meanwhile, melt butter over low heat in a large skillet. Sauté onion and curry powder for three minutes. Stir in flour, salt, sugar, and ginger, and cook until bubbling and smooth. Add chicken broth and milk and bring to a boil, stirring. Boil one minute, then add cooked chicken and lemon juice. Cook for three minutes.

Distribute rice to serving plates, then pour curry mixture over, and serve.

≈~

# Real Greek Salad

No lettuce or heavy dressing on this salad, just fresh, fresh vegetables, creamy Feta, and briny Kalamata olives. Looking for a light meal? Serve this with bread and you're done.

Prep time: 10 minutes  •  Serves 4 to 6

2 large sweet green peppers, seeded and chopped into 1-inch pieces

2 large fresh, firm tomatoes, chopped into 1-inch pieces

1 large or two small cucumbers, striped, sliced lengthwise, and pieces cut into ½ inch thickness

½ large sweet onion, chopped into ½-inch pieces

5 leaves of fresh basil, chopped (optional)

3 TB. extra virgin olive oil

2 TB. red wine vinegar

8 oz. Feta cheese, crumbled

½ cup Kalamata olives

Salt and pepper

Put peppers, tomatoes, cucumbers, onions, and basil (if using) in a large serving bowl. Drizzle with olive oil, then with red wine vinegar, and toss to coat. Top with feta and Kalamata olives and serve, seasoning with salt and pepper.

### Cuisine Context

Of the many vacation memories we brought back from the Greek island of Crete, the food was perhaps the most important to our kitchen-oriented lifestyle. At small restaurants, called *tavernas*, we ate outside on wooden tables under the summer sky. The food, featuring fresh local vegetables, herbs, and seafood, made dinner the most anticipated part of every day.

# Black Bean and Corn Stew

Evocative of Mexican and border-states cuisine, this rich vegetable stew is the antidote for cold weather.

Prep time: 3 minutes • Cook time: 20 minutes • Serves 8

| | |
|---|---|
| 2 TB. olive oil | 1 (10- or 16-oz.) pkg. frozen corn kernels |
| 1 large onion, chopped | ½ cup fresh cilantro, chopped (optional) |
| 1 TB. chili powder | 1 (15.5-oz.) can vegetable broth |
| 1 tsp. cumin | ⅔ cup sour cream |
| 1 (28-oz.) can chopped tomatoes, with juice | Salt and pepper |
| 1 (16-oz.) can black beans, drained | |

### Flare-Up

Black Bean and Corn Stew is one recipe just made for cilantro. However, if you've met cilantro before and it's not your friend, use less or just leave it out.

Heat oil in a large skillet over medium heat, and sauté onion for three minutes. Add chili powder and cumin and cook two minutes, stirring constantly. Add tomatoes, black beans, corn, cilantro (if using), and broth, and cook for 15 minutes.

Serve in large bowls topped with sour cream and seasoned with salt and pepper.

# Hummus Platter

A fast, tasty, and healthy Middle Eastern dish.

Prep time: 12 minutes  •  Serves 4

1 TB. crushed garlic

Juice of 1 lemon

1 tsp. salt

1 can chickpeas, drained

2 TB. olive oil

½ cup tahini (sesame paste—available in most grocery stores)

4 pieces of fresh pita sliced pizza-style into 8 wedges

1 cucumber, striped, ends removed, cut into sticks

8 oz. baby carrots

1 cup black olives

Put garlic, lemon juice, and salt in a blender and pulse to finely chop garlic. Set the blender on purée, and slowly add chickpeas, allowing them time to purée. Add oil and then tahini, and blend until the texture is fine and creamy. If hummus is too thick, add a little more olive oil.

Put hummus in a bowl, set on a large platter, arrange pita, cucumber sticks, carrots, and olives around the platter, and serve.

# Beef and Broccoli Stir-Fry

A flavorful, crunchy dish making quick use of traditional Chinese ingredients and methods.

Prep time: 5 minutes  •  Cook time: 7 minutes  •  Serves 4

1 TB. canola oil

1 lb. flank steak, cut into thin strips

½ tsp. salt

¼ tsp. pepper

1½ tsp. fresh ginger, grated (available in the vegetable section of most grocery stores)

2 cups chopped Chinese cabbage or bok choy, thick stem pieces separated from leaves

2 cups broccoli florets

2 TB. soy sauce

2 TB. sesame oil

4 cups cooked rice

Heat canola oil in a wok or large skillet over high heat. Sprinkle strips of steak with salt and pepper, and cook in oil with ginger, stirring constantly, for three minutes or until almost done. Add thick stem pieces of cabbage (or bok choy) and broccoli *florets*, and cook for two minutes. Add cabbage leaves, and continue cooking for two more minutes, or until leaves wilt and soften.

Add soy sauce and sesame oil, toss to coat, and serve over rice.

> **Cook's Glossary**
>
> A **floret** is the part of broccoli or cauliflower that holds all the flower or bud ends.

# Nuts About 20-Minute Cuisine

The next several recipes, inspired by cuisine from across Asia, use one or two ingredients that might be new to you (although you'll find them at most grocery stores), as well as some familiar ingredients (such as peanut butter) used in ways you've probably never seen before.

Fasten your seat belts and put your tray tables in an upright and locked position.

## Za's Peanut Sauce and Rice

The unusual (to us) combination of ingredients in this dish shows what we can learn from the cuisine of other countries.

Prep time: 5 minutes • Cook time: 8 minutes • Serves 4

3 tsp. crushed garlic

3 TB. creamy peanut butter

¼ cup white wine vinegar

¼ cup soy sauce

¼ cup warm water

2 TB. sesame oil

Pinch of cayenne pepper

½ tsp. fennel seeds

1 tsp. dried basil

4 cups cooked rice

Whisk together garlic, peanut butter, vinegar, soy sauce, water, sesame oil, cayenne, fennel seeds, and basil and heat in a saucepan over medium heat until just boiling. Remove from heat and let sit for one minute. It's ready!

Serve over rice for a flavor explosion.

**Cook to Cook** _____

If you're not accustomed to foods cooked with hot peppers or chili paste, try the recipes in this section first with half the suggested amount of the hot ingredient.

# Korean-Style Fried Rice

Prep time: 5 minutes   •   Cook time: 15 minutes   •   Serves 4

4 TB. canola oil (2 TB. for each skillet)

1 cup green beans, cut into 1-inch pieces

½ cup carrots, scraped and cut into ½-inch pieces

2 cups cooked rice

2 tsp. peanut sauce (available in the ethnic food section of most grocery stores), or to taste

1 TB. soy sauce

½ TB. sesame oil

3 TB. sesame seeds

¼ cup cashews

¼ cup pickled hot vegetables and liquid from jar (available at most grocery stores in the ethnic food section)

4 eggs

Hot pepper sauce

Heat 2 tablespoons oil in a large skillet. Sauté beans and carrots until just done (five minutes). Add rice, peanut sauce, soy sauce, sesame oil, sesame seeds, cashews, and pickled vegetables with juice. Mix thoroughly, heating. Distribute to four plates.

Heat remaining 2 tablespoons oil in a small skillet and fry eggs one by one. When done, put one egg on top of each plate of fried-rice mixture. Season with hot pepper sauce to taste.

# Derek's Nutty Chicken Stir-Fry

Prep time: 5 minutes   •   Cook time: 13 minutes   •   Serves 4

2 TB. vegetable oil

1½ TB. crushed garlic

1½ tsp. fresh ginger, grated (available in the fresh produce section of most grocery stores)

1 tsp. Chinese chili paste

4 TB. soy sauce

2 TB. peanut butter

1½ lbs. boneless, skinless chicken breasts, cut into ¾-inch cubes

3 cups green beans, cut in half

Heat oil in a wok over medium heat, and add garlic, ginger, chili paste, soy sauce, and peanut butter, stirring. Turn heat up to medium high and stir until peanut butter melts into sauce. Stirring constantly, add chicken. Cook until browned all over (about five minutes). Add beans and cook until slightly crisp (about five minutes). Serve over rice.

**Cook to Cook**

Fresh ginger root is a fresh, strong seasoning used in many ethnic recipes from Asia. Buy a piece and keep it in the freezer, grating a bit of it as needed.

# Ethnic Easy Timesavers

Even, or perhaps especially, when it comes to ethnic cooking, there are many 20-minute opportunities. After all, many countries rely on quick-cooking staples and vegetables—ingredients we've already found to be the friend of the busy cook. Here are a few that are quicker than most.

## Thai Couscous Salad

Prep time: 5 minutes • Cook time: 10 minutes • Serves 4

1 cup couscous

1 cup water

2 TB. butter

½ tsp. salt

1 (16-oz.) can sweet corn, drained

1 large red pepper, chopped

2 medium-size tomatoes, chopped

½ cup diced cucumber

½ cup scallions, finely chopped

½ cup dried fruit, such as raisins, currants, figs, or cranberries

1 tsp. Thai peanut sauce (optional)

**Cook's Glossary**

**Couscous** is a wheat-based staple similar in usage and nutritional value to pasta, bread, or rice.

Cook couscous per package instructions. The method will differ according to the brand, but often the method, for 1 cup couscous, is to boil water with butter and salt and then turn off the heat. You then pour dry couscous into water, stir, cover, and let stand for five minutes.

After couscous is ready, add corn, pepper, tomatoes, cucumber, scallions, fruit, and peanut sauce, and mix thoroughly. Vegetables will be warmed by couscous but will still be crisp.

# Bacon, Eggs, and Rice

A purely right-brain interpretation of rice, a worldwide staple. If you've got rice in the fridge (as a 20-minute cook, of course you do!) you're 10 minutes from this flavorful dish. It can be as simple or complex, bland or spicy as you want. This basic recipe will start you on your (culinary) way.

Prep time: 5 minutes   •   Cook time: 14 minutes   •   Serves 4

| | |
|---|---|
| ½ lb. bacon | 4 eggs |
| 1 large onion, chopped | 4 cups cooked rice |
| ½ tsp. crushed red pepper | Salt and pepper |

In a large skillet over medium-high heat, cook bacon until crispy. Remove bacon to paper towels. Add onion and red pepper to the skillet and cook for three minutes. While onion is cooking, whisk eggs. Add them to the skillet, stirring, and cook until done, about four minutes. Crumble bacon. Stir in bacon and rice. Heat thoroughly. Serve with salt and pepper.

# Down Under Burger

People might raise their eyes at this twist on the all-American food, but an ostrich burger is easy to cook, delicious, and fun. Ostrich (and its cousin, the emu) makes a healthy, low-fat meat with great beeflike flavor.

Prep time: 5 minutes   •   Cook time: 8 minutes   •   Serves 4

| | |
|---|---|
| 1½ lbs. ground ostrich meat (available at many grocery stores) | ½ tsp. salt |
| | ¼ tsp. pepper |
| ½ onion, finely chopped | Hamburger buns |
| 1 egg | Lettuce and tomato slices for serving |

Preheat the grill to medium, or heat a large skillet with a little butter over medium-high heat. In a bowl, combine ostrich meat, onion, egg, salt, and pepper. If the mixture is too moist to form patties, add a little dried bread crumbs. Form into patties three inches across.

Grill or skillet-fry burgers for eight minutes or until done, turning once. Serve on toasted burger buns with lettuce, tomato, and ketchup.

**Cook to Cook**

You can make ostrich burgers with cheese, but I find the cheese tends to hide the flavor, thus masking a new taste experience.

## The Least You Need to Know

◆ Many dishes popular in other countries are well suited to quick cooking.

◆ Experimenting with cuisines from different parts of the world is a learning experience … in 20 minutes!

◆ Familiar ingredients, like peanut butter, can be used in new and exciting ways.

◆ A slight twist on a familiar dish adds flavor—and interest—to an everyday meal.

# Chapter 20

# Healthy ... and Delicious!

## In This Chapter

- ◆ Healthy is second nature
- ◆ Favorite high nutrition recipes
- ◆ Favorite low-fat recipes

At times in my life I've eaten a lot of processed foods—fast food, instant soups, packaged foods with a shelf life of 40 years. I bought these things because I perceived them as inexpensive and convenient, and did not pay particular attention to that little ingredient box that shows I was devouring fat and salt. No wonder some of that stuff gives you a stomachache a day later. Now that I'm a little older and perhaps a little wiser, I've realized that processed is not necessarily quicker or less expensive than fresh, healthy ingredients. And as for the taste of a freshly prepared dish or one out of a can? Well, there's just no comparison.

Many recipes in this book already easily fall into the "healthy" category for the reasons we've discussed. Seafood (see Chapter 9) and certain cuts of chicken and pork (see Chapter 10) can be very low fat. Vegetarian dishes (see Chapter 12) are extremely healthy and most could easily fit into this chapter. The same goes for many vegetable dishes listed in Chapter 14. In this chapter, we'll review some tips and tricks for healthy eating, and, of course, take a look at some new, tasty, and healthy recipes.

# Low Fat Does Not Mean Tasteless

Low calorie does not mean bland, exactly the opposite, as a matter of fact. Healthy food, by nature, tends to be fresher and rely on unprocessed or less processed ingredients. Flavor comes from herbs and spices (0 calories, 0 fat!) rather than from salt and fat. Open a newspaper on most days and you'll find an article either touting the benefits of fresh ingredients or blaring news of some newly discovered hazard associated with preservatives used to extend the shelf life of highly processed foods. It's enough to make me start eating better (most of the time ... the occasional mac and cheese out of a box is part of life!).

Under the "health" umbrella, the information and recipes that follow focus on maximizing nutrition and minimizing fat intake. Nutrition is enhanced, as we mentioned, through the use of fresh, wholesome ingredients. Fat intake is reduced through careful selection of these ingredients, such as choosing lean cuts of meat and lots of vegetables. Fat intake is also reduced through choosing cooking methods that use minimum amounts of fat. (You may remember these from Chapter 3: broiling, grilling, steaming, and boiling.) These distinctions are not exclusive; something that is listed as "nutritious" may also be (bonus!) low in fat.

**Cook's Glossary**

Not all fats are created equal. "People living on the Greek island of Crete have very low rates of heart disease even though their diet is high in fat. Most of their dietary fat comes from olive oil, a monounsaturated fat that tends to lower levels of 'bad' LDL-cholesterol and maintain levels of 'good' HDL-cholesterol."

—From Eleanor Mayfield's "A Consumer's Guide to Fats," published in the *FDA Consumer*, by the Federal Consumer Information Center (www.pueblo.gsa.gov/cic_text/food/fatguide/fatguide.html)

# Nutritious and Quick

Here are several of my favorite recipes for their balance; they offer lots of nutrition without unnecessary fat or calories.

# Whole-Wheat Penne with Summer Squash, Tomato, and Mushroom

Prep time: 5 minutes  •  Cook time: 15 minutes  •  Serves 6

½ tsp. salt

2 tsp. + 2 TB. olive oil

1 TB. chopped garlic

1 tsp. crushed red pepper

1 tsp. dried basil

½ tsp. dried tarragon

8 oz. sliced fresh mushrooms

1 small yellow (summer) squash, sliced lengthwise and cross cut in ½-inch-thick pieces

2 large fresh tomatoes, chopped into 1-inch pieces, or 1 (16-oz.) can chopped tomatoes with juice

1 lb. whole-wheat penne pasta (available at many grocery stores)

Parmesan cheese, salt, and pepper

Boil water for pasta with salt and 2 teaspoons oil.

Meanwhile, heat 2 tablespoons oil in a large skillet over medium-low heat. Sauté garlic, crushed red pepper, basil, and tarragon for two minutes. Add mushrooms, yellow squash, and tomatoes and cook for six minutes, covered, stirring a couple times while cooking.

Distribute pasta to serving plates, top with tomato and pepper mixture, and season with Parmesan cheese, salt, and pepper.

**Cuisine Context**

Whole wheat in breads and pasta brings much higher nutritional value than white flour. Whole-wheat flour also brings a characteristic rich, nutty taste that many people prefer.

# Freddie's Spanish Eggs

Eggs, in *moderation*, are back in favor for their terrific nutritional value. This flavorful dish serves four, and can easily be scaled higher or lower.

Prep time: 5 minutes   •   Cook time: 10 minutes   •   Serves 4

| | |
|---|---|
| 6 eggs | 1 clove garlic, minced |
| ½ cup skim milk | 1 sweet red pepper, chopped into ½-inch pieces |
| Salt and pepper | |
| 2 TB. + 1 TB. olive oil | 2 fresh tomatoes, chopped into ½-inch pieces |
| 1 onion, chopped | 2 tsp. basalmic vinegar |

In a bowl, whisk eggs and milk with a dash of salt and pepper and set aside. Heat 2 tablespoons oil in a skillet and sauté onion, garlic, and peppers for 10 minutes over medium heat. Add tomatoes and balsamic vinegar, and salt and pepper to taste. Cook for another eight minutes.

Meanwhile, after adding tomato and vinegar to onion mixture, heat remaining teaspoon olive oil to another skillet and pour in egg mixture. Turn the heat to low and cook eggs, stirring, for five minutes or until cooked to your desired consistency. (Remember, the more you cook eggs, the firmer they will get.)

Divide eggs between four plates and top each with ¼ tomato-pepper mixture. Season with salt and pepper. As breakfast, this might be served with crisp whole-wheat toast. For dinner, serve with salad and hunks of baguette.

# Baked Acorn Squash

This is another dish Mom used to make. Very easy, tasty, and nutritious. Best served as a side dish, perhaps with bread and a grilled chicken breast.

Prep time: 4 minutes   •   Cook time: 14 minutes   •   Serves 4

| | |
|---|---|
| 2 small acorn squashes (4 to 5 inches long), halved lengthwise, seeds scooped out | 2 TB. butter or margarine |
| ¼ cup molasses (4 TB.) | Salt and pepper |

Pour ¼ inch water into a microwave-safe baking dish. Place squash halves, cut side down, side by side in the dish, and cook seven minutes on high. Remove dish from microwave, turn squash over (careful, it's hot!), and put 1 tablespoon molasses and 1½ teaspoons butter or margarine in the cavity of each squash. Microwave on high for seven minutes or until squash is soft and can scoop out with a fork, rotating dish to ensure even cooking. Serve with salt and pepper, using a fork to mash flesh of squash with any remaining molasses and margarine.

# Broiled Lemon Rosemary Chicken

Prep time: 5 minutes    •    Cook time: 8 minutes    •    Serves 4

1½ lbs. boneless, skinless chicken breasts

2 TB. olive oil

Juice of 1 lemon

½ tsp. dried rosemary

Salt and pepper to taste

Preheat the broiler. Place chicken breasts in a bowl. In a measuring cup, combine olive oil and lemon juice. Pour mixture over chicken breasts, turning to coat thoroughly. Sprinkle rosemary, salt, and pepper over chicken. Place chicken on an oven-safe baking pan and broil for four minutes. Drizzle any extra juice over chicken when turning, and broil for four more minutes, or until done.

Serve with rice and salad for a simple, flavorful meal.

**Cook to Cook**

A chicken breast is perhaps a near-perfect low-fat, quick-cooking ingredient. Be sure to use skinless, boneless breasts, as the skin contains most of the fat, and without the bone, the meat cooks much faster.

# Chicken and Paprika Cream

A spicy-creamy dish (a variation on the classic Hungarian Chicken Paprika) that is fun for dinner and suitable for guests. Serve with steamed vegetables and rice.

Prep time: 5 minutes    •    Cook time: 15 minutes    •    Serves 4

2 TB. olive oil

1½ lbs. boneless, skinless chicken breasts, each breast cut into three strips lengthwise (about ¾-inch thick)

1 tsp. paprika

¾ tsp. salt

Pinch of pepper

1 cup fat-free chicken broth

1 tsp. paprika

½ tsp. salt

⅔ cup fat-free or low-fat sour cream

Heat oil in a large skillet over medium-high heat. Sprinkle chicken breasts with paprika, salt, and pepper. Cook chicken for eight minutes or until done, turning once. When chicken is done, remove to a serving plate and cover with foil to keep warm.

Turn heat to high. Add chicken broth, paprika, salt, and more pepper to the skillet where chicken was cooked and heat to boiling. Cook for seven minutes (broth will reduce by approximately ¾). Turn off heat and stir in sour cream.

Arrange chicken slices on serving plates, pour sauce over, and serve.

# Low Fat and Quick

Eating food that contains a lot of fat needn't be a default way to live. For most high-fat dishes, there are tasty low-fat alternatives. Often, the shift to a healthy, low-fat recipe from a high-fat one is possible through seasoning. A slight change makes all the difference.

The following tip list from the National Institutes of Health provides several examples of how to reduce fat. Many of these suggestions are already an important part of healthy recipes in this book.

- Use reduced-fat or nonfat salad dressings.
- Use nonfat or lower-fat spreads, such as jelly or jam, fruit spread, apple butter, nonfat or reduced-calorie mayonnaise, nonfat margarine, or mustard.
- Use high-fat foods only sometimes; choose more low-fat and nonfat foods.
- To top baked potatoes, use plain nonfat or low-fat yogurt, nonfat or reduced-fat sour cream, nonfat or low-fat cottage cheese, nonfat margarine, nonfat hard cheese, salsa, or vinegar.
- Use a little lemon juice, dried herbs, thinly sliced green onions, or a little salsa as a nonfat topping for vegetables or salads.
- Use small amounts of high-fat toppings. For example, use only 1 teaspoon butter or mayonnaise; 1 tablespoon sour cream; 1 tablespoon regular salad dressing.
- Switch to 1 percent or skim milk and other nonfat or lower fat dairy products (low-fat or nonfat yogurt, nonfat or reduced-fat sour cream).
- Cut back on cheese by using small (1 ounce) amounts on sandwiches and in cooking or use lower fat and fat-free cheeses (part-skim mozzarella, 1 percent cottage cheese, or nonfat hard cheese).
- Try small amounts of these low-fat treats: fig bars, vanilla wafers, ginger snaps, angel food cake, jelly beans, gum drops, hard candy, puddings made with low-fat (1 percent) skim milk, nonfat frozen yogurt with a fruit topping, or fruit popsicles. Try pretzels or popcorn without butter or oil for an unsweetened treat.
- Save french fries and other fried foods for special occasions; have a small serving; share with a friend.
- Save high-fat desserts (ice cream, pastries) for special occasions; have small amounts; share a serving with a friend.
- Choose small portions of lean meat, fish, and poultry; use low-fat cooking methods (baking, poaching, broiling); trim off all fat from meat and remove skin from poultry.

- Choose lower-fat luncheon meats, such as sliced turkey or chicken breast, lean ham, lean sliced beef.

- What's a recommended serving size for meat? Experts suggest three ounces of cooked meat (which is the size of a deck of cards or a hamburger bun).

*Source: "Action Guide for Healthy Eating" from the Federal Consumer Information Center. The full text can be found at www.5aday.gov, and at the Federal Consumer Information Center website: www.pueblo.gsa.gov/cic_text/food/guideeat/Actiongd.html.*

Here are some of my favorite recipes. They bring flavor and nutrition without a lot of fat.

# Chicken, White Bean, and Vegetable Stew

This is reminiscent of Italian farmhouse dishes, rich with vegetables, herbs, and nutrition. Leftovers will taste even better the next night.

Prep time: 5 minutes • Cook time: 20 minutes • Serves 4 to 6

| | |
|---|---|
| 4 TB. olive oil (divided) | ½ tsp. dried basil |
| 1½ lbs. boneless, skinless chicken breasts, chopped into ½-inch cubes | ½ tsp. dried oregano |
| ¼ tsp. salt | 4 cups (2 cans) fat-free chicken broth |
| Pinch of pepper | 1 (16-oz.) can white (cannellini) beans, drained |
| 1 onion, chopped | ½ tsp. salt |
| 1 TB. chopped garlic | 1 cup 20-Minute Tomato Sauce, or 1 cup crushed tomatoes |
| 2 large carrots, scraped and cut into ¼-inch rounds | Parmesan cheese |
| 4 large celery sticks, washed and cut into ¼-inch slices | Salt and pepper |

Heat 2 tablespoons oil in a large skillet over medium-high heat. Sprinkle chicken pieces with salt and pepper, and cook for six minutes or until done, turning once. Remove chicken from the skillet and place on a plate. Cover with foil to keep warm.

Add remaining olive oil to skillet over medium-high heat. Cook onion for two minutes. Add garlic, carrots, and celery and cook for two more minutes. Then add basil, oregano, chicken broth, beans, salt, tomato sauce, and cooked chicken. Cook, stirring, for 14 minutes. Serve in large bowls with Parmesan cheese, salt, and pepper.

# Anya's Turkey Salad

Prep time: 10 minutes • Serves 4

1½ lbs. white turkey meat, cubed

2 TB. olive oil

2 TB. sherry

1 TB. sugar

2 TB. low-fat or fat-free sour cream

½ tsp. salt

½ lb. seedless grapes, cut in half

4 oz. walnut pieces

Place turkey pieces in a bowl. Combine olive oil, sherry, sugar, sour cream, and salt, and pour over turkey. Gently stir in grapes and walnuts.

# Country Potato Chowder

Prep time: 5 minutes • Cook time: 15 minutes • Serves 4 to 6

1½ lbs. baking potatoes, peeled and cut into 1-inch cubes, or new potatoes, unpeeled, scrubbed and cut into 1-inch chunks

3 TB. olive oil

1 large onion, sliced thin

1 cup skim milk

1½ cups fat-free chicken broth

¼ cup sherry or cooking wine

2 tsp. salt

Salt and pepper

½ cup fat-free or low-fat sour cream

### Cook to Cook

For a flavor and visual variation to Country Potato Chowder, I like to stir in a handful of fresh arugula or spinach, washed and chopped, stems removed, a minute before cooking is finished. This addition makes a big change to the texture of the chowder, however, which is not to everyone's taste!

Peel and slice potatoes. Arrange slices in a microwave-safe baking dish and microwave on high for 10 minutes or until soft.

While potatoes are cooking, heat oil in a large skillet over medium-low heat and cook onion until potatoes are finished cooking.

Working in batches, add cooked potatoes, cooked onion, and a little milk and broth to a food processor. Purée until smooth and creamy. If chowder is too thick, add a little more milk and broth. Return chowder to the skillet, add sherry and salt and any remaining milk and broth, cook for five minutes, and serve. Serve with salt and pepper, and a spoonful of sour cream.

# Broiled Zucchini

This is delicious and surprisingly rich for a vegetable dish.

Prep time: 8 minutes • Cook time: 6 minutes • Serves 4 to 6

3 zucchini squash, striped, ends removed, and cut into quarters lengthwise

Whites from 2 eggs

⅓ cup skim milk

1 tsp. salt

Pinch cayenne pepper powder (optional)

1 cup dried bread crumbs

Preheat the broiler. Place zucchini sticks in a flat tray. Whisk egg whites and milk and pour mixture over squash, turning to coat. Mix salt and cayenne pepper with bread crumbs and pour bread crumb mixture onto a plate. Roll squash sticks one by one in bread crumbs and arrange on a lightly oiled, oven-proof baking tray. (Use a canola-oil spray for best results.) Broil squash for six minutes or until done, turning sticks to ensure even cooking. Drizzle cooked squash with balsamic vinegar, and serve.

**Flare-Up**

Be extra careful of splashes and splatters when transferring hot liquids.

# Pasta with Broiled Tomatoes and Garlic

Broiled tomatoes gain a richness that stands up to hearty whole wheat.

Prep time: 5 minutes • Cook time: 15 minutes • Serves 6 to 8

1 lb. whole-wheat spaghetti

3 large tomatoes

1 TB. chopped garlic

1 tsp. dried basil

1 tsp. dried oregano

½ tsp. dried thyme

½ tsp. salt

Pinch pepper

Cook spaghetti. Preheat broiler. While spaghetti is cooking, chop tomatoes into ½-inch pieces and place in a bowl. Mix with garlic, basil, oregano, thyme, salt, and pepper. Spread mixture in a glass baking tray, and broil for 10 to 12 minutes, stirring every few minutes. Toss sauce with pasta and serve.

## The Least You Need to Know

- One of the reasons we are attracted to fat is for the flavor. Knowing this, we can substitute other ingredients rich in flavor but low in fat.
- Healthy 20-minute cuisine is possible through careful selection of ingredients that are low in fat.
- Healthy 20-minute cuisine is also possible through cooking methods that require minimum added fat, such as grilling, broiling, steaming, and boiling.
- Healthy cooking is another opportunity to explore new ingredients and cooking methods.

# Chapter 21

# Whirlwind Romantic ... Food!

## In This Chapter

- ◆ What makes a meal romantic?
- ◆ Meals with luxuriant flavor and texture
- ◆ Quick romantic recipes

Of course, the question "What is romantic?" could fill a series of books. The concept of romantic food or romantic meals alone is a topic for an entire book by itself (now there's an idea). Fortunately, we focus here on a subset of that group, quick dishes and meals that inspire love and affection.

## What Is It About Food That Inspires Romance?

The romance of a meal comes in equal parts from the food and from our attitude toward the food and each other. A peanut butter sandwich, a glass of milk, and Oreo cookies might not be romantic to you, but to the couple whose first shared meal was PB&J 20 years ago in college, that might be the very epitome of a romantic anniversary dinner.

◆ **Magic by association.** A date often centers around a meal. Whether it's a burger and fries or filet mignon and lobster tails, as you gaze into your beloved's eyes, some of that magic rubs off on the food. That magic is still there, waiting for the occasion when you call upon it again over a dish that is either special in its own right, or made special by the occasion.

◆ **Demonstration of care.** Whether a simple quick meal or a long and complex one, when you cook for someone you are demonstrating that you care. Part of human nature is that we all want to be loved. As we eat that burger or that casserole, we're eating more than just food, we're absorbing and appreciating the attention that went into making it.

◆ **Aphrodisiac connotations.** Whether true or not, some foods (oysters, truffles, chocolate) contain ingredients that are associated with an improved love life.

◆ **Flavor and texture.** Ripe, juicy fruit. Smooth, velvety sauces. Rich chocolate. For most of us, these are not only appealing characteristics, they are welcome elements of a dish intended to be romantic.

◆ **Appetite.** A recurrent theme in literature from classics to paperbacks. To devour something is to absorb it, to make it part of you. Call me crazy, but there might just be a common element of appetite in both romance and a romantic meal.

### Cuisine Context

I once read a quote that one movie star's favorite meal is a cheeseburger and a bottle of Lafite-Rothschild (an expensive red Bordeaux). Talk about the little black dress of 20-minute cuisine. We might have to substitute a slightly less expensive Cabernet, but I'll take a page out of that recipe book.

◆ **Environment.** The setting of a meal is incredibly important to how it is perceived, from a brightly lit cafeteria to a candlelit table for two. We'll go into this more later (see Chapter 28), but keep in mind the stage on which you set your romantic meal.

◆ **Circumstances.** Sometimes we simply need fuel or want to celebrate. At other times we simply want, and need, quiet time with people we love. What's the occasion that leads to the meal? An anniversary, a promotion, a day at the beach, a hard day's work. Each circumstance naturally affects your attitude. Planning a romantic meal for romantic circumstances helps make the meal a success.

# Luxurious Meals

These quick recipes bring some of the flavors and textures of a romantic meal.

## Bowties with Sherry Pepper Cream

Luxuriant cream with distinctive sherry richness make this a special dish.

Prep time: 3 minutes • Cook time: 17 minutes • Serves 6 (or just the two of you more than once!)

1 lb. bowtie pasta

2 TB. butter

1 TB. crushed garlic

3 large tomatoes, chopped, or 1 (28-oz.) can whole Italian tomatoes, chopped

½ tsp. crushed red pepper

1½ tsp. dried basil

¼ tsp. freshly ground black pepper

⅔ cup heavy cream

½ cup cooking sherry

Parmesan cheese

Cook pasta for five minutes. Heat butter in a large skillet over medium-low heat. Sauté garlic two minutes. Cut tomatoes in can. Add tomatoes, red pepper, basil, black pepper, cream, and sherry. Cook five minutes, then add partially cooked pasta. Cook five minutes more.

Serve with Parmesan cheese, Italian bread, and steamed asparagus.

# Romantic Veal

This piccata variation is simple and luxuriant, and unusual enough to add something special to a meal. This will also make enough to serve the kids beforehand without the sauce. Tell them it's chicken nuggets.

Prep time: 5 minutes • Cook time: 15 minutes • Serves 4

1½ to 2 lbs. veal leg cutlets or scaloppini (The key here is that the veal needs to be thin, ¼ to ½ inch thick, to enable quick cooking.)

Salt and pepper

2 TB. + 1 TB. butter or olive oil

⅔ cup dry white wine

⅓ cup chicken broth

1 lemon, ⅔ cut into thin round slices, the other ⅓ whole for squeezing

Dry veal with a paper towel, sprinkle with salt and pepper. Heat the sauté pan over medium heat and add 2 tablespoons butter or olive oil, heat until a drop of water sizzles when dropped in to the pan, then add pieces of veal. Depending on the size of the pan, you may need to cook veal in batches so veal pieces are separate from each other while cooking. Cook veal approximately three minutes per side (checking for doneness). Remove to serving plates.

**Flare-Up**

Depending on the size of the pan, you might need to cook the veal in batches so that the veal pieces are separate from each other while cooking.

Pour wine and chicken broth into the skillet, and deglaze the pan (reducing wine while scraping the pan with a rubber spatula to capture meat juices) over high heat. Once liquid is reduced by ⅓ or so, squeeze ⅓ lemon into sauce and add remaining 1 tablespoon butter or oil, and cook for a few more minutes, until mixed thoroughly.

Pour sauce over veal, and garnish with lemon slices. Accompany with rice or pasta and green beans.

# Anya's Smoked Salmon Penne Pasta

Sweet red (or yellow) peppers work beautifully with the rich taste of smoked salmon.

Prep time: 5 minutes • Cook time: 15 minutes • Serves 4 to 6

1 lb. penne pasta

3 TB. olive oil

2 large sweet red peppers, sliced thin

1 small red onion, sliced very thin

¾ cup whipping cream

1½ TB. cloves garlic minced

2 TB. cream cheese (or more to thicken sauce)

2 TB. capers

Freshly ground black pepper to taste

6 to 8 oz. smoked salmon, chopped into bite-size chunks

⅓ cup chopped fresh parsley

¼ cup grated Parmesan cheese

Cook pasta. While penne is cooking, heat oil in a large skillet over medium heat and sauté sliced peppers and red onion, covered, for five minutes to wilt and soften vegetables. Set vegetables aside and add cream and garlic to skillet. Boil one to two minutes to soften garlic and reduce cream 25 percent. Add cream cheese. Stir gently to ensure cream cheese melts into sauce and thickens it. Sauce should coat back of spoon. Add another tablespoon cream cheese, if necessary, to thicken.

Drain pasta. Toss with cream sauce, capers, pepper, salmon, parsley, and Parmesan cheese. Serve immediately.

**Flare-Up**

Shorten this recipe even more by using a 16- to 20-ounce jar of roasted red peppers, sliced. If you're using a jar of roasted red peppers in this smoked salmon dish, make sure they are not pickled or preserved in vinegar. *Don't pick a pint of pickled peppers for this pasta* (say that five times fast!). Pickled peppers will not taste good.

# Paul's Quick and Easy Mac and Cheese

Prep time: 5 minutes • Cook time: 15 minutes • Serves 4 to 6

16 oz. macaroni

3 TB. butter

3 TB. flour

1 tsp. dry mustard

1 tsp. Tabasco

½ tsp. Worcestershire sauce

1 cup milk

Dash of your favorite beer (optional but a great secret ingredient)

2½ cups grated sharp cheddar cheese

Freshly ground black pepper to taste

In large pot, bring water to boil for pasta. Add salt. Add pasta and cook. While pasta is cooking, melt butter in a large skillet over medium-low heat. Add flour and dry mustard and stir in with a fork or whisk until blended. Let cook gently for one minute. Add Tabasco and Worcestershire sauce, still stirring. Add ¼ cup milk while stirring with whisk. Stir constantly to work out lumps. Add another ¼ milk and stir to incorporate. Repeat two more times. Raise heat a little and let simmer one minute. Add beer, if using. Let cook off. Lower heat, add grated cheese, and stir. If sauce seems too thick, add a little more milk and stir to thin.

Drain macaroni and add to cheese sauce. Add black pepper to taste. Stir gently to mix everything and serve immediately with a tossed salad and a glass of light red wine.

Cheddar aged at least 18 months is they key ingredient of this rich and savory macaroni and cheese dish. Aged cheddar is available in the cheese shop of most grocery stores.

✍

# Romantic Easy Timesavers

Talk about the ultimate hope for the cook: to create something rich, luxuriant (and romantic) in less than 20 minutes. Well, these recipes aim to please ….

# Fondue

Melted cheese is somehow the definition of romance. This dish is easy to make and exotic.

Prep time: 5 minutes  •  Cook time: 10 minutes  •  Serves 4

½ lb. shredded or grated Gruyere cheese

½ lb. shredded or grated Swiss cheese

2 tsp. crushed garlic

1½ cups dry white wine

½ tsp. nutmeg

Pinch black pepper

1 loaf crusty white bread, cut into 1-inch cubes

Mix shredded Gruyere and Swiss cheeses.

In a medium saucepan, heat garlic and wine to a bare simmer over low heat. When wine reaches a simmer, slowly stir in cheese mixture a spoonful at a time, stirring until melted, then adding the next spoonful. When mixture is melted, smooth, and just beginning to bubble, stir in nutmeg and black pepper. Distribute bread pieces, dunk in cheese, and enjoy.

### Cuisine Context

There was a time when a fondue set was an unavoidable wedding or house-warming gift. If you have such a set gathering dust in the closet, bring it out for this recipe! The secret of the fondue set is the ability to deliver, usually through canned heat or a candle, a small amount of continuous heat to keep the mixture liquid. If you use a saucepan, you'll need to periodically reheat the fondue. The long thin forks that come with a fondue set will be useful, too, although a regular fork works okay for dunking bread.

# Muffy's Pumpkin Mousse

Simple and rich.

Prep time: 5 minutes  •  Serves 4

2 cups milk

1 cup canned pumpkin

2 (3.8-oz.) pkgs. vanilla pudding mix

1 tsp. baking mix or pumpkin pie spice (or use ½ tsp. cinnamon, ¼ tsp. nutmeg, pinch of cloves and a pinch of allspice)

1 cup whipped topping

Combine milk, pumpkin, pudding mix, and spices. Stir in whipped topping and serve.

# Pan-Broiled Bacon, Scallops, and Rice

Use an oven-safe skillet (such as cast iron) for this flavorful dish.

Prep time: 5 minutes • Cook time: 15 minutes • Serves 4

3 cups cooked rice

½ lb. bacon

2 TB. sherry

½ tsp. dried thyme

¼ tsp. ground sage

1 *bunch* scallions, dark green parts removed, white and light green parts thinly cross-sliced

1 lb. sea scallops

½ cup shredded Swiss cheese

Salt and pepper to taste

Cook rice. Preheat the broiler. Meanwhile, cook bacon in a large skillet over medium-high heat for five minutes or until done. Remove bacon to paper towels. Add sherry, thyme, sage, and scallions to the skillet and cook for three minutes. Remove about half the scallions to a small bowl, using a slotted spoon, and add scallops to the skillet and cook two minutes on each side, or until done, stirring. While scallops are cooking, crumble bacon. Add rice and crumbled bacon to the skillet and stir to thoroughly combine. Sprinkle cheese over top of the mixture in the skillet, and sprinkle reserved scallions over cheese.

**Cook's Glossary**

A **bunch** is another generic term for long, slender vegetables. In the case of scallions, it usually means 5 to 10 stalks.

Place skillet under the broiler for three minutes or until cheese melts. Remove from oven, season with salt and pepper, and serve.

# Eggs for Two, Scrambled with Sun-Dried Tomato and Sweet Onion

Finally, here's a fast, rich egg dish. After you try this, you'll know the answer when someone asks you how you like your eggs.

Prep time: 3 minutes • Cook time: 10 minutes • Serves 2

| | |
|---|---|
| 2 TB. olive oil | Pinch dried thyme |
| ½ cup finely chopped sweet onion (such as Vidalia or Spanish Sweet) | Pinch crushed red pepper |
| | 3 eggs |
| ⅓ cup oil-packed sun-dried tomato, chopped into 1-inch pieces | ⅓ cup skim milk |
| | Salt and pepper |

Heat oil in a small skillet over medium heat and sauté onion, tomato, thyme, and red pepper for seven minutes. Whisk eggs and milk in a bowl. Turn heat to low and add egg-milk mixture. Stir slowly for three minutes or until egg mixture is cooked but still soft and velvety. Serve to two plates with salt and pepper.

Accompany with crisp wheat toast, freshly squeezed orange juice, and coffee, and you've got a candidate for the perfect breakfast.

## The Least You Need to Know

- A romantic meal is as much about the occasion as it is about the food.
- Prepare a meal with care, and you're halfway there.
- A romantic meal needn't be complex or time-consuming.
- A special occasion is a good time to experiment with one or two indulgent or unusual ingredients ... honor a memorable occasion with a memorable meal.

# 22

# Entertain, Sane

## In This Chapter

- ◆ Secrets of sane entertaining
- ◆ Quick appetizer recipes
- ◆ Crowd-pleaser recipes
- ◆ Make-ahead recipes

A gathering of friends and family presents a unique challenge for those who aspire to good cooking. Magazines, newspapers, and television cooking shows are filled with images of perfect tables, arrayed with carefully prepared, gorgeous gourmet dishes.

Holidays present a similar challenge—and opportunity. Holidays bring a disproportionate focus on family time, and family time often centers around the table. Family members who might be apart during the rest of the year are now together for days (or weeks!). For those of us with a family, the kids are home more often.

When we entertain, more so than any at other time, we have a huge desire to impress our friends and loved ones with the gift of good food, yet for all these reasons, we've got even less time than normal in which to prepare it. This chapter will help relieve some of the pressure.

# Fast and Fabulous

Entertaining with terrific food, prepared in limited time, is not only possible, it's critical if you are to enjoy your own gathering. These tips and web resources will help you shine, while at the same time maintain composure.

- **Be realistic.** We have steadily reduced the number of offerings at our own party table. With two or three main dishes, rather than six or seven, we now focus on preparation and quality while at the same time keeping blood pressure in check. Guest compliments have only increased.

- **Pay close attention to ingredients and cooking methods.** The same wisdom we've applied throughout this book, choosing quick-cooking ingredients and quick-cooking methods, applies more than ever when planning a party menu. When considering ingredients, also consider choosing not only quick-cooking items, but also foods that are ever-so-slightly out of the ordinary to add interest.

- **Prepare in advance.** Many irresistible menu items lend themselves to advance preparation, such as casseroles and pasta dishes, and many actually improve with time to allow the flavors to meld. Others are delicious in their simplicity, from casual chili to elegant salmon. Imagine how impressed your guests will be; they arrive, you chat for an hour, and then suddenly you produce a succulent master-piece … that you've prepared beforehand.

- **Familiar themes, unusual twists.** People bring expectations. These expecta-tions can be respected, and delighted, by variations on a theme. Keep in mind that you should appeal to most (if not all) of your guests, so this may not be the time to unveil raw octopus. If your group loves salmon, however, a quick search on Epicurious.com turns up a whopping 284 possibilities.

- **Keep cool.** Or at least keep room temperature. Serving up a combination of dishes that need to be hot for a long period of time means that you will be checking temperature rather than enjoying yourself at your own party.

- **Many hands make light work.** *Ouch*, so it's cliché. It's also true. Guests, friends, and family often want to contribute by bringing or making something, or helping in the kitchen. Let them.

- **Learn from history.** If you hold an event each year, record what was a hit, what wasn't, and how much to make. The hits become your "tradi-tions." Discard what didn't work, and replace it with something new. File the list away in real files or on your computer.

> **Cook to Cook**
>
> Myriad dishes are delicious served at room tempera-ture … and you get to socialize. One of my favorites is cold poached salmon, a delicious

◆ **Don't reinvent the wheel.** When you need ideas, inspiration, and practical "how-to" guidance take advantage of the timesaving tips, recipes, and collective experience of friends, family, and the web. For a listing of some of my favorite food-related web resources, read on.

**Cook to Cook**

For specific recipes, you can keep a "recipe box" of your favorites on many cooking websites, including Epicurious and

# Recipes for Fast Appetizers

I have deliberately not included in this book a lot about appetizers: For a busy household on a weeknight, hors d'oeuvres are just not in the 20-minute cards—unless they *are* the dinner, of course.

## ══════ Jean's Mexican Dip ══════

This delicious recipe takes full and quick advantage of commercially available ingredients.

Prep time: 10 minutes   •   Serves 8

½ envelope taco seasoning

1 cup sour cream

1 (17-oz.) can refried beans

1 cup guacamole

2 cups shredded Mexican cheese (available pre-shredded at many grocery stores)

3 small tomatoes, chopped

3 scallions, dark green parts removed, chopped

1 (8-oz.) can sliced black olives, drained

Mix taco seasoning with sour cream. In a quiche pan or pie plate, layer ingredients, starting with refried beans on the bottom, then sour cream, guacamole, cheese, tomatoes, scallions, and ending with black olives on top.

Serve with tortilla chips for dipping.

## Derek's Curry Ball

An unusual, flavorful appetizer that benefits from making ahead, but can be eaten right away if it just looks too good (or if you don't have the time to wait!).

Prep time: 10 minutes • Serves 8

1 (8-oz.) pkg. cream cheese (softened)

2 TB. sour cream

2 tsp. curry powder

½ cup chopped green onion

½ cup coarsely chopped dried peanuts

½ cup raisins (optional)

Dried/flaked coconut

1 cup mango chutney

In a medium bowl, combine cream cheese and sour cream. Blend in curry powder. Add chopped green onions, peanuts, and raisins. Mix thoroughly and form into a ball.

To serve: Roll ball in coconut and pour chutney over the top. Serve with crackers as hors d'oeuvre.

# Recipes to Please the Toughest Crowd

Entertaining brings the opportunity for a few quick treats to prepare for a group, even with the most discerning palates. Here are a couple of my favorites.

## Tuna Broccoli Pasta Salad

Easy to make and tasty. Not a bad choice for a family dinner, either.

Prep time: 5 minutes • Cook time: 15 minutes • Serves 4

½ lb. pasta shells

1 bunch broccoli

3 medium tomatoes, cubed

1 can solid white water-packed tuna, drained.

¼ cup red wine vinegar

¼ cup olive oil

2 tsp. dried basil

1 tsp. dried oregano

Salt and pepper to taste

Cook pasta, drain, and rinse under cold water. Set aside.

Meanwhile, chop broccoli into small bite-size florets (about one inch in length). In a vegetable steamer or large saucepan with one inch boiling water, steam broccoli until still crisp but starting to become tender. Drain and rinse under cold water.

In a large bowl, combine pasta, broccoli, tomatoes, and tuna. In a bowl, whisk vinegar, oil, basil, and oregano. Pour dressing over salad and toss to coat. Season with salt and pepper to taste.

# Quick and Easy Angel Hair Pasta with Shrimp and Feta

This recipe, from my wife's cousin Anya (a super cook) is a real crowd-pleaser.

Prep time: 5 minutes   •   Cook time: 15 minutes   •   Serves 4 to 6

16 oz. angel hair pasta (capellini)

2 to 3 TB. olive oil

1 tsp. minced garlic

1 tsp. red pepper flakes (optional but adds nice zing)

1 tsp. dried oregano

¼ cup clam juice (optional)

1 (28-oz.) can chopped plum tomatoes, drained with juice reserved

2 TB. tomato paste (optional if using clam juice)

2 TB. capers

1 lb. raw medium shrimp, shelled and deveined

Black ground pepper to taste

Salt to taste

¼ to ⅓ lb. feta cheese, crumbled into good-size chunks (not small chunks)

In large pot, bring salted water to boil for pasta. Lower water to simmer until ready to cook pasta five minutes before serving.

Heat olive oil in a large skillet over medium heat and sauté garlic until translucent. Add pepper flakes, oregano, clam juice, and reserved tomato juice. Turn heat to high. Reduce liquid by half. Add tomatoes, tomato paste, and capers. Reduce heat and simmer five minutes. Add shrimp and simmer an additional five minutes. Add salt, pepper, and feta cheese and gently mix. (Make sure to stir feta gently: The goal is not to dissolve cheese in sauce but to have chunks of warm, soft feta floating.)

Once shrimp is added to tomato sauce, turn up pasta water and cook capellini until *al dente*.

Drain and serve with shrimp feta tomato sauce.

Garnish with addition crumbled feta (Parmesan is inappropriate for this dish) or serve finely crumbled feta alongside for garnish. With bread and salad, this is an elegant meal.

If you like saucier pasta for this recipe, double the chopped tomatoes, garlic, and capers (easy on the oregano and pepper flakes; they are potent, so don't necessarily double them). Clam juice is optional but adds a nice depth to the sauce. No salt needed as the feta, clam juice, and capers are salty.

## Cook's Glossary

**Al dente** is Italian for "against the teeth." In the context of cooking, it refers to pasta (or another ingredient) that is neither soft nor hard, but just slightly firm against the teeth. This, according to many pasta aficionados, is the perfect way to cook pasta.

# Stir-Fried Orange Beef

Prep time: 4 minutes   •   Cook time: 10 minutes   •   Serves 4

1 TB. sesame oil (can use all canola oil if necessary)

1 TB. canola oil

1 lb. steak tips, sliced thin (approximately ¼ inch)

½ tsp. salt

1 large onion, sliced thin (approximately ⅛ inch)

1 tsp. crushed garlic

6 oz. peapods, fresh or frozen

1 (6-oz.) can water chestnuts (optional)

½ cup orange juice

1 TB. soy sauce

1 TB. orange zest

2 TB. brown sugar

¼ tsp. black pepper

Orange slices to garnish

Heat sesame and canola oils in a wok or large skillet over medium-high heat. Sprinkle beef slices with salt, and cook four minutes or until done. Remove beef to a separate plate and reduce heat to medium. Cook onion for two minutes. Add garlic and cook for one minute. Add peapods and water chestnuts, and cook for an additional two minutes or until pods are still crisp but turning tender. Return beef to wok or skillet, add orange juice, soy sauce, orange zest, brown sugar, and pepper. Cook, stirring, for one minute.

Serve over white rice, garnished with thinly sliced orange cross-sections.

# Ham and Swiss Casserole

Quick, hearty, and flavorful.

Prep time: 2 minutes   •   Cook time: 18 minutes   •   Serves 4

2 TB. oil

1 large onion, chopped

1 chicken breast, approximately 6 oz., cubed

10 oz. broccoli florets, fresh or frozen (if fresh, about ½ head)

4 slices bread (I like rye.)

6 oz. cubed ham steak (½-inch cubes)

1 (10.5-oz.) can cream of mushroom soup

1 (8-oz.) pkg. shredded Swiss cheese

½ tsp. paprika

Heat oil in a small skillet over medium heat, and cook onion and chicken together until chicken is done, about six minutes.

Meanwhile, if broccoli is frozen, rinse to thaw. Line an 8 × 8 × 2 microwave-safe dish with bread. Top with chicken-and-onion mixture, ham, and broccoli. Pour soup over all, top with shredded Swiss, and sprinkle on paprika. Cook on medium in microwave for approximately 12 minutes, turning a quarter turn every 3 minutes (cooking time will vary depending on the microwave).

### Cook to Cook

Cream soups, such as cream of chicken, broccoli, or mushroom are a traditional secret of the busy cook looking for an ingredient that will add flavor and creamy texture.

# Spicy Mayonnaise

Prep time: 4 minutes   •   Serves 4 to 8

½ cup mayonnaise

2 TB. Worcestershire sauce

2 TB. Dijon mustard or brown mustard (not a too strong Dijon and not a yellow mustard)

1 tsp. Tabasco sauce

1 tsp. paprika

¼ tsp. freshly ground black pepper

Juice of 1 lemon

Whisk mayonnaise, Worcestershire sauce, mustard, Tabasco, paprika, pepper, and lemon juice and use in recipes or as a spicy spread on hearty grilled seafood.

# Dorst Family Crab Cakes

This is an impressive and delicious dish to serve guests. Serves four as dinner or eight as an appetizer. Lobster or salmon can also be used and the results will reflect the different nuances of flavor.

Prep time: 9 minutes • Cook time: 11 minutes • Serves 4

1 bunch parsley, cut off at stems

11 slices inexpensive, soft white bread, torn up into pieces

1 red bell pepper

½ small onion

1 lb. lump crab meat drained, picked over to remove shells

Spicy Mayonnaise (see preceding recipe)

4 TB. butter for sautéing

Preheat oven to 425°F. In food processor, chop parsley until fine. Measure out ⅓ cup and put in a large mixing bowl. Put remaining parsley in a big, wide salad bowl. In same food processor (without cleaning out leftover parsley) add torn bread. Process a few seconds until finely chopped. Dump into salad bowl with parsley and mix together. Measure 1 cup bread crumbs and add to a large mixing bowl.

Chop pepper and onion fine in food processor (no need to clean out bread crumbs). Put in the mixing bowl with the 1 cup parsley bread crumbs. Gently add crab meat (or lobster or salmon) and mix carefully to distribute ingredients but not break up seafood too much. Add Spicy Mayonnaise to crab mixture.

Form into 8 cakes (use a ⅓ cup measure to scoop out a single serving size). Roll cakes in bread crumbs in big salad bowl and put on plate.

Melt 4 tablespoons butter in large ovenproof nonstick pan over medium heat and place 8 cakes in pan. After one minute, gently flip cakes over. Put immediately in oven and bake 10 minutes at 425°F or until heated through.

Serve directly with lemon wedges (and tartar sauce, if desired.)

### Cook to Cook

Don't be intimidated by the number of steps—most of it is simply using the food processor in succession without cleaning! Two other quick accelerators: Use canned seafood or prepared seafood from the fish counter, and store-bought mayonnaise mixed with spicy seasonings rather than homemade mayonnaise.

# Why Not Make Some Things Ahead of Time?

These recipes take less than 20 minutes to make, but then require chilling, hence the "make-ahead" description. The advantage, of course, is that when guests arrive, these dishes are ready to go.

# Marcia's Shrimp Mold

Prep time: 5 minutes    •    Cook time: 10 minutes    •    Serves 8

1 can (10.5-oz.) tomato soup

¼ cup water

1½ envelopes gelatin

9 oz. cream cheese

1 cup mayonnaise

¾ cup onion, finely chopped

1 cup celery, finely chopped

2 (4.5-oz.) cans shrimp, rinsed

½ tsp. salt

¼ tsp. ground black pepper

In a saucepan over medium heat, boil soup and water. Stir in gelatin.

Turn heat to low. In pieces, stir in cream cheese, stirring after each piece until it melts. Stir in mayonnaise, onion, celery, shrimp, salt, and pepper.

Pour into a well-greased *mold* and refrigerate overnight.

### Cook's Glossary

A **mold** is a decorative shaped metal pan in which contents, such as mousse or gelatin, firm and take the shape of the pan.

# Friedkin Family Salmon Mousse

Serve with cocktail pumpernickel bread or crackers. The ingredients are listed for each stage in this blender-intensive dish. Although this needs to set in the fridge, making it takes 10 minutes or less.

Prep time: 10 minutes    •    Serves 8 as an appetizer

1 envelope gelatin

2 TB. lemon juice

1 TB. minced onion

½ cup boiling water

½ cup mayonnaise

⅛ tsp. Tabasco sauce

Dash salt

¼ tsp. paprika

Dash Worcestershire sauce

Dash garlic powder

1 lb. canned salmon (drained and boned)

1 cup heavy cream

Combine gelatin, lemon juice, onion, and water in a blender and blend 40 seconds at high speed.

Add mayonnaise, Tabasco sauce, salt, paprika, Worcestershire sauce, garlic powder, and salmon to the blender and blend 20 seconds on high.

Blend in cream ⅓ cup at a time, blending after each addition. Blend 30 seconds longer when all ingredients have been added, and pour into a well-oiled mold. Chill until set.

# Cold Poached Salmon

One memorable vacation in the highlands of Scotland, we were served cold poached salmon. It was elegant and delicious, and remarkably quick to make, although this does fall into the category of a make-ahead timesaver because of the cooling time.

Prep time: 10 minutes  •  Cook time: 15 minutes  •  Serves 8

1 (3-lb.) salmon filet

**Broth:**

1 bottle white wine (a dry white, such as a sauvignon blanc or chardonnay)

Water sufficient to cover the salmon after addition of wine, about 10 cups

1 TB. salt

2 onions, chopped

3 bay leaves

2 tsp. dill

2 tsp. celery seed

½ tsp. ground black pepper

Thoroughly rinse fish.

Using a fish poacher or large pan with lid, combine wine, water, salt, onions, bay leaves, dill, celery seed, and black pepper, bring to a boil, and simmer for five minutes.

Lower fish into broth (if you are not using a rack to hold fish in broth, cheesecloth is a good idea, wrapped around filet, to keep it from breaking apart when you lift it out). Add more water if needed to cover fish. Put on the lid and simmer 10 to 15 minutes, or until done.

Remove fish carefully from broth, and cool in the refrigerator. I cool it on a platter, and then slide it onto the serving tray atop a bed of greens (like kale) and garnished with lemon wedges and dill.

**Cuisine Context**

Many enthusiasts are satisfied with lemon alone, but there are many sauces that are also delicious with poached salmon, including homemade tartar sauce.

# The Least You Need to Know

- ◆ Entertaining with 20-minute cuisine is not only possible; it's critical if you are to enjoy your own gathering.
- ◆ Pay close attention to quick-cooking ingredients, such as seafood and thin cuts of white meats and beef.
- ◆ Experiment with slightly unusual preparation or seasoning to add interest … but don't go too far.
- ◆ Consider 20-minute recipes that can be made ahead of time, so at the actual event you can focus on your guests, rather than the food.

# Chapter 23

# Leftovers

## In This Chapter

- ◆ Make the most of your time
- ◆ Rice-based recipes
- ◆ Pasta-based recipes

Throughout this book, I've referred to the concept of the make-ahead Easy Timesaver. This concept covers two types of food: completed dishes and cooked ingredients.

*Completed dishes* means they are ready for future use and nothing else needs to be done. This includes many pasta dishes, such as lasagnas, and vegetable dishes, such as ratatouille or minestrone. Many of these dishes not only taste great the next time around, they often taste better. *Cooked ingredients* are the key ingredients in many recipes, including the staples (rice, pasta) and main ingredients (meats). With a supply of these ingredients on hand, a quick meal is minutes away.

This chapter focuses on how to used cooked ingredients, sometimes called "planned leftovers" to accelerate a second meal. These dishes can often be prepared in 10 minutes or less. I've organized these dishes by staple (rice and pasta), although as you'll see, they could also be organized by other common ingredient (white meat, richer meat, and so on).

**Cook to Cook** _____

If you've got the space in your refrigerator, consider making it a regular habit to make double batches of these ingredients to take advantage of the time savings the next night. Each of these recipes will use those extras to create a tasty dish in well less than 20 minutes.

# Rice Dishes

As if wearing a new suit of clothes, rice takes on a new character with each seasoning variation—here, Italian, Mexican, Asian, and Middle-Eastern. Does this get your imagination cooking?

## Chicken, Tomato, and Rice

Prep time: 4 minutes   •   Cook time: 12 minutes   •   Serves 4

1 TB. olive oil

½ onion, chopped

¾ lb. cooked chicken, chopped into 1-inch pieces

1 cup 20-Minute Tomato Sauce (or pasta sauce)

3 cups cooked rice

Salt, pepper, and Parmesan cheese as seasoning

Heat oil in a large skillet over medium heat. Sauté onion for five minutes. Add chicken and cook for two minutes. Then add tomato sauce and cook for three minutes more. Finally, stir in rice and heat through, about two minutes.

Season with salt, pepper, and Parmesan cheese.

# Salsa Rice

Prep time: 6 minutes  •  Cook time: 8 minutes  •  Serves 4

1 TB. olive oil

2 scallions, dark green parts removed, white and light green parts sliced into ¼-inch pieces

¾ lb. cooked chicken, chopped into 1-inch pieces

1 cup salsa

3 cups cooked rice

Salt and pepper to taste

½ cup sour cream

Heat oil in a large skillet over medium heat and sauté scallion pieces for two minutes. Add chicken and cook for two minutes. Add salsa and rice, and cook for four minutes more.

Distribute to serving plates, season with salt and pepper, and spoon a *dollop* of sour cream on each serving.

### Cook's Glossary

A **dollop** is yet another fun cooking term that roughly corresponds to a spoonful. It is most appropriately used with ingredients where quantity varies widely according to taste, such as a dollop of sour cream. (One would probably not refer to a dollop of crushed red pepper.)

# Stir-Fried Teriyaki Beef, Pea Pods, and Rice

Prep time: 5 minutes  •  Cook time: 12 minutes  •  Serves 4

1 cup cooked steak, cut into ½-inch pieces

3 TB. teriyaki sauce

4 cups cooked rice

1 TB. olive oil

1 onion, chopped

1 (9-oz.) box frozen snow peas or sugar snap peas (or fresh)

Place steak pieces in a bowl and cover with teriyaki sauce, turning steak to coat each piece. Set aside.

Heat rice in a microwave for three minutes or until hot.

Meanwhile, heat oil in a large skillet over medium heat and sauté onion for five minutes. Add peas and cook for four minutes. Then add steak pieces with teriyaki sauce, and cook for three minutes or until heated through.

Distribute rice to serving plates and top with steak and snap pea mixture.

# Curried Rice

The flavorful, somewhat unusual treatment of these ingredients is a delicious wake-up for the taste buds.

Prep time: 5 minutes   •   Cook time: 9 minutes   •   Serves 4

4 cups cooked rice

2 TB. olive oil

1 onion, chopped

2 tsp. curry powder

½ lb. cooked chicken, cut into ½-inch pieces

½ cup raisins

1 crisp apple, cored and cut into small (¼-inch) pieces

1 tsp. salt

¼ tsp. black pepper

Heat rice in a microwave for three minutes or until hot.

Meanwhile, heat oil in a large skillet over medium heat and sauté onion and curry powder for five minutes. Add chicken pieces and raisins and cook for three minutes longer. Finally, add apple pieces, salt, and pepper, and heat for one minute longer, stirring to mix seasoning.

Distribute rice to serving plates or bowls, and top with curried chicken mixture.

# Rice with Mozzarella, Bacon, and Scallions

This rich, hearty dish is quick to make but will disappear even more quickly.

Prep time: 4 minutes   •   Cook time: 14 minutes   •   Serves 4

6 strips bacon

4 scallions, dark green parts removed, white and light green parts sliced into ¼-inch pieces

4 cups cooked rice

⅓ cup shredded mozzarella cheese

Salt and pepper

Cook bacon in a large skillet until crisp. Remove bacon to a plate covered with paper towels. Discard all but about 3 tablespoons bacon fat in the skillet.

Add scallion pieces and cook in bacon fat for two minutes. Add rice and cook, stirring, for four minutes. Add mozzarella cheese, stir to mix, turn off heat, and serve, seasoning with salt and pepper.

# Pasta Recipes

Leftover pasta can be reheated in several ways. My favorites are to quickly submerge it in boiling water, or to sauté the pasta in a skillet, where it takes on a unique, browned quality and regains some of that al dente texture. Although not my favorite method, the microwave can do the job quickly, although the result can be clumpy pasta.

## Skillet-Broiled Double Cheese Casserole

Prep time: 5 minutes　•　Cook time: 14 minutes　•　Serves 4

1 lb. ground beef

1 onion, chopped

1 tsp. salt

¼ tsp. black pepper

1 tsp. crushed red pepper

1 cup 20-Minute Tomato Sauce

1 *half-batch* (5 cups) cooked macaroni

1 cup shredded mozzarella

3 slices provolone cheese

Preheat the broiler. Heat a large oven-safe skillet over medium heat and cook ground beef, onion, salt, black pepper, and red pepper until beef loses its pink color, about seven minutes. Pour off excess fat. Add tomato sauce and macaroni and cook, stirring, for five minutes more.

Turn off heat, stir in mozzarella, and top mixture with slices of provolone. Slide the skillet under the broiler and cook for three minutes, or until cheese melts and bubbles.

### Cook's Glossary

A 1-pound package of pasta will cover two meals for my family of four (with small children). I always cook the entire package to enable an even quicker meal the following night. The leftover cooked pasta, what I call a **half batch,** is the quantity I refer to in some of these recipes. A half batch of spaghetti is about 5 cups and will vary for other pasta shapes.

# Romano Pasta

Simple can be delicious.

Prep time: 4 minutes • Cook time: 6 minutes • Serves 4

| | |
|---|---|
| 4 TB. olive oil | 1 tsp. salt |
| 2 TB. chopped garlic | ¼ tsp. black pepper |
| 1 half-batch (5 cups) cooked spaghetti | ½ cup shredded or grated Romano cheese |

Heat oil in a large skillet over medium heat and sauté garlic for two minutes. Add spaghetti and sprinkle with salt and pepper. Heat, stirring, for three to four minutes until pasta is heated to your preferred temperature.

Serve, topping generously with Romano cheese.

# Black Tie and a Red Dress

The "black" comes from sliced olives, the "tie" from bowtie pasta, and the "red" from sweet grape tomatoes.

Prep time: 5 minutes • Cook time: 8 minutes • Serves 4

| | |
|---|---|
| 2 TB. olive oil | 2 cups grape tomatoes, each sliced in half |
| 2 TB. chopped garlic | 1 half-batch (5 cups) bowtie pasta |
| ⅔ cup sliced black olives | Salt and pepper |
| ½ tsp. crushed red pepper | Parmesan cheese |

Heat olive oil in a large skillet and sauté garlic for two minutes. Add olives and red pepper and sauté for two more minutes. Add tomatoes and pasta, and cook until heated through, about four minutes.

Season with salt, pepper, and Parmesan cheese.

# Penne with Sweet Sausage and Tomato Sauce

Prep time: 5 minutes • Cook time: 15 minutes • Serves 4

1 lb. sweet Italian sausage, sliced into ¼-inch sections

1 onion, chopped

1 tsp. chopped garlic

3 cups 20-Minute Tomato Sauce

1 half-batch (5 cups) penne pasta

Parmesan cheese

Cook sausage in a large skillet with onion for eight minutes. Add garlic and continue cooking until sausage is done. Drain excess fat. Add tomato sauce to the skillet and cook over medium heat for five minutes.

Meanwhile, heat pasta and distribute to serving plates. Pour sauce over each serving and serve topped with Parmesan cheese.

### Flare-Up

Fatty meats, such as sausage, bacon, and ground lamb and beef release fat when they are cooked. This fat can be used as a flavorful cooking medium for other ingredients, such as onion and garlic in the accompanying recipes. Just keep in mind that, although delicious, this is saturated fat we're talking about, to be enjoyed in moderation. Discard extra fat to minimize your saturated fat intake.

# Lamb and Feta Orzo

Prep time: 5 minutes  •  Cook time: 7 minutes  •  Serves 4

| | |
|---|---|
| 1 lb. ground lamb | ½ tsp. crushed red pepper |
| 1 TB. garlic | 1 half-batch cooked orzo pasta |
| 1 tsp. oregano | 6 oz. crumbled feta cheese |
| ½ tsp. rosemary | |

Cook lamb, stirring, in a large skillet over medium-high heat with garlic, oregano, rosemary, and red pepper. Cook for seven minutes or until done.

Meanwhile, heat *orzo* in the microwave. Distribute pasta to serving plates, and top with seasoned lamb and feta cheese.

### Cook's Glossary

**Orzo** pasta, with its tiny oblong shape, might be mistaken for rice. It provides an interesting variation on the pasta theme, and mixes well with other small ingredients.

## The Least You Need to Know

- ◆ Key ingredients for leftovers, such as rice and pasta, often take no extra time to prepare in large quantities.
- ◆ Using planned leftovers enables extra-quick preparation at the next meal, often 10 minutes or less for a tasty dish.
- ◆ Rice and pasta are extremely flexible and can be used to create a dish using many leftover meats and seasonings.

# Part 5

# Behind the Scenes

A work of art is often better appreciated when placed in the right frame; a frame that helps focus attention on that which it contains.

Here we review some of the background to a meal—helpful tips and tricks that you might keep secret, but that help provide inspiration, set the right tone, and generally put a meal more under your control, including the web and your own friends as sources of inspiration, food and wine, and gardening for 20-minute cuisine.

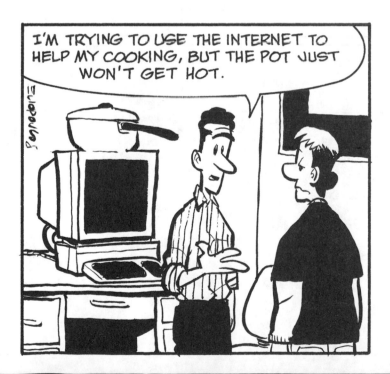

# Chapter 24

# Cyber Soufflé: 20-Minute Cuisine on the Web

## In This Chapter

- ◆ How the web can speed you on your way
- ◆ Favorite sites
- ◆ Reviews of cooking websites

We've all heard the cliché "It's not what you know, but that you know where to find it." Nowhere is that more true than on the Internet. The web offers up a vast, savory stew of cooking information, and an endless gush of products. Help is out there; the challenge is finding it without wasting time.

As the "gourmet expert" on an Internet guide site, I sift the web's many food resources for those few worth recommending in my weekly 'zine. As the subscriber list has grown, I've realized that smart cooks use the web for many purposes, read this chapter to find out where to begin.

## The Newest Kitchen Appliance ... Your Mouse

There are thousands of food-related sites out there. Some are purely commercial, only of interest if you're looking to buy what they sell. Others have missing pages or strange parts that won't work; like with the search for the ancestors of humanity, no one can find the missing link. Some are homemade and filled with typos and irrelevant information on Pez dispensers or stories about "what I did on my vacation." Some are just forgotten, neglected sites that once were great, but now are sad shadows.

Amongst this mass of time-wasters, there are some gems. These sites are fast-loading and inviting, have a minimum of annoying ads, are easy to navigate, and are filled with useful information. Those are the ones we want.

I've spent the past year and a half reviewing food-related websites for my "gourmet cooking on a budget" e-mail newsletter. I've seen many sites of all kinds in my culinary "surf" for the ideal cooking website.

I've learned from experience that the interests of my newsletter subscribers (at times more than 75,000 of them) are wide and varied. Entertaining subscriber questions are standard fare. How do you cook a walleye? Can you help me find a recipe for Dutch honey? How about South African Bobotie? Dandelion wine? A romantic meal featuring pork chops? Or an increasingly common theme, "I'm in an Iron Chef competition next week, and I need creative things to do with *X*. Can you help?"

The scope is nothing if not entertaining, but each question illustrates the potential of the web for the busy, inquisitive cook. I found that resources do indeed exist that provide guidance for walleye (I had to learn first that it was a fish!), for Bobotie (delicious), romantic chops, dandelion wine, and just about any bizarre ingredient you can cook up for Iron Chef. The responses are gratifying: "The recipes for Dandelion wine were exactly what I was looking for. Many thanks!"

### Cuisine Context

Searching for cooking help on the web is a terrific example of the potential value—and the hassle—of the Internet in the everyday life. Without knowing where to go, it's just too easy for the casual surfer to get buried in useless or irrelevant information.

I wish I could claim true expertise in exchange for that praise; the fact is I just know where to find things on the Net.

So does the web provide value for busy cooks? The answer is a resounding "yes." The web can provide a new and exciting vehicle to use to improve food knowledge, but as chefs, restaurants, vendors, and enthusiasts keep adding to the vast smorgasbord of foodie sites, the need for help grows. For this reason, it's helpful to know where to start.

# À La Carte Web

When you need ideas, inspiration, and practical guidance to prepare for holiday meals, using the web can be a delight. Here are terrific web resources that go a long way toward enabling a delicious meal with limited time. For others, take a look at Appendix B.

## General Recipe Sites

**AllRecipes, All the time:** AllRecipes draws on a massive database of recipes, and provides advice on techniques, meal planning, and more. The "by ingredient" search engine enables mix-and-match creativity; think shrimp and pasta, or apples and cream. Tap them in, the inspiration flows, and you can save your favorites to your personal recipe box. (www.allrecipes.com)

**Sam Cooks:** Longtime gourmet columnist for *Wine Spectator*, Sam Gugino has constructed a clean, information-packed site for the intelligent cook. Check out "Cooking to Beat the Clock," and "Eat Fresh, Stay Healthy: An A to Z Guide to Fruits and Vegetables." (www.samcooks.com)

**Vivisimo:** This is, of course, the same great search engine you've used before, but the "clusters" of categories on the left can be particularly useful for the cook. Enter "Porcini Recipes," and the groups are separated into "Italian," "Mushroom," "Salad," "Risotto," "Wine, Food," even "Recipes from Famous Chefs and Restaurants." There is the danger of having too much fun and spending hours here. (www.vivisimo.com)

**Flare-Up**

A simple web query will often return an avalanche of information. Try "gourmet cooking" on one of the major search engines. One of my searches—and I'm not kidding—came up with a hopeless 516,000 "hits."

## Healthy Cooking and Vegetarian Sites

**Cooking Light:** Tips, recipes, and themes (French, Italian, celebration menus, and so on), for those of us who want taste and quality, but who also might be concerned with what we eat. Who, me? (www.cookinglight.com)

**Cook to Cook**

Find an interesting site? If you like the information you've found on a site, look to see if the site offers a "recommended links" page. Often there you'll find more of the same.

**Delicious Decisions:** This site is serious about health (it's part of the American Heart Association). I find this useful primarily for detailed advice on substitutes and healthy cooking methods (see the "heart health chef's tour"). (www.deliciousdecisions.org)

*Vegetarian Times:* Vegetarian never looked so good as the collection of mouth-watering recipes here. (www.vegetariantimes.com)

## Comfort Food

*Southern Living:* Comfort food with a regional slant from *Southern Living*. Tantalizing recipes throughout make it tough to decide where to start. Well, I guess it will be Apple Pancakes for me. (www.southernliving.com—click on "foods")

# Selected Site Reviews

Here are several more of my favorite sites, as excerpted from my subscriber newsletter "Gourmet Cooking on a Budget" found at www.wz.com. (Copyright WZ.com Inc., reprinted with permission. Ongoing reviews of this type of website are available at wz.com/food/GourmetCookOnBudget.html.) I've picked out one or two of my favorites from several categories of ingredients or themes (again, even more in Appendix B).

## Sites Focused on Quick Cooking

**Cook's Recipes:** An archive of fruit-based dessert recipes, most of them quick, all of them tempting. (www.cooksrecipes.com/desserts/fruit-dessert-recipes.html)

**Diana's Kitchen:** It must be the "skillet recipes" theme that kept me poking through the choices. Easy, quick, flavorful. Skillet Beef Burgundy? (www.dianaskitchen.com/page/skillet.htm)

**Lo Cal Diner:** A tidy collection of low-calorie desserts, some quite quick to prepare. Strawberries and Cream Pie sounds like the place to start. (lowcaldiner.com/Desserts/desstoc.html)

**Minutemeals** challenges the assertion that cooking quickly requires sacrifice of quality and taste. The listing of complete holiday menus is especially soothing. (www.minutemeals.com/pages/recipes/holiday.htm)

> **Cook to Cook**
>
> When you've found a great site, one you want to visit again, use your browser to mark it with a "bookmark" so you can come back to it quickly.

**My Meals:** A selection devoted to recipes requiring 30 minutes or less. Some are very basic; others decidedly less so. Hot Carameled Apples with Pie Crust Dippers? (www.my-meals.com/Search/SearchResults.aspx?cat=19,103)

**Quick Menu Organizer:** Choose between "Weeknight," "30 Minutes or Less," "Healthy," and more. Plenty of simple menus enable creativity from the fatigued weeknight gourmet. (www.ivillage.com/food)

## General Recipe Sites

These sites also have plenty of information on quick cooking.

*The Cook's Thesaurus* contains a truly massive gourmet glossary. Ever wonder where that cut of beef is from? Voilà—there it is, with diagrams. Each section provides guidance on substitutions (very useful if you cook with what's on hand). (www.foodsubs.com)

**Epicurious.com:** Epicurious claims more than 13,000 recipes, drawing from years of *Gourmet* and *Bon Appetit*, among other sources. Try visiting the search engine with random ingredients you have on hand that need a "common destiny." You'll be surprised what you come up with: Ground Turkey and Sun-Dried Tomato Meatloaf is a surprising delight I make every winter. Assemble your favorites and create your own personal recipe file. (www.epicurious.com)

**Flare-Up**

Many cooking-related sites offer free e-mail newsletters. They can be fun and useful, but be careful signing up for too many, otherwise you'll find yourself with a full mailbox. Also check carefully how frequently the newsletter (or 'zine) is delivered. Do you really want it every day? Finally, look at a sample on the site. Will you have to sift through a page of ads to get to the information you actually signed up to see?

**Global Gourmet** will draw you in to articles on everything from "Holiday Helpers" to "I Love Chocolate" (let's get to the point already). (www.globalgourmet.com)

## Miscellaneous

**All Green:** A clearinghouse of Irish recipes. Who can object to the concept that, for Beef with Guinness, the beer "has the same function as the wine in Coq Au Vin"? (www.irelandseye.com/aarticles/culture/recipes/index.shtm)

**Burpee:** Yes, the famous seed catalog has a helpful section on vegetable-intensive recipes (the best kind). Check out Easy Risotto with Garlic and Parsley. (www.burpee.com)

**EatDrinkDine:** What a great site! Sommelier Evan Goldstein offers a wonderfully complete yet easy to use page that you can approach from "Start with Food" or "Start with Wine." Chicken cacciatore goes with …. (www.eatdrinkdine.com)

**Hershey's:** Simple, fun desserts featuring—what else—chocolate, from a small company in Pennsylvania. Classic Chocolate Mousse might just do it for me. (hersheykitchens.com)

**Holiday Menus:** A terrific site! Christmas, Chanukah … a menu for Van Gogh? Talk about theme cuisine. Emphasis is on simplicity, taste, and "scalability" (quantities can be increased for large gatherings). Menus requiring time can be made a day or so ahead. Talk about impressing your guests—they arrive, you chat for an hour, then suddenly you produce a masterpiece that's been prepared beforehand. (Check out Braised Beef with Anchovies and Oranges, part of the "Menu for Van Gogh.") (www.foodstyles.com/Indices/menu_index.htm)

**I Love Pasta!:** The National Pasta Association offers a clean, easy to navigate site that is packed with information on all kinds of pasta dishes, from super quick to super low fat. Roasted Vegetable Lasagna? (www.ilovepasta.org/recipes.html)

### Cuisine Context

As you know just from reading the paper, the Internet is in an ongoing state of flux. Sites appear and disappear regularly. Many of the sites that have been around for the longest are closely linked or owned by non-Internet organizations. That's often where they get their stability, their funding, and their ability to be around in an industry that's changing so rapidly.

**I wish they all could be California Fish …:** The California Seafood Council puts in a plug for seafood from the Golden State. You can safely substitute fish from other waters. Check out Steamed California Halibut on Rice Pillow (entrées). Barracuda Burgers?! (www.ca-seafood.org/recipes/index.htm)

**Penzey's Spices:** Each recipe makes use of one or more assertive, characteristic spices. Check out Grilled Asparagus, using bold cracked pepper. I'm a big fan of these guys. (www.penzeys.com)

**Seafood Watch:** Worth a click to check the list of recommended seafood, and learn what to avoid due to overfishing. (www.montereybayaquarium.org/efc/cr/seafoodwatch.asp)

**Spiceopedia:** A who's who of spices and usage. (chef-of-the-month.com/recipes/katzer)

**Spicy Cooking:** This nifty site ties together diverse cooking styles through the common element of heat and spice. From Mexican to Thai, with several stops in between, it's all here. (www.spicy-cooking.com)

***Southern Living:*** Comfort food with a regional slant from *Southern Living*. Tantalizing recipes throughout make it tough to decide where to start. (www.southernliving.com/food/comfort_food.asp)

**TastingTimes:** My site offers a growing section on food and wine pairing, wine menus, and recipes. It also features a free e-mail newsletter, *The Wine Minute*, with "hot pick" recommendations under $15. (www.tastingtimes.com)

**Tienda.com:** If you've ever wondered where to find tapas recipes or how to make the perfect flan, this is the place. Tienda, a vendor of all things Spanish, offers a well-organized shortlist of Spanish recipes, from appetizers and tapas to desserts. Castilian Garlic Soup, anyone? (www.tienda.com/recipes.htm)

## The Least You Need to Know

- If you know where to look, the web can enable the busy cook to quickly find information on fast cooking.
- Identify your favorite websites, and bookmark them for frequent use.
- Be picky about the sites you rely on. There are many out there, so choose ones that are visually appealing, clean and easy to use, and trustworthy.
- Use the web to test out new uses for ingredients you have on hand and make a quick meal fun, new, and interesting!

# Chapter 25

# Inspiration from Unexpected Places

## In This Chapter

- ◆ Old and new traditions
- ◆ Barbershop special
- ◆ Memory lanc cuisine

Certain topics of conversation like sports and the weather are generally considered safe while having universal appeal. These topics, unless you're a sports fanatic or weather hobbyist, however, can get pretty stale pretty quick. And that's where food and cooking come in. We might not all be sports fans, and we might not want to think about the weather (especially in New England), but we all have to eat, and most of us would prefer to eat something tasty and interesting. That is what this chapter is all about.

## It's a Tradition!

All of us meet new people, whether it's by the grill, at school, or over lunch at work. I've seldom met a person who doesn't warm up to the topic of food, and more often than not, I'll find out that the person is proud of a recipe, whether it is a creation of their own or a family tradition.

The opportunity here is tremendous, because every person's culinary interests are a result of their own family traditions, which are sure to be different from mine. Different traditions mean …

- **New ingredients.** I can't count the number of ingredients I've learned from others, but just to name a few: cannellini beans (see recipes to follow), feta cheese, buttermilk, arugula, lentils. At one point these were all discoveries, ingredients that I could add to my repertoire that brought texture, flavor, and interest to dishes I made.

- **New seasonings.** Seasonings evoke memories and provide windows into new styles of cooking from around the world. Each has a distinct personality. Where would we be without the fire and richness of cumin, the spiciness of black pepper, the warmth of cinnamon? All of these spices are "from" somewhere, and they bring history with their flavor.

- **New combinations.** New combinations are a wake-up for the palate. They might not all be our favorite, but it's all learning. And some of those combinations are pure magic. Nutmeg and spinach? It works.

- **New cooking methods.** There's more for the 20-minute cook than just a fry pan.

- **Even new methods of eating.** In Chapter 11, I relayed a meatball recipe my wife originally obtained from her hairdresser. What was new about this (Sandra's Easy Meatballs) was not only the ingredients, but that her family tradition was to eat meatballs plain, one by one, enjoying them for their flavor all by themselves. Meatballs to me came attached to sauce and spaghetti, so this was a learning experience. Not an epiphany, perhaps, but learning nonetheless. So I've tried these homemade meatballs, and they're delicious when they're not obscured by tomato sauce. So I learn.

### Cuisine Context

Every ingredient, of course, is "new" to us at some point. That's part of the joy of cooking. The universe of possibilities is almost unlimited, so we can look forward to ongoing interest and excitement. Not bad for a humble meal.

### Flare-Up

There's a big difference between someone's favorite recipe and someone's "favorite meal ever." A recipe is something a human being can actually make, and that your friend has likely made many times (and can reel off instructions for you). A *favorite-something-ever* might be tough to duplicate, especially if it's a notable memory because it was eaten at a fancy restaurant.

What is the value of a new recipe? Something new, whether it's a new car or a new recipe, brings a little bit of interest and learning to our lives. We're experiencing something new, and we're expanding. I don't know about you, but to me learning and expanding are what life is all about.

# A New Haircut and Old-Country Recipes

My barber provides one personal example of how the people we meet can provide unexpected inspiration. One winter conversation yielded a wealth of information … for the kitchen.

On a cold late winter afternoon, the weather outside is no match for the heated debate in Bruno's Barber Shop. The perfect minestrone is no small matter, and participants are emotional. "Use homemade chicken broth"—snip—"store-bought tomatoes have no flavor!"—snip, snip. "Don't add the pasta too soon"—whir.

A visit to Bruno's is a comforting journey; conversation without pressure, warmth and camaraderie from all parts of town, between all ages. The shop is an institution in Natick, Massachusetts, a historically working-class town 10 miles from Boston. Energetic opinions on local news, politics, sports, movies (I'll be forever thankful for the tip about *The Secret of Santa Vittoria*), and music are all standard topics. The audience, from my three-year-old to town elders generally agree (one does not argue with a man holding scissors). I've taken the movie recommendations, looked for the soccer games on TV, and checked out the music events; although I've left politics at the door.

The surprises, however, are the old-country recipes and gardening advice served up with my short-back-and-sides. Bruno and his brother Italo came to this country in the 1950s, but they proudly continue the traditions they remember from childhood in Calabria. From seedling to simmering, the brothers savor every step of growing a meal. Within weeks of my midwinter cut, the front window of the shop will fill with plastic trays. Basking in the early spring sun, tomato, eggplant, and pepper seedlings will grow faster than they would in any commercial greenhouse I know. Gardeners in town take their cue from the appearance of these trays. I've tried to keep up myself and have failed miserably.

The myriad tiny plants are a natural conversation starter. Many years ago I asked Italo what he did with all these tomatoes. I quickly learned that while sports, politics, and news might form the grist for barber shop conversation, the heart is reserved for gardening and cooking. I learned the secrets of cooking dark greens, of garlic and olive oil, of cannellini beans, and of course of fresh, juicy tomatoes. What I couldn't remember I would scribble down between snips, notes about cooking rooted in a hard life on a dry farm. Vegetables are at the core, and nothing is wasted.

Call it Italian Farmhouse 101.

I started with the basics, and prepared what Italo calls *Minestra*. I know, I know, this is old news to you, but to me, Minestra was a revelation. It is no soup, but rather a simple dish of garden greens. So simple, in fact, that I was skeptical. In dutiful waste-not compliance, I used trimmed garden Brussels sprout leaves. I sautéed them to a dark green in olive oil and garlic, added cannellini beans, and sprinkled the glistening greens with freshly shredded Parmesan. My wife and I found ourselves devouring the

rich and flavorful dish as though we hadn't eaten in days. Served with fresh Italian bread and a glass of good Chianti, this surprisingly hearty, flavorful dish is one we look forward to again and again.

**Cook to Cook**

One valuable lesson I learned from my barber: *Waste nothing.* That lesson made me look at some of my garden with a different perspective. Many of the cole crops, for example (cabbage relatives such as broccoli, cauliflower, and Brussels sprouts) produce tasty, nutritious leaves that most people just throw away. I still haven't found any use for those slugs, though.

With this success under my belt, I went back for minestrone soup, for vegetable stews, for sauce, for pasta dishes that showcase vegetables and seafood. I found that as my repertoire improved, so did my appreciation for the simple, rich flavors from an Italian farm.

So where do you go for cooking inspiration? Some people have a favorite magazine or cookbook. Others use the Internet. As for me, I go to my barber.

# Italian Farmhouse Vegetable Stew

Hearty and healthy and perfect for a cold day. Got leftover chicken? Put that in, too. Good for two meals.

Prep time: 5 minutes • Cook time: 20 minutes • Serves 8

2 TB. olive oil

1 large onion

2 tsp. crushed garlic

2 large potatoes, peeled and cut into ½-inch cubes

3 to 4 large kale, collard, or similar leaves, washed and coarsely chopped

1 cup cabbage, thinly sliced

8 cups chicken broth

1 (15.5-oz.) can cannellini beans, drained

1 zucchini squash, rinsed, ends removed, sliced into ¼-inch medallions

½ tsp. dried basil

½ tsp. salt

¼ tsp. ground black pepper

Heat oil in a large soup pot and sauté onion for three minutes. Add garlic and cook for one minute. Add potatoes and cook for three minutes, stirring. Then add kale and cabbage and cook for five more minutes. Finally, add broth, cannellini beans, squash, basil, salt, and pepper, and cook for eight more minutes, or until potatoes are soft. Season with additional salt and pepper, if desired.

# Minestrone

This is the soup. Delicious, quick, and this batch will give you seconds.

Prep time: 5 minutes   •   Cook time: 15 minutes   •   Serves 8

8 cups chicken broth

2 cups 20-Minute Tomato Sauce

1 cup cabbage, thinly sliced

1 tsp. dried oregano

1 tsp. dried basil

¼ tsp. crushed red pepper (optional)

1 tsp. salt

1 cup spaghetti, broken into 2- to 3-inch pieces

2 large carrots, scraped and sliced into ¼-inch medallions

2 large sticks celery including leaves, rinsed and sliced into ¼-inch pieces (Keep leaves separate in 1-inch pieces.)

1 (15.5-oz.) can (or 2 cups soaked dry) cannellini beans

2 TB. olive oil

1 large onion

2 tsp. crushed garlic

1 zucchini squash, rinsed, ends removed, sliced into ¼-inch medallions

Parmesan cheese, salt, and pepper to season

Heat broth, tomato sauce, cabbage, oregano, basil, crushed red pepper, and salt to a simmer. Add spaghetti pieces, carrot, celery, and beans and cook for 10 minutes.

Meanwhile, heat oil in a large skillet and sauté onion for six minutes. Add garlic and cook for one minute.

## Cook to Cook

This fast version of Minestrone requires a large soup pot and a large skillet going at once, in order to finish quickly. The bonus: It's even better the second day (and no additional time necessary other than to heat it up!).

Add onion and garlic to soup and cook for five minutes, stirring occasionally. Add zucchini and cook for three more minutes, or until pasta is al dente.

(I've suggested cooking onions separately in this recipe to cut down on cooking time. If you have an extra 10 minutes, you can save cleaning and enhance flavor by sautéing onion and garlic in the soup pot, *then* adding liquid and vegetables.)

Top with Parmesan, salt, and pepper and serve with fresh Italian bread for a simple, healthy meal.

# Minestra

This flavorful, simple, and healthy recipe is not a soup, but a sautéed vegetable dish.

Prep time: 4 minutes  •  Cook time: 11 minutes  •  Serves 4

4 TB. olive oil

1½ TB. crushed garlic

1 bunch greens such as chard, kale, escarole, even broccoli or Brussels sprouts leaves

1 (15½-oz.) can (or 2 cups soaked dry) cannellini beans

Salt and pepper to taste

Freshly shredded Parmesan

In a large sauté pan, heat olive oil over medium-low heat and sauté garlic for three minutes.

Chop greens coarsely and blanch in boiling water for one minute. Drain and add greens to garlic in the sauté pan. Sauté for about five minutes, until greens soften (the time required will vary according to the greens you use). Add cannellini beans and heat for two to three minutes, stirring. Serve immediately with salt, pepper, and Parmesan.

**Cook to Cook**

Rich vegetable soups like minestrone are the very essence of an easy time-saver. They can be quick to prepare and bring the added benefit of providing a second (or third!) meal from that same effort. The dish tastes great, and with that extra day for the ingredients to meld, it tastes even *better*.

# Cuisine Can Take You Down Memory Lane

Have a favorite vacation or trip you love to remember? Was the food part of that great memory? Use those great memories as inspiration (within reason) and take a crack at re-creating a culinary memory. Don't forget that if you remember a great meal at a casual restaurant, it's possible that that dish, as in the restaurant, can be prepared quickly.

# Sautéed Scallops

I'm told this is similar to a dish a friend of mine enjoyed in the South of France. I'm willing to take his word for it.

Prep time: 4 minutes   •   Cook time: 5 minutes   •   Serves 4 to 6

¼ cup olive oil

¼ cup flour

2 lbs. bay scallops

1 TB. garlic

½ tsp. dried basil

½ tsp. dried oregano

Salt and pepper

Heat oil in a large skillet over medium heat. *Flour* scallops and add to hot oil in the skillet and salt and pepper to taste. Stir occasionally. When scallops are nicely browned, about four minutes, add garlic, basil, and oregano. Continue to cook for one minute, stirring, then serve with rice. Delicious.

### Cook's Glossary

To **flour** something is to coat it on all sides with flour. With scallops, this is best done by placing the scallops in a large bowl, sprinkling the flour over, and stirring with a wooden spoon until evenly coated.

# Grapes Rockefeller

Talk about simple and delicious; double at will.

Prep time: 5 minutes   •   Serves 2

½ lb. seedless grapes, cut in half

½ cup low-fat sour cream

⅛ cup brown sugar

Mix grapes, sour cream, and brown sugar and serve. Can be served cold or at room temperature.

### Flare-Up

Be realistic: Don't expect the dish you make to taste *exactly* like you remember it! Memory has a way of changing, and the place where you enjoyed a dish has a lot to do with the pleasure you took from it. The goal here, with a re-creation, is not an exact match, but to have some fun and perhaps bring back part of the memory.

# Baked Cherry Miel

*Miel* is French for "honey." This will provide two nights' dessert unless you *really* like cherries.

Prep time: 5 minutes  •  Cook time: 18 minutes  •  Serves 8

1 lb. fresh ripe cherries, sliced in half and pitted

1 TB. flour

¼ cup + 1 TB. honey

4 TB. butter, melted

1 cup uncooked oatmeal

¼ tsp. cinnamon

Pinch nutmeg

Preheat oven to 425°F. In a bowl, sprinkle cherries with flour, stir to coat. Pour ¼ cup honey over cherries, stir again, and pour cherries into an 8 × 8 greased baking dish.

Combine butter, 1 tablespoon honey, oatmeal, and cinnamon, and spoon over cherries. Sprinkle with nutmeg.

Bake for 18 to 20 minutes, or until mixture is bubbling and the top is crispy.

Distribute to serving plates and eat as is, or if you want to be decadent, add a scoop of vanilla ice cream. But who wants to be decadent?

**Cook to Cook** _____

On vacation in France years ago, our rental house had two huge cherry trees. While we were there, we discovered the branches dripping with white cherries. The kids spent an hour eating them, with plenty to spare. Without a fully stocked pantry, we took a crack at whipping up a dessert. Baked Cherry Miel is a slightly improved version.

## The Least You Need to Know

♦ Everyone you know is likely to have a favorite recipe. Learn just a few of them, and you'll strengthen friendships, have fun, and learn new things.

♦ Recipes can be found where you least expect them.

♦ Be open-minded about cooking. There are many methods, seasonings and combinations out there just waiting to be tried.

♦ Use your favorite memories as inspiration for a meal!

# Chapter 26

# Wine and 20-Minute Cuisine

## In This Chapter

- ◆ Wine with food, a natural pair
- ◆ Food and wine chart
- ◆ Wine menus
- ◆ Favorite food wines

This chapter lists suggestions for different types of wine and the foods that go well with them. Remember that chicken can be served in infinite varieties, from a simple breaded cutlet (fine with chardonnay), to a marinated grilled capon (hmm, pinot noir). Sauces also impact the weight of the wine you should choose. Finally, personal preference trumps everything. The whole point of wine with a meal is fun—pleasure and taste. If you like a wine-food combination (lamb and chardonnay?) that the "experts" don't recommend, it might be worth trying the so-called ideal match, but after that stick with what you like!

## Wine Guidelines

The old wisdom used to be "white wine with fish and red wine with meat." The conventional wisdom now seems to be to drink what you like; with whatever you want to eat. This freedom to match is appealing, not because I totally agree (the advice is still generally valid), but because it means that personal taste is now acceptable, and a person doesn't have to follow a decades-old rule.

Nevertheless, food affects the taste of wine, and some guidelines still apply. Have any of the following happened to you?

♦ Before dinner you might enjoy a glass of fruity, rich pinot noir. Then bring out pasta with plenty of tomato and garlic, and suddenly the luscious red wine vanishes, leaving in its place a tart and tough imposter. How can this happen? The acid in the tomato sauce has mugged your soft wine.

**Cuisine Context**

The simple awareness that eating food with wine affects its taste (and vice versa) is valuable. Use this awareness to learn and experiment with what you like.

♦ Those German white wines, gewürztraminer and riesling, that we thought were too sweet are suddenly refreshing and delicious when paired with curry, or a spicy Thai dish. The slight sweetness of these wines brings some weight and balance that fits well with the food's spice.

♦ A delicious chardonnay suddenly turns to water after a bite of lamb. Why? The wine was no match for the fat, salt, and seasoning of this rich meat.

## Pairings

The hazard of any pairings list is that it provides *general* guidance. Keep in mind that every wine, and every food, has its own characteristics that will impact how well a food/wine pairing works. Adding a sauce to a fish dish, for example, brings in elements that might improve the recipe but change the type of wine that will match. Treat this as general guidance, and let your own taste be the judge.

### Basic Wine and Food Pairing

|  | Light White | Rich White | Light Red | Rich Reds | Sweet |
|---|---|---|---|---|---|
| Appetizers | X | X | X | | |
| Light seafood | X | X | | | |
| Rich seafood | X | X | X | | |
| White meats | X | X | X | | |
| Rich meats | | | | X | |
| Spicy dishes | X | X | | | |
| Dessert | | | | | X |

The following is a list of the types of food (using general definitions from this book and the previous pairings table):

- ◆ **Appetizers.** All over the flavor map, appetizers can be light and mild or rich and spicy. The general rule, however, is that appetizers precede a meal, and as a result will usually not be so spicy or heavy that they will obscure the main courses. Because of this, they should be lighter, and the corresponding wines (white wines or light reds) should be lighter, too

- ◆ **Light seafood.** Light fish with mild seasoning, such as Sole Meuniere (see Chapter 9).

- ◆ **Rich seafood.** Seafood with rich cream or tomato sauces, such as Salmon Aux Herbs (see Chapter 9).

- ◆ **White meats.** Pork and poultry dishes with a variety of seasonings (see Chapter 10).

- ◆ **Rich meats.** Beef and lamb dishes with a variety of seasonings (see Chapter 11).

- ◆ **Spicy dishes.** Highly seasoned dishes of all types, included in most chapters in this book.

- ◆ **Dessert.** Sweet dishes with a high sugar and (sometimes) fat content.

When you're entertaining, consider giving people the option of a white and a light red. Many people have a favorite, and will stick to it regardless of the food being served. And no matter what the "experts" say, if it tastes good to you, *it's a match!*

**Cuisine Context** _____

One general truth about matching food and wine is that you're usually not really matching the wine with the food at all; rather you're dealing with the *seasoning*. A plain chicken breast, for example, will go well with just about any wine. Add a spicy chili component, and you're talking about a completely different pairing (for me, that would call for a white with heft that's slightly sweet, such as a riesling or gewürztraminer, that will stand up to the spice).

# Types of Wine

As with the observation about different manifestations of a food ingredient, there are also ranges of wine characteristics within each area. The following, however, are general characteristics:

- **Light white wines.** Sauvignon blanc, pinot grigio, and others are often available at a low price relative to other white wines, and offer characteristically refreshing, tart flavors of grapefruit and green apple. These are often great wines for relatively light foods.

- **Rich whites.** Chardonnay is the prime suspect here (also riesling and gewürztraminer, although these last two tend to be in a category by themselves because of their usually higher residual sugar). Chardonnay is often characterized by buttery, even creamy notes, and is a generally good match for lighter fare, such as seafood and mildly seasoned poultry and pork.

- **Light and medium-bodied reds.** Gamay (in Beaujolais), some merlot, some pinot noir, sangiovese (the grape in Chianti), and others are, in the under-$15 range, generally pleasant and easy drinking with characteristics of ripe cherries, chocolate, toffee, and vanilla. These versatile wines are good with a range of foods, with the sweet spot (no pun intended) being with lighter meats.

> **Cook to Cook**
>
> Here's a classic match to keep in mind: chianti and tomato-sauce dishes. Chianti, the sangiovese-based wine of Italy, is often a light red with pleasant acidity (that's the bite and tartness you taste), an acidity that matches the acidity in tomatoes. Pasta and Chianti ... a natural match!

- **Rich red.** Grapes like cabernet sauvignon, syrah/shiraz, and zinfandel are flavor-packed, assertive wines with characteristics of ripe fruit, spice, even chocolate and oak. They can overpower many foods, but often are good matches for rich meats or meat dishes such as steaks and stews.

- **Sweet wines.** These are wines vinified with a high amount of residual sugar, and can be made from many varietals of grape, from otherwise light whites (sauvignon blanc makes the world-famous sweet white wine of Sauternes) to rich reds. These powerful wines need careful pairing, and are often at their best with correspondingly sweet foods.

> **Cook's Glossary** _____
>
> A **varietal** is the type of grape used to make a wine, such as cabernet sauvignon, merlot, or chardonnay. Many producers (often in Australia, South America, and the United States) bottle primarily varietal-based wine. Other producers (often in Europe) produce primarily blends, which contain several different varietals in one wine (a Bordeaux blend, for example, often contains both cabernet sauvignon and merlot).

# Food and Wine Menus

I've organized some of the recipes in this book according to wines I would choose. Try these on for size:

**Light White:**

- ◆ Boiled Lobster (Chapter 3)
- ◆ 10-Minute Chicken and Herb Pasta (Chapter 6)
- ◆ Pasta Aux Trois Herbs (Chapter 8)
- ◆ Sole Meuniere (Chapter 9)
- ◆ Pan Broiled Scallops and Shrimp (Chapter 9)

**Rich White:**

- ◆ Tuscan Chicken Breasts (Chapter 6)
- ◆ Spaghetti Carbonara (Chapter 8)
- ◆ Shrimp and Feta Pasta (Chapter 8)
- ◆ Broiled Halibut (Chapter 9)
- ◆ Microwave Poached Salmon (Chapter 9)
- ◆ Bill's Arugula Pasta (Chapter 12)
- ◆ Lightning Chicken Curry (Chapter 17— use a riesling or gewürztraminer)
- ◆ Beef and Broccoli Stir Fry (Chapter 17— use a riesling or gewürztraminer)
- ◆ Chicken and Paprika Cream (Chapter 18)

> **Cook to Cook** _____
>
> The seasoning can decide the pairing. With a rich white wine, such as chardonnay, I've suggested Tuscan Chicken Breasts. Take that same chicken, however, and up the seasoning, and I'd prefer a red.

**Light Red:**

- Quick Pork Stir-Fry (Chapter 3)
- Lasagna (Chapter 6)
- Grilled Salmon Steaks (Chapter 9)
- Broiled Pork Tenderloin (Chapter 10)
- Rosemary's Quick Enchiladas (Chapter 12)
- Minestrone Pasta (Chapter 12)
- Tomato and Mushrooms with Whole Wheat Penne (Chapter 18)
- Minestra (Chapter 22)

**Cook to Cook**

When looking for a match, don't forget the weather. My area is famous in the summer for hot, muggy evenings. Even if I'm grilling a steak on a night like that, I'll sometimes reach for a glass of cold, refreshing white. Rather than a food-wine pairing, I suppose you could call that a weather-wine pairing.

**Rich Reds:**

- Fleisch Kuchle (Austrian Meat Cakes) (Chapter 11)
- Grilled Rosemary and Garlic Lamb Chops (Chapter 11)
- Burgers with a Twist (Chapter 11)

**Sweet:**

- Strawberries and Thick Cream (Chapter 16)
- Poached Pears (Chapter 16)

To give you a decent shot at a sure winner, here are several dependable sources—wine producers I've found to sell good quality, reasonably priced wines across the board:

**Flare-Up**

Unless you know what you're looking for, don't feel the need to spend more than $15 per bottle. There are plenty of tasty, high-quality wines out there that can be purchased for less than $15, and often less than $10 per bottle. The wines highlighted in this chapter generally fall within this range.

- Penfolds (Australia)
- Rosemount (Australia)
- Tyrrell's (Australia)
- DuBoeuf (France)
- Louis Jadot (France)
- Ruffino (Italy)
- Bogle (United States)
- Chateau St. Michelle (United States)
- Coppola (United States)
- Hogue (United States)

- J. Lohr (United States)
- Rabbit Ridge (United States)

# Favorite Wines

I've listed some of my favorite wines here. To make your search easier, I've listed wines by country (wines are often listed by the country in wine stores). These notes are obviously related to specific wines, and by the time you take a look at your local wine store, it's entirely likely you'll be looking at a 2002, say, rather than a 2001 *vintage*. With these producers, that should be okay. Wine from a different vintage won't taste exactly the same, but the characteristics should be similar.

You won't find all of these wines in every store, which is why I've included a decent list. Keep in mind the previous list of reliable producers! (Copyright Tod Dimmick and TastingTimes.com, reprinted with permission. Ongoing wine reviews like these are available at the author's website: www.tastingtimes.com.)

**Cook's Glossary**

The **vintage** is the year in which the grapes were harvested and, usually, in which the wine was produced. A 2002 sauvignon blanc means that the grapes were harvested in 2002. One interesting twist on vintages is the difference in harvest date between the Southern and Northern Hemispheres. An Australian 2002 vintage, for example, was picked in their fall, which is actually spring for those of us who live up North.

Prices listed were current at the time of this writing.

We tasted these wines with food, as the notes often reflect. The "grade" is a subjective measure of quality and price (I've only included wines here I highly recommend): A = yum, worth *searching* for; B = very good, worth buying again; C = fine, but not worth buying again.

| Winery/ Producer | Region of Origin | Varietal | Year | Price | Description |
|---|---|---|---|---|---|
| *Australia* | | | | | |
| Tyrrell's | Southeastern Australia | Cabernet, Merlot | 1999 | $10 | Juicy ripe fruit cherries very tasty and in this case perfect with pizza. B+ |

*continues*

*continued*

| Winery/ Producer | Region of Origin | Varietal | Year | Price | Description |
|---|---|---|---|---|---|
| **Australia** | | | | | |
| Marquis Philips | Southeastern Australia | "Sarah's Blend" | 2000 | $15 | Wow. Cornucopia of jammy ripe fruits, chocolate, butter, and cream. Gorgeous. A |
| Tyrrell's | McLaren Vale-King Valley-Padthaway | Cabernet, Merlot | 1999 | $10 | Licorice, caramel, berries, and cream Opulent. A- |
| Oxford Landing | Southeastern Australia | Grenache | 1998 | $11 | Smoky, gamy, and mulled fruits. Pleasure in a glass. B+ |
| **New Zealand** | | | | | |
| Sacred Hill | Hawkes Bay | Sauvignon Blanc | 2000 | $11 | Tangerine rind, tart peach, tart fruits, refreshing and delicious. A- |
| Cat's Phee on a Gooseberry Bush | East Coast | Sauvignon Blanc | 2000 | $11 | Grapefruit and grassy flavors in a refreshing tart wine. The label claims (tongue in cheek?!) a hint of cat. I didn't get that. B |
| Higfield | Marlborough | Merlot | 1998 | $10 | Cloves, cinnamon, and oak. Tasty, medium-bodied. B |
| **Argentina** | | | | | |
| Norton Blanc | Mendoza | Sauvignon | 2001 | $9 | Grapefruit, melon, peach, nutmeg. Gorgeous. Run don't walk to get this. A- |
| Argenta | Mendoza | Malbec | 1999 | $4 | Sinewy leather and dried cherry. An enjoyable weeknight glass and yes, the price is right. B |

| Winery/ Producer | Region of Origin | Varietal | Year | Price | Description |
|---|---|---|---|---|---|
| *Chile* | | | | | |
| Santa Rita | Lontue Valley | Merlot | 2000 | $7 | Ripe cherries and vanilla, pleasant and easy drinking. This is a good wine for the price. B |
| San Fran-cisco de Mostazal | Cachapoal | Merlot | 1999 | $10 | Charcoal-grilled cherries (presents an unusual mental image), vanilla clove. An interesting tasty wine. B |
| *France* | | | | | |
| J & F Lurton | D'Oc Vin De Pays | Sauvignon Blanc | 2000 | $6 | Clean, fresh, citrus, and lemon. Very tasty and perfect with seafood. B+ |
| Louis Jadot | Beaujolais-Villages | Gamay | 2000 | $10 | Leather, clove, earth, and strawberry. Delicious. A- |
| E. Guigal | Cotes du Rhone (white) | Blend | 2000 | $10 | Creamy tropical fruits, pineapple, vanilla, and orange peel. This is very tasty stuff. I will buy it again. B+ |
| Hugel | Alsace | "Gentil" Blend | 1999 | $9 | Clean mineral, mandarin orange, and juicy peach. Wow this is good. B+ |
| *Italy* | | | | | |
| Le Bocce | Chianti Classico | Sangiovese | 1997 | $14 | Leaf mold, baked earth, stewed fruits, cloves, and puckery. Sensuous and deli-cious. B+ |

*continues*

*continued*

| Winery/ Producer | Region of Origin | Varietal | Year | Price | Description |
|---|---|---|---|---|---|
| **Italy** | | | | | |
| Ruffino | Chianti | Sangiovese | 2000 | $7 | Juicy cherry, juicy fruits. Hard not to drink it quickly. Factor in the price and this is an A-. |
| Castello di Poppiano | Chianti Colli Fiorentini | Sangiovese | 1997 | $13 | Chocolate, earth, (yes, baked again) mouth-coating deep ripe fruit, caramel cream. Delicious. A- |
| **Portugal** | | | | | |
| Famega | Vinho Verde | Blend | 2001 | $7 | Citrus effervescence. Perfect with pasta tossed with scallops. B |
| **Spain** | | | | | |
| Borsao | Campo de Borja | Blend | 1998 | $8 | Focused fruit, dried cherry, whiff of cloves. Very good wine for the price. B |
| **United States** | | | | | |
| Jamesport | North Fork of Long Island | Merlot | 1998 | $15 | Rich smoky cherry, licorice. Delicious. A- |
| Chateau St. Michelle | Columbia Valley | "Horsehead Vineyard" Sauvignon Blanc | 2000 | $9 | Grapefruit, kiwi Succulent. A- |
| Coppola | California | "Bianco" Blend | 2000 | $9 | Vanilla, oak, citrus. Very tasty and remarkably consistent tasting notes over time. B+ |

| Winery/ Producer | Region of Origin | Varietal | Year | Price | Description |
|---|---|---|---|---|---|
| **United States** | | | | | |
| Rabbit Ridge | California | Zinfandel | 1999 | $10 | Bright raspberry, fruity, even a little effervescent. Enjoyed with grilled steak. B |
| Cline | California | Zinfandel | 2000 | $10 | Raspberry syrup, Twizzlers, cough drops. This is a "big" tasty wine. The poem on the back is the perfect slightly risqué toast. A- |
| Camelot | California | Pinot Noir | 2000 | $12 | Super-ripe velvety cherries, velour on the tongue (in a good way). B+ |
| Dry Creek Vineyards | California | Chenin Blanc | 2000 | $10 | Gardenia notes tropical fruits, gulpably delicious. Perfect with seafood. B+ |
| Columbia Crest | Columbia Valley | Merlot | 1998 | $12 | Focused, luscious fruit, Chocolate toffee. This is gorgeous stuff. A- |
| Pepperwood Grove | California | Pinot Noir | 1998 | $10 | Perfumed violets, floral, anise, plum. Try it with minestrone & frankfurters. B |
| Rabbit Ridge | California | Merlot | 1999 | $11 | Ripe Cherry, cloves, mild tannins, this is a velveteen rabbit. B+ |

*continues*

*continued*

| Winery/ Producer | Region of Origin | Varietal | Year | Price | Description |
|---|---|---|---|---|---|
| ***South Africa*** | | | | | |
| Southern Right | Western Cape | Sauvignon Blanc | 2000 | $10 | Floral, citrus, pineapple. Refreshing and tasty. B |
| Charles Back | South Africa | "Goats Do Roam" Blend | 2001 | $8 | Fleshy, fruity. A perfect weeknight glass with grilled sausages. Rated B with a "+" for price |

As I hope you've seen from this chapter, wine, like food, is about fun. A glass of wine is a natural with a meal, and can help turn dinnertime into a quiet celebration. Weeknights are busy, and something that can make dinnertime relaxing and special, like wine, is okay in my book. To enjoy wine with a 20-minute meal, don't get preoccupied with vintages, varietals, and all the details. Take some of the basic advice of "what goes with what," and test it out at your own dinner table. Then, after you've tested a few different choices (I can't stress this enough), *stick with what you like*!

## The Least You Need to Know

♦ General guidelines, such as lighter wines with lighter foods, are valuable when choosing a wine to go with your meal.

♦ Delicious, food-friendly wines can be found without spending a lot of money.

♦ Charts might be helpful, but let your own taste be the guide. If a wine-food pairing works for you, *it's a good match*.

♦ If you familiarize yourself with a short list of dependable wine producers, all you'll need to do is look for them at the wine store.

# Chapter 27

# The 20-Minute Garden

## In This Chapter

- ◆ Why grow 20-minute food?
- ◆ Easy-growing garden favorites

Perhaps you are wondering how can I possibly include growing vegetables in a book about quick cooking? It is true that vegetable gardening is not for everyone (living in a city with no space outside comes to mind!). You've also got to enjoy being outdoors and have the hobby time and discipline to plan a garden and take care of it.

If you've got the space, however, there are several reasons to consider growing vegetables for quick cooking, and we're going to cover them in this chapter.

# Nature's Recipe

Recipes from the garden spotlight fresh vegetable and herb flavors. Cooking time is strictly limited, or even eliminated. Seasonings are straightforward. Fresh vegetables bring the added benefit of the highest possible nutritional value, and incomparable taste. Grocery stores have mastered many things, chief among them convenience, but they have yet to come anywhere near a tomato that tastes as good as that one I just picked from my garden.

Some have to do with eating them, but not all:

◆ **Taste.** Fresh, crisp lettuce. Pungent, minty basil. Carrots with a crunchy sweetness that's almost unrecognizably better than the store variety. Snap beans so fresh they taste, well, *green*. Mountains of rich, creamy squash. Tomatoes that are the definition of sweet. The only thing these delicacies ask is to be prepared quickly, so as not to lose their delicate flavors and textures. Talk about tailor-made, er, *grown*, 20-minute food.

◆ **Satisfaction.** As a hobby, there are few things more satisfying than growing things. You orchestrate the plan, the execution, and the rewards of your own little piece of earth. Even weeding (an unavoidable part of gardening!) brings a strange satisfaction; a bit of work and immediate, soothing results. After a tough day at the office, 20 minutes of aggressive weeding is the perfect stress-relief valve. If only it were so easy at the office.

◆ **Health.** Remember the food pyramid? Vegetables feature prominently, only when you grow them they are more fun to eat, tasty, often even more nutritious than vegetables that have lived on a display shelf. Growing vegetables can even save you money. And all those vitamins, antioxidants, and minerals help to keep the doctor happy.

◆ **Control, or lack thereof.** Closely related to the health benefits of growing vegetables, control in this context means you know how something was grown, and the amount of pesticides that were used (possibly none!). When I'm eating a fresh salad using vegetables I've grown, or even more importantly, when my kids are eating that salad, it's great to know where it comes from.

◆ **Quantity.** Each season, there's a wonderful time, usually about mid-August, when certain vegetables such as tomatoes, beans and squash, together conspire to all ripen simultaneously, overloading the table with all the fixings for huge batches of 20-minute sauce. I fill the freezer with sauce, and reap the rewards all winter with an Easy Timesaver (the work's done!) and a terrific midwinter taste of fresh vegetables.

◆ **Learning.** One vegetable analogy I heard once is "When you're green, you're growing. When you're ripe, you're rotten." We all get more out of life when we're learning and experiencing new things. Growing vegetables is a delightful activity I look forward to season after season. Planning a garden in the depths of winter is to believe in warmth and sunshine. And for kids, the pleasure of watching their own beans sprout, or of carving their own pumpkin, is an experience they never forget.

◆ **Convenience.** Yes, you read right. In the summertime I don't think about what vegetables to eat with dinner. From the end of June through September, I go see what's ready in the garden, pick it, and get started.

**Cuisine Context** _____

If you don't know where to start for growing vegetables, there are two general options, buying seedlings (small plants) from your local nursery, or buying seeds from a catalog. Some of my favorite catalogs (both seeds and a free catalog can be ordered online): Park Seed (www.parkseed.com), Burpee (www.burpee.com), Harris (www.harrisseeds.com), Pinetree (www.superseeds.com), and Territorial (www.territorialseed.com).

# The Dirt on Sure Winners

Here are some of my easy-growing garden favorites:

◆ **Tomatoes.** Summer Sweet and Juliet are grape tomatoes. Small and oblong, they produce hundreds of amazingly sweet fruit that are perfect cut in half in salads, tossed with pasta, on pizza, or eaten alone. Beefy Boy is a large, beefsteak tomato that is great for tomato salads, burgers, and even sauce.

◆ **Summer squash.** Zucchini and yellow crookneck squashes provides loads of flavorful fruit.

◆ **Beans.** From Blue Lake (a tall pole bean) to Pencil Pod (a bush bean), beans can be used in many recipes, or as a delicious side dish. They are a kid favorite for growing and eating.

◆ **Chard.** Large, dark green, rippled chard leaves are nutritious, flavorful, and versatile; they can be used raw in salads, cooked as a side dish, and in recipes that call for spinach. Bright Lights is my favorite, the multicolored stems are tasty and look almost like they have been dyed.

◆ **Herbs.** Dill and basil are fast-growing, easy-care herbs that can be picked and used liberally in many vegetable dishes. Fresh herbs bring great flavor, and a touch of elegance, to any dish.

◆ **Salad.** I'm a fanatic about garden greens. I've grouped them into the general category of salad here. Included in this green mass are lettuces, cress, arugula, spinach, and a variety of plants that cross that gray zone between edible and ornamental, or both, such as nasturtiums (delicious flowers), signet marigolds (flowers), and shungiku (edible Chrysanthemums—a delicious novelty). Most of these are easily grown, and the challenge is eating them as fast as they grow.

**Cuisine Context**

If you're limited on space, and want to grow ornamental plants, it is still possible to grow tasty, attractive edibles for the table. Some herbs, such as basil, are attractive in pots, and practical when it comes to cooking. Certain flowering plants are both attractive and delicious, providing a doubly satisfying small garden.

And here are some of my favorite recipes ….

# Fresh Tomato Salad

This treat gives a flavor burst from tomatoes and Italian dressing, all packed in a five-minute or less recipe.

Prep time: 5 minutes  •  Serves 4

2 large fresh tomatoes, chopped into ¾-inch chunks, or 20 grape tomatoes, halved

1 tsp. dried basil (or handful of fresh basil leaves)

¼ cup shredded mozzarella cheese

¼ cup Italian dressing (your favorite)

Mix tomatoes, basil, cheese, and Italian dressing in a bowl and serve.

# Sautéed Herbed Summer Squash

Prep time: 3 minutes  •  Cook time: 7 minutes  •  Serves 4 to 6

2 TB. olive oil

4 small summer squash, 2 yellow and 2 zucchini, *striped* and sliced into ¼-inch pieces

½ tsp. dried thyme

½ tsp. dried dill

1 TB. balsamic vinegar

Salt and pepper

Heat olive oil in a large skillet over medium heat. Spread squash pieces in the skillet and sprinkle with thyme and dill. Sauté for approximately seven minutes, stirring and turning frequently, until softened but not completely mushy (to your taste). When done, drizzle with balsamic vinegar, and serve with salt and pepper. Fresh garden taste is a great thing.

**Cook's Glossary** _____

**Striped** refers to half-peeling a vegetable (or fruit) so that half of the skin remains in alternating strips, providing a striped appearance.

# Sautéed Garden Beans

Watch these disappear, and you'll be convinced to grow them yourself (the beans, not the almonds)

Prep time: 3 minutes  •  Cook time: 4 minutes  •  Serves 4 to 6

2 TB. butter

1 lb. fresh green beans, stems removed, sliced into 2-inch sections (longer if the kids like to pretend they're swords)

¼ cup slivered almonds

½ tsp. dill (or 1 TB. fresh)

Salt and pepper to taste

Melt butter in a large skillet over medium heat, and sauté beans, almonds, and dill for four minutes, stirring. They will still be a bit crunchy. Cook a little longer if you like them soft.

Serve and season with salt and pepper.

**Cook to Cook** _____

To avoid overcooked beans, periodically take a bite as they cook. When one is just a bit crispy for your taste, turn off the heat. The beans will continue to cook in the residual skillet heat for a minute, bringing them to the perfect texture.

# Chard with Balsamic Vinegar

Prep time: 4 minutes  •  Cook time: 6 minutes  •  Serves 4

2 TB. olive oil

8 to 10 large chard leaves, washed and chopped, stem sections separated

1 TB. balsamic vinegar

Salt and pepper

Heat oil in a large skillet over medium heat and sauté chard stem pieces for three minutes. Add leaves, cover, and cook for three more minutes, removing the cover to stir every minute, or until leaves are wilted. Drizzle with balsamic vinegar, and serve, seasoning to taste with salt and pepper.

# Flower Bed Salad

This salad changes with the season, but these ingredients are a fair representation. This colorful mixture is filled with flavor and just shouts "Be healthy!" Italian or oil-based dressing may be used in place of the vinegar and oil.

Prep time: 10 minutes • Serves 4 to 6

2 medium fresh romaine plants, about 12 large leaves, washed and dried, leaves chopped into 2-inch pieces

10 spinach leaves, washed, dried, and chopped

10 grape tomatoes, halved

1 *handful* arugula leaves, washed and dried

2 TB. balsamic vinegar

1 TB. extra virgin olive oil

8 fresh, young edible nasturtium flowers

Mix romaine, spinach, tomatoes, and arugula in a large serving bowl. Drizzle with vinegar and olive oil, arrange flowers on top, and present for multiple compliments.

### Cook's Glossary

A **handful** is yet another (unscientific!) term that refers to as much of a material as you can hold in your hand. As for the difference between a *large handful* and a *small handful*, well …

# Rhubarb Sauce

Many gardeners have a patch of rhubarb, quietly growing those elephantine leaves and thick red stalks. This sauce is dead simple, tart, and sweet, and delicious warm or cold.

Prep time: 6 minutes • Cook time: 14 minutes • Serves 4 to 6

½ cup water

3 stalks (about 1 lb.) rhubarb, scrubbed and cut in to 1-inch segments

1 cup sugar

### Cook to Cook

Try warm rhubarb sauce over vanilla ice cream.

Heat water in a large saucepan over medium heat. Place rhubarb in a large bowl, pour sugar over, and mix. Scrape into the saucepan and cover. Cook for 14 minutes or until rhubarb pieces are completely soft and mixture is more like a thick liquid.

Serve in bowls with a little bit of cream stirred in.

# Fresh Herb Pizza

Prep time: 5 minutes   •   Cook time: 15 minutes   •   Serves 3 to 4

1 ball pizza dough

1 TB. olive oil

⅔ cup 20-Minute Tomato Sauce

6 to 8 oz. mozzarella cheese, shredded

1 handful small arugula leaves

1 handful small basil leaves

1 small handful (perhaps 12), young edible flowers, such as nasturtium

Follow the pizza preparation directions for 20-Minute Pizza (see Chapter 8). Upon removing from the oven, arrange arugula, basil, and edible flowers across pizza.

**Flare-Up**

Don't end up with dried, flavorless greens on your pizza. The key to fresh herbs on pizza is to add them as the pizza comes out of the oven, so they soften, but still retain their color and flavor.

# Ratatouille

This traditional French vegetable dish just bursts with rich vegetable flavors. This batch should last for two meals.

Prep time: 5 minutes • Cook time: 18 minutes • Serves 8

3 TB. olive oil

1 onion, chopped

1 TB. crushed garlic

1 large green pepper, seeded, stem removed, and chopped into ½-inch pieces

1 large zucchini squash, ends removed, cut in half lengthwise, and sliced into ½-inch pieces

1 medium-size eggplant, peeled and cut into ¾-inch chunks

2 cups 20-Minute Tomato Sauce (or a 15 oz. can chopped tomatoes with 1 tsp. basil and ½ tsp. oregano added)

2 large fresh tomatoes, chopped into ¾-inch chunks, or 20 grape tomatoes, halved

1 tsp. salt

1 cup shredded mozzarella cheese

**Cook to Cook**

Ratatouille is another dish that will taste as good, if not better, the next day.

Heat oil in a large skillet over medium heat and sauté onion for two minutes. Add garlic, sauté for one minute. Then add pepper, squash, eggplant, tomato sauce, tomatoes, and salt, and cook, stirring occasionally, for 15 minutes.

Serve to individual plates or bowls and top with mozzarella cheese.

## The Least You Need to Know

♦ Fresh garden-grown vegetables and herbs require little in the way of seasoning, and short, if any, cooking, making them perfect ingredients for 20-minute cuisine.

♦ A vegetable garden provides a surprisingly convenient source of quick-cooking vegetables.

♦ Fresh produce not only tastes better than store-bought, but it's also often better for you.

♦ Growing vegetables is not for everyone, but for many people the hobby not only provides food, but learning, interest for children, and even after-work therapy.

# Glossary

**al dente**   Italian for "against the teeth." In the context of cooking, it refers to pasta (or another ingredient) that is neither soft nor hard, but just slightly firm against the teeth. This, according to many pasta aficionados, is the perfect way to cook pasta.

**bake**   To cook in a dry oven.

**baking pan**   Baking pans round out the 20-minute kitchen. They also are versatile and can be used for tasks ranging from baking potatoes to chicken, cookies to croutons. Cake pans are of course used for cakes; related tools, such as cookie sheets, are also a nice addition; however, in a pinch the cake pan will do the job. The usage of a muffin pan is primarily limited to muffins, although there are a few creative uses I've found for savory muffin-shaped entrees.

**barbecue**   This is a loaded word, with zealous, and different, definitions in different parts of the country. In some cases it is synonymous with grilling (quick cooking over high heat), in others to barbecue is to cook something long and slowly in a rich liquid.

**baste**   To keep foods moist during cooking by spooning, brushing, or drizzling with a liquid.

**beat**   To quickly mix substances and air.

**blend**   To mix one substance with another, more slowly than beating.

**boil**   To heat a liquid to a point where water is forced to turn into steam, leading to all those bubbles. To boil something is to insert it in boiling water. A rapid boil is when lots of bubbles are foaming the surface of the water.

**bok choy**   A member of the cabbage family, with thick stems, crisp texture, and fresh flavor. Perfect for stir-frying (often referred to as Chinese cabbage).

**braise**   To cook with the introduction of some liquid, usually over extended time.

**broil**   To cook under the high heat element.

**brown**   To quickly cook the surface of all sides of a piece of food, with the intent of locking in the juices.

**brush**   To coat food with a liquid.

**casserole dishes**   Primarily used in baking, they hold liquids and solids together, and keep moisture around ingredients that might otherwise dry out.

**chop**   To cut something into pieces. Usually qualified by an adverb (one bluefish, coarsely chopped).

**core**   To core a piece of fruit or a vegetable is to remove the unappetizing middle membranes and seeds.

**cream**   The operational image for "creaming" something is with a blender, resulting in a soft, creamy liquid or substance.

**cream soups**   Cream soups, such as cream of chicken, broccoli, or mushroom are a traditional secret of the busy cook looking for an ingredient that will add flavor and creamy texture.

**cuisine**   A style of cooking. *The Complete Idiot's Guide to 20-Minute Meals* is all about 20-minute cuisine; delicious, quick, and fun.

**dash**   A dash is a traditional cook's term that means a "small amount"—anywhere from a few drops to a tablespoon. A right-brain cook's term if there ever was one. For this recipe, a dash is about a tablespoon.

**dice**   To cut into small cubes (about ¼-inch square). (Diced potato)

**double boiler**   A double boiler is a set of two pots designed to nest together, one inside the other. The bottom one holds water (not quite touching the bottom of the top pot) and the top one holds the ingredient you are trying to heat. A double boiler provides consistent heat for things that need delicate treatment.

**dredge**   Covering a piece of food with a dry substance like flour or corn meal. (Dredge a piece of chicken through flour.)

**drizzle**   Like when it's almost raining, to lightly sprinkle drops of a liquid over food. (Drizzle a salad with olive oil.)

**Easy Timesavers**   Methods and recipes that take full advantage of prepared foods, marinades, and other timesaving tricks.

**filet**   A filet is a piece of meat (including fish and poultry) with the bones removed.

**fish basket**   A fish basket is a grill-top metal frame that holds your fish intact when turning.

**fish poacher**   For a seafood lover, a fish poacher is a great member of the 20-minute kitchen. A poacher is a long, rectangular pot with a separate metal basket designed to hold a fish inside the pot, either above boiling water for steaming, or in simmering liquid for poaching. They come in varying sizes up to 24 inches, although an 18 inches version will cover all but the largest meals. The method is quick and easy, resulting in a delicious, flaky fish that disappears in minutes from our dinner table.

**floret**   A floret is the part of broccoli or cauliflower that holds all the flower or bud ends.

**fry**   Pan cooking over high heat, usually with butter or oil.

**fusion**   "Fusion" cuisine is a method or style that marries two or more styles of cooking, such as Chinese and French. The concept has been quite trendy at times at some restaurants.

**garnish**   To decorate food with something to add color and flavor, and to make it look more appealing (parsley on a dish of tomatoes).

**grate**   To break up into tiny pieces (grated cheese).

**grill**   To cook over high heat, usually over charcoal or gas.

**handful**   Yet another (unscientific!) term that refers to as much of a material as you can hold in your hand.

**haute cuisine** (French for "high cooking")   Refers to the painstakingly prepared, sometimes exotic, delicious, often complex meals one might find at an upscale restaurant.

**herb**   For cooks, herbs are generally the leaves of flavorful plants characterized by fresh, pungent aromas and flavors, such as parsley, sage, rosemary, and thyme.

**hors d'oeuvres**   Appetizers. Canapés are hors d'oeuvres made up of small toasts topped with your favorite ingredients (commonly cheese, vegetables, and herbs).

**julienne**   To slice something into very thin pieces.

**leftover**   A leftover is extra food not eaten at a meal. "Leftovers" are also a frame of mind. To some people they are somehow lessened in value, like a new car the minute you drive it off the lot. To many others, leftovers are a timesaving opportunity to take prepared ingredients to explore a new way of serving.

**macerate**   Mixing sugar or another sweetener with fruit initiates a process called maceration; the fruit softens and a delicious juice is released.

**marinate**   To cover an ingredient with an herb or seasoned sauce over time to both spread the flavor and tenderize.

**medallion**   A small round cut, usually of meat.

**mesclun**   Mixed salad greens, usually containing lettuce and assorted greens, such as arugula, cress, endive, and many others.

**mince**   To cut something into very small pieces.

**mold**   A mold (not the kind that grows) is a decorative shaped metal pan in which contents, such as mousse or gelatin, firm and take the shape of the pan.

**paella**   A feast for the eyes as well as the stomach, a grand Spanish mélange of rice, shellfish, onion, meats, rich broth, and herbs.

**pantry**   A pantry is a storage space (a small room, a closet, a series of shelves) for basic cooking ingredients. To a cook, a pantry might be the favorite room in the house!

**parboil**   To partially cook in boiling water or broth.

**pinch**   A pinch (maybe the oldest cook's measure around?) is the amount of a substance that can be held between your thumb and forefinger.

**pizza stone**   A pizza stone is the secret for the knowledgeable pizza chef. Preheated with the oven, the stone cooks a crust to a delicious crispy pizza parlor texture. It also holds heat well, so that a pizza removed from the oven on the stone will stay hot for as much as half an hour at the table.

**poach**   To simmer very gently.

**potato masher**   A potato mashing tool is a useful gadget to have around for the mashed-potato lover. A thick wire grill held by a handle, it allows the user to, well, mash potatoes into an unlumpy mass.

**reduce**   To reduce is to heat a broth or sauce to remove some of the water content, resulting in more concentrated flavor and color.

**refried beans**   Refried beans are cooked pinto beans softened into a thick paste, and often seasoned with peppers and spices. Refried beans are a side dish in their own right, but also a terrific way to thicken chili.

**right-brain cooking**   A right-brain cook might use general guidelines, but will not hesitate to experiment with new ingredients and new methods.

**sauté**   Pan cooking over lower heat than frying. (Sautéed onions.)

**search engine**   A search engine is a website that, based on key words you supply, helps to find related resources on the internet. Typing in "Italian Recipes," for example, will result in a multitude of sites that list those words. A good search engine will help suggest those sites that are really close to what you seek.

**shellfish**   Shellfish comprises a broad range of seafood, including clams, mussels, oysters, crabs, shrimp, and lobster.

**shred**   What accounting firms are not supposed to do, to shred is to cut something into many long thin slices.

**simmer**   To boil so gently that the liquid barely bubbles.

**skillet**   A skillet, or frying pan, is generally a heavy, flat metal pan with a handle, designed to cook food over heat, from a stovetop to a campfire.

**slice**   To cut something into thin pieces. (Slices of fudge!)

**spice**   For cooks, spices are generally the seeds, seed pods, shells, or even woody parts (cinnamon bark) of plants, characterized by intense flavors and aromas.

**splurge**   Hardly a cook's term, a splurge is a slightly indulgent purchase, a purchase that one would not normally make. Perhaps you have never "splurged"?

**steam**   Generally to suspend something over boiling water and allowing the heat of the steam to cook the food. (Steamed carrots, steamed clams.)

**terroir**   The elements that affect a grape vine in the vineyard, the sun, the wind, the soil, the climate, the weather. All the external factors that affect how that vine grows are respected for the role they play in the grapes used to make a wine.

**varietal**   The type of grape used to make a wine, such as cabernet sauvignon, merlot, or chardonnay. Many producers (often in the "New World"—such as Australia, South America, and the United States) bottle primarily varietal-based wine.

**veal**   Veal is meat from a calf, generally characterized by mild flavor and tenderness. Certain cuts of veal, such as cutlets and scaloppini, are well suited to quick cooking.

**vegetable broth**   Vegetable broth is a liquid that adds body and flavor to many dishes, and serves as an alternative to chicken or beef broth in many recipes.

**vegetable steamer**   A vegetable steamer takes two main stovetop forms—as an insert for a large saucepan, and as a special pot with tiny holes in its bottom designed to fit on another pot with boiling water.

**vintage**   The vintage is the year in which the grapes were harvested and, usually, in which the wine was produced. A 2002 sauvignon blanc means that the grapes were harvested in 2002.

**whisk**   To rapidly mix something, introducing air to the mix (whisk eggs).

**wok**   A wok is a wonderful tool for quick cooking. Unfortunately it is only suitable for use on a gas cooktop, unless you purchase an electric version, which may not have the important capability of rapid heating characteristic of a wok over a gas flame. Large enough to hold an entire meal, different enough to inspire interest, a wok brings fun to a meal.

**yeast**   A teaspoon of yeast is made of many millions of tiny fungi, which react with water, sugar, flour, and heat to release carbon dioxide bubbles. These bubbles raise your bread. The yeast also provides that wonderful warm, rich smell, and flavor.

**zest**   Zest is small slivers of peel, usually from a citrus fruit like lemon, lime, or orange. Lemon zest is used in many recipes to add a tart taste of citrus. A zester is a small kitchen tool used to scrape lemon zest off a lemon (a grater, one of my recommended kitchen tools, also works fine).

# References, Resources, and Vendors

## Books

This listing includes not only cookbooks (devoted to recipes), but also books *about* food (and wine).

Bales, Suzanne Frutig. *Ready, Set, Grow!*. Macmillan, 1996.

Barrett, Judith. *From an Italian Garden*. Macmillan, 1992.

Chalmers, Irena. *Good Old Food*. Barron's, 1993.

Child, Julia. *Cooking With Master Chefs*. Ballantine, 1998.

———. *The French Chef Cookbook* (30th Anniversary Edition). Ballantine, 1998.

Creasy, Rosalind. *The Edible Flower Garden*. Periplus, 1999.

Cunningham, Marion. *The Fanny Farmer Cookbook*. Alfred A. Knopf, 1990.

Gardiner, Anne, and Sue Wilson. *The Inquisitive Cook*. Henry Holt, 1998.

Green, Henrietta. *Farmer's Market Cookbook*. Kyle Cathie, 2001.

Grunes, Barbara. *The Beef Lover's Great Grill Book*. Contemporary Books, 1991.

Grunes, Barbara, and Phyllis Magida. *Fish On The Grill*. Contemporary Books, 1986.

Harlow, Joan S. *The Loaf and Ladle Cookbook*. Down East Books, 1983.

Katzen, Mollie. *Moosewood Cookbook*. Ten Speed Press, 1977.

Kropotkin, Igor and Marjorie Kropotkin. *The Inn Cookbook*. Castle, 1983.

Lanchester, John. *The Debt to Pleasure*. Henry Holt, 1996.

Loomis, Susan Herrmann. *Farmhouse Cookbook*. Workman Publishing, 1991.

MacMillan, Diane D. *The Portable Feast*. 101 Productions, 1984.

McNair, James. *Pizza*. Chronicle Books, 1987.

Mayes, Francis. *Under the Tuscan Sun*. Broadway Books, 1997.

Mayle, Peter. *A Year In Provence*. Vintage Books, 1991.

Murphy, Margaret Deeds. *The Boston Globe Cookbook* (Third Edition). Globe Pequot Press, 1990.

Ojakangas, Beatrice. *Whole Grain Breads By Machine Or Hand*. Macmillan, 1998.

Oliver, Jamie. *The Naked Chef*. Michael Joseph, 1999.

de Pomiane, Edouard. *French Cooking in Ten Minutes (1930)*. North Point Press, 1994.

Richardson, Ferrier, ed. *Scotland On A Plate*. Black & White Publishing, 2001.

Rosso, Julee, and Sheila Lukins. *The New Basics Cookbook*. Workman Publishing, 1989.

Child Rosso, Julee, and Sheila Lukins. *The Silver Palate Cookbook*. Workman Publishing, 1982.

———. *The Silver Palate Good Times Cookbook*. Workman Publishing, 1985.

Seranne, Ann, ed. *The Western Junior League Cookbook.* McKay, 1979.

Tudor, Tasha. *The Tasha Tudor Cookbook.* Little, Brown, 1993.

Urvater, Michele. *Monday to Friday Cookbook.* Workman Publishing, 1991.

Visser, Margaret. *Much Depends on Dinner.* Macmillan, 1986.

# Favorite Publications

*Bon Appetit*—www.bonappetit.com

*Cooking Light*—www.cookinglight.com

*Cook's Illustrated*—www.cooksillustrated.com

*La Cucina Italiana*—www.italiancookingandliving.com/store/magazines/la_cucina_italiana.html

*Fine Cooking*—www.taunton.com/finecooking/index.asp

*Food & Wine*—www.foodandwine.com

*Saveur*—www.saveur.com

*Wine Spectator*—www.winespectator.com

The Busy Person's Guide to Gourmet Cooking on a Budget—wz.com/food/GourmetCookOnBudget.html—This is the author's own cooking site, devoted to finding and publicizing the most user-friendly cooking sites on the web. "Budget" in this context includes making the best use of time, and many of the sites promoted focus on quick cooking.

Selected cooking-related pages are reviewed by Tod Dimmick in his email newsletter for WZ.com. (Copyright WZ.com, Inc., reprinted with permission. Ongoing reviews of this type of website are available at wz.com/food/GourmetCookOnBudget.html.) Some of these links will bring you to a general site, others to a specific, entertaining article or recipe.

# Theme Cuisine

The sites listed in this section are particularly strong on a particular cooking topic or theme. For some, that topic is all they cover. For others, the link will bring you right to the food section that I think is the most useful.

### Seafood

All Fins, All the Time—www.seafoodrecipe.com—This subset of the AllRecipes site has got it all, organized by cooking method, ethnic origin, specific undersea creature.

I wish they all could be California Fish …—www.ca-seafood.org/recipes/index.htm— The California Seafood Council puts in a plug for seafood from the Golden State. You can safely substitute fish from other waters. Check out Steamed California Halibut on Rice Pillow (entrées). Barracuda Burgers?!

Seafood Watch—www.montereybayaquarium.org/efc/efc_oc/dngr_food_watch.asp— Worth a click to check the list of recommended seafood, and learn what to avoid due to overfishing.

## Food and Wine Sites

Start Simple—www.adwfoodandwine.com—Here's a basic chart, courtesy of Clos du Bois, explaining matches that work, and why.

Wine and the good life—www.winespectator.com—One of the largest wine-related sites on the web, offers a mountain of information on wine, travel, restaurants, and more.

TastingTimes—www.tastingtimes.com—The author's own site offers a growing section on food and wine pairing, wine menus, and recipes. It also features a free email newsletter with "hot pick" recommendations under $15.

## Healthy Cooking

Delicious Decisions—www.deliciousdecisions.com/cb/index.html—This site is serious about healthy (it's part of the American Heart Association). I find this useful primarily for detailed advice on substitutes and healthy cooking methods (see the "heart health chef's tour").

Eat Smart—www.usaweekend.com/food/carper_archive/index.html—A collection of articles from Jean Carper, the well-known columnist for *USA Weekend*, covering everything from vitamins and whole grains to avoiding carcinogens when grilling. I need those tips.

Tastes Great, Less Fat—lowfatcooking.about.com—Trevy Little hosts a detailed page of resources on the low-fat theme. Categories include the expected salads, as well as imaginative entries for beef, pasta, lamb, and more.

## Vegetarian

AllVegetarian—www.vegetarianrecipe.com—A vegetarian collection drawing upon the extensive AllRecipes database and featuring, of course, ratatouille.

Vegetarian across the globe—www.ivu.org/recipes/regions.html—The International Vegetarian Union offers a multitude of recipes divided by region of the world, and by type of cuisine. From tofu to curry, chili to portabella bruschetta, it's here, plus everything you ever wanted to know about the vegetarian movement.

## Savor the Season

And from the West Coast—www.bestapples.com/recipes—A stunning range of apple recipes from the Washington Apple board. Think Apple Ratatouille on Crostini (under the entrees link). Wow.

Chef's Garden—www.chefsgarden.com/recipes.htm—Salads, dressings, a simple yet tempting Garden Casserole.

Cook's Garden—www.cooksgarden.com—Click on the Favorite Recipes link. This is a short list, but Sesame Asparagus looked so good I had to stop there.

Feeling Blue—www.wildblueberries.com—The Wild Blueberry Association of North America (yes, there is such a group) serves up history, stories, and an array of recipes on the theme. Blueberry Crisp, mmm.

Garlic Grin—www.garlicgoddess.com/index.html—The Garlic Goddess is fun on the web. While not polished (not every site has a design budget), it's nevertheless filled with information on that favorite flavorful ingredient. Enjoy the photograph on the home page, then click the link for recipes. Shrimp and Celery Bisque is "it" for me.

GourmetGarden—www.gourmet-garden.co.uk/recipe/recindx.htm—These simple tasty recipes focus on specific herbs. There's a bit of "divided by a common language" on this British site (you can substitute whipping cream for "double cream") but that adds to the fun.

Grapes!—www.tablegrape.com—If you consider grapes something to eat with lunch, visit the "grape recipe search" for grape entrées. Grape Rosemary Focaccia? Use this link, click on In the kitchen.

More than just pie—www.apples-ne.com/newrecipes.html—From Red Delicious Apple Oatmeal to Apple Halibut Kebabs, there's nothing flashy about this site, just creative approaches to the fruit of the fall.

On the radio …—www.here-now.org/topics/_news/nws_020423b.asp—Here's part of National Public Radio's "Here and Now" show featuring "food evangelist" Dun Gifford. I encourage a visit both to listen to the story, and to read the spring menu. You might even enjoy a quick revisit to the food pyramid.

Yankee Gardener—www.yankeegardener.com/recipe.html—Okay, I've got a soft spot for Rhubarb Cobbler.

## Comfort Food

Breadworld—www.breadworld.com/recipes—Bread recipes for conventional oven and machine. This link takes you to "healthy & hearty" bread machine recipes (check out Oatmeal Molasses Bread); other options are on the left.

Cooking Method—www.gumbopages.com/food/sauces—Here are the Sauce Facts, there will be a quiz tomorrow. In his cheerful personal site, Chuck Taggart provides an engaging, detailed overview of the five basic sauce methods. Nicely done.

Top 10—pasta.allrecipes.com/topten/top10.asp—Market research by way of the stomach, here's the top 10 from AllRecipes. What's the Comfort connection? While the list changes, Lasagna is usually at the top.

## Meats

Barbecue or Grill?—www.culinarycafe.com/Barbeque.html—Both methods are outlined with tantalizing recipes.

Brining!—www.turkeyhelp.com/cookingproblembrining.htm—If you love flavorful, moist turkey, consider brining. The basic concept is that soaking turkey in a saline and seasoning solution prior to cooking enhances flavor and augments moisture. This selection from *Cooks Illustrated* gives the science, the method, and several basic recipes.

Fowl Fanatic—www.eatchicken.com—This is a chicken lover's paradise, with information from technique to recipes and poultry statistics. Follow the "show a little leg" link to Peruvian Grilled Chicken Thighs with Tomato Cilantro Sauce.

## Restaurant Recipes

RSVP—eat.epicurious.com/bonappetit/restaurant_recipes—This is my favorite section of *Bon Appetit*. Recipes from famous restaurants, some adapted for the home kitchen that doesn't have the more unusual ingredients. Hmm. How about Crab Bisque with sweet red bell pepper? (Under the "Soups/Salads" menu).

StarChefs—starchefs.com/Quickmeals.html—StarChefs is worth the visit for several entertaining reasons. In this case I've guided you specifically to the "quick meals" page, featuring a range of really interesting recipes from famous white hats. Check out Veal and Artichokes Baked Casserole?

# Spices

Granddaddy of Hot—www.tabasco.com—Across the world Tabasco is consumed, well, with relish. This playful site features menu and recipe ideas, including unexpected applications of the elixir of cayenne. Check out Cool Fruit and Vegetable Salad with Hot Tomato Dipping Sauce.

Just for fun—www.herbies.com.au/newsletters.html—Herbies Spices (based in Australia) carries many seasonings unique to Down Under, and a healthy helping of many others. The newsletters are an entertaining and fun gold mine of information.

Penzey's Spices—www.penzeys.com—Each recipe makes use of one or more assertive, characteristic spices. Check out Grilled Asparagus, using bold cracked pepper. I'm a big fan of these guys.

Pepperfool?—www.pepperfool.com/recipe_home.html—Here's a wealth of hot pepper recipes, from mouthwatering Australian Grilled Fish (seafood), to vegetables and—you read right—desserts. The photo section is terrific, but the peppers in my garden never look that good. Another slice of Chocolate Chile Cake, anyone? Hello?

# Culinary Travel

Elephant Stew?!—wind.prohosting.com/outabout/recipes.html—Here's an informal and entertaining selection of African recipes. Thanks to Doug Hendry, a member of the South African Chefs' Association, for the referral. The Bobotie is a head-turning variation of good old-fashioned meatloaf. The Elephant Stew I'll leave to readers to test.

French Chefs—www.delices-defrance.com/index-gb.htm—Some of these recipes are actually healthy, not to mention delicious. "Sunny" veal stew?

Gourmet Heaven—www.cuisineinternational.com/index2.html—Cuisine International arranges cooking school education in such mundane venues as Portugal, England, France, and Italy. *Sigh.* For those of us on a budget, selected examples from these courses bring us along via palate express. Follow the Food Link, and whatever you do, don't look at the pictures of the chateaux.

Holy Guacamole—recipes.alastra.com/Mexican—Wow. Talk about Encyclopedia Mexicana. There are 39 kinds of Guacamole here, and that's just for starters.

Spicy Cooking—www.spicy-cooking.com—This nifty site ties together diverse cooking styles through the common element of heat and spice. From Mexican to Thai, with several stops in between, it's all here.

Wines and Food from France—frenchwinesfood.com/html/entertaining_recipes.htm—Goat cheese stuffed tomatoes. Need I say more.

## Famous Chefs

"Brilliant Career"—www.salon.com/people/bc/1999/11/16/waters/index.html—This Salon article by Leslie Crawford tells Chef Alice Waters' story through the eyes of respected industry leaders. Why is she called the "Mother of American Cooking"?

Just a taste …—www.onlinechef.com/chez.recvege.html—A few recipes from Chez Panisse, for a sense of the approach.

# Favorite Vendors

Here are a few of my favorite vendors:

◆ Trader Joe's at www.traderjoes.com—This national chain offers an eclectic yet tempting array of ingredients helpful to the 20-minute cook.

◆ King Arthur Flour at www.kingarthurflour.com—This mail and Internet-order company provides a huge range of specialty flours and baking ingredients. Add a little buckwheat flour to quick pancakes, and you'll never go back.

◆ Penzey's Spices at www.penzeys.com—Another mail and Internet-order company with a huge selection of top quality herbs and spices, and a recipe-filled catalog to salivate over.

◆ Your Local Farmer's Market at www.ams.usda.gov/farmersmarkets/map.htm—You'll know the one down the street from you better than I. A farm stand is the place to go for the freshest, tastiest farm produce, key ingredients of healthy 20-minute cuisine. This link takes you to a U.S. map, where you can find the market nearest you.

# Index

## Symbols

10-Minute Chicken and Herb
  Pasta, 60
20-Minute Homemade Pizza, 85
20-Minute Tomato Sauce, 54

## A

al dente, 237
AllRecipes.com, 255
allspice, 20
Always Delicious Pasta, 61
Anya's Smoked Salmon Penne
  Pasta, 227
Anya's Turkey Salad, 220
appetizers
  canapés, 161
  Derek's Curry Ball, 236
  dinner parties, 235-236
  Friedkin Family Salmon
    Mousse, 241
  Greek Cucumber Dip
    (Tsatsiki), 130
  Hot Artichoke Dip, 192
  Hummus Platter, 207
  Jean's Mexican Dip, 235
  Quick Grilled Cheese
    Dipping Sauce, 195
  Quick Guacamole, 182
  Sun-Dried Tomato Canapés,
    160
  "Uncle" Marcia's Cheese
    Puffs, 192
  wines, 271
apples
  Right-Brain Chicken and
    Apples, 62
  textures, 170
  warm apples, 170

artichokes
  Hot Artichoke Dip, 192
  Roasted Red Pepper and
    Artichoke Pizza, 87
asparagus
  Penne with Asparagus and
    Ham, 80
  Steamed Asparagus, 31
Aunt Jean's Dijon Chicken, 106

## B

Baby Spinach and Feta Penne,
  81
Bacon, Eggs, and Rice, 211
Bacon and Cabbage, 147
Bacon and Swiss Tortilla Melt,
  181
bake pans, 39
Baked Acorn Squash, 216
Baked Cherry Miel, 268
Baked Sole, 96
baking accoutrements, stocking
  your kitchen with, 13
baking goods
  baking soda, 25
  baking spice, 158
  flour, 13
  meals, 13
baking soda, 25
baking spice, 158
Banana-Oatmeal Breakfast
  Bread, 158
bananas, Banana-Oatmeal
  Breakfast Bread, 158
Barry's Taco Salad, 49
Basic Pizza Dough, 84
Basic White Bread, 155
basil, 17
batches, half, 247

Bay View House Sourdough
  Pancakes, 67
beans
  Black Bean and Corn Stew,
    206
  growing, 283
  Sautéed Garden Beans, 285
  Sautéed Green Beans and
    Scallions, 145
beef
  Barry's Taco Salad, 49
  Beef and Broccoli Stir-Fry,
    207
  Beef Wraps, 115
  Burgers with a Twist, 116
  Easy Timesavers, 117-118
  Fleisch Kuchle (Austrian
    Meat Cakes), 113
  John Q's Mac and Cheese
    (with Slight Variation), 198
  Make-Ahead Lasagna, 58
  Quick Cajun Kebabs, 114
  Romantic Veal, 226
  Sandra's Easy Meatballs, 116
  seasoning, 111-113
  Skillet-Broiled Double
    Cheese Casserole, 247
  Stir-Fried Orange Beef, 238
  Stir-Fried Teriyaki Beef, Pea
    Pods, and Rice, 245
  Unbelievably Good Chili,
    117
Beef and Broccoli Stir-Fry, 207
Beef Wraps, 115
Bill's Arugula Pasta, 129
Black Bean and Corn Stew, 206
black olives
  Black Tie and a Red Dress,
    248
  Feta and Black Olive Pizza,
    86

Black Tie and a Red Dress, 248
blenders, 43
Boiled Lobster, 30
Boiled New Potatoes, 136
Boiled Rice (Both White and
    Brown), 135
boiling, 29-30
bok choy, 146
*Bon Appetit* magazine, 50
Bowties with Sherry Pepper
    Cream, 225
box graters, 40
breads
    Banana-Oatmeal Breakfast
        Bread, 158
    Basic White Bread, 155
    benefits of, 151-152
    Bruschetta, 159
    Buttermilk Biscuits, 153
    Buttermilk Oat Bread, 155
    canapés, 161
    Crostini, 185
    Crostini with Roasted Red
        Pepper, 185
    Delicious Whole-Wheat, 157
    Easy Timesavers, 158
    Healthy White Bread, 156
    Jamie's Welsh Rarebit, 160
    knives, 41
    machines, 43
        adding ingredients, 155
    quick, 152-153
    Rich Breakfast Bread, 156
    Scones, 152
    Skillet-Baked Cornbread, 153
    Sun-Dried Tomato Canapés,
        160
    tortillas, 180
    Wheatena Bread, 157
    yeast breads, 154
breakfast, 65-66
    Banana-Oatmeal Breakfast
        Bread, 158
    Bay View House Sourdough
        Pancakes, 67
    Breakfast Yogurt, 75
    Buttermilk Biscuits, 153
    Buttermilk Health Waffles, 69

Buttermilk Pancakes, 66
Colette's Bacon and Egg
    Buttie, 73
Cottage Griddlecakes, 67
Eggs for Two, Scrambled
    with Sun-Dried Tomato
    and Sweet Onion, 231
Eggy Mess, 72
Freddie's Spanish Eggs, 216
fruit, 75
Garden Herb Eggs, 71
George Ames's Blueberry
    Muffins, 68
Highland Eggs, 202
Instant Mix Tune-Up, 74
instant mixes, 73
Orange French Toast, 70
Orchard Fruit Mélange, 75
Quick and Healthy French
    Toast, 69
Scones, 152
Scrambled Eggs, 71
toast, 76
Tropical Fruit Mélange, 76
yogurt, 74
Breakfast Yogurt, 75
Brendan's Penne Pasta Salad,
    139
Brewpub Fried Fish, 95
Brigitte's Speedy Chicken, 109
broccoli
    Beef and Broccoli Stir-Fry,
        207
    Cheesy Broccoli, 148
    Quick Stir-Fry Medley, 27
Broiled Halibut Steaks, 92
Broiled Lemon Rosemary
    Chicken, 217
Broiled Soy Salmon, 91
Broiled Zucchini, 221
broiling, 31-32
broth, vegetarian, 121
Bruschetta, 159
bunches, 230
Burgers with a Twist, 116
Burpee.com, 258
Buttermilk Biscuits, 153
Buttermilk Health Waffles, 69

Buttermilk Oat Bread, 155
Buttermilk Pancakes, 66
Butternut Squash Soup, 123

# C

cabbage
    Bacon and Cabbage, 147
    Chinese cabbage, 146
    Jean's Oriental Cabbage
        Salad, 144
    Quick Chinese Cabbage
        Stir-Fry, 146
can openers, 41
canapés, 161
caraway, 17
cardamon, 20
Carol Ann's Tortellini Salad, 140
casserole dishes, 38
catfish, Whisker-Licking
    Catfish, 95
chard
    Chard with Balsamic
        Vinegar, 285
    growing, 283
Chard with Balsamic Vinegar,
    285
Charles River Mud Pie, 174
cheese, Parmesan, 5
Cheesy Broccoli, 148
chef's knives, 41
Chef-of-the-month.com, 259
cherries, Baked Cherry Miel,
    268
chicken
    10-Minute Chicken and
        Herb Pasta, 60
    Aunt Jean's Dijon Chicken,
        106
    Brigitte's Speedy Chicken,
        109
    Broiled Lemon Rosemary
        Chicken, 217
    Chicken and Paprika
        Cream, 217
    Chicken and Shrimp Paella,
        203

Chicken Chunk Pasta, 81
Chicken Kebabs, 104
Chicken Marsala, 107
Chicken, Spinach, and Rice
  Soup, 193
Chicken, Tomato, and Rice,
  244
Chicken, White Bean, and
  Vegetable Stew, 219
Chive Chicken, 108
Derek's Buffalo Wings, 105
Derek's Nutty Chicken Stir-
  Fry, 209
Drumroll Chicken, 105
Easy Timesavers, 108-109
Grilled Cheddar Chicken
  Sandwich, 196
Grilled Chicken and Sweet
  Onion, 188
Lightning Chicken Curry,
  204
Pasta with Chicken,
  Mozzarella, and Sweet Red
  Peppers, 5
Quick Home-Style
  Barbecued Chicken, 103
Right-Brain Chicken and
  Apples, 62
"Tarragarlic" Chicken, 107
Tortilla Roma, 182
Tuscan Chicken Breasts, 60
U. B.'s Salsa Chicken, 106
Chicken and Paprika Cream,
  217
Chicken and Shrimp Paella, 203
Chicken Chunk Pasta, 81
Chicken Kebabs, 104
Chicken Marsala, 107
Chicken, Spinach, and Rice
  Soup, 193
Chicken, Tomato, and Rice, 244
Chicken, White Bean, and
  Vegetable Stew, 219
chili powder, 18
Chinese cabbage, 146
Chive Chicken, 108
chives, 18
  Chive Chicken, 108

cilantro, 21
cinnamon, 20
cloves, 20
cod, Poached Black Pepper
  Cod, 93
colanders, 40
Cold Poached Salmon, 242
Colette's Bacon and Egg
  Buttie, 73
*Complete Idiot's Guide to Cooking
  Techniques and Science, The*, 25
completed dishes, 243
condiments, stocking your
  kitchen with, 13
containers, 42
Cook's Recipes.com, 256
*Cook's Thesaurus, The*, 257
cookbooks, 50
cooked ingredients, 243
cookie cutters, using drinking
  glasses as, 172
cookies
  Joe Frankenfield's Brickle,
    172
  Oatmeal Chocolate-Chip
    Cookies, 171
*Cooking Light* magazine, 50
Cooking Light.com, 255
cooking pots, large, 37
cooking utensils, 39
  box graters, 40
  can openers, 41
  colanders, 40
  corkscrews, 41
  garlic presses, 40
  kitchen shears, 41
  knives, 41-42
  lime squeezers, 40
  measuring cups, 40
  measuring spoons, 40
  melon scoops, 41
  pasta spoons, 39
  peelers, 41
  rubber spatulas, 39
  salad spinners, 40
  sieves, 40
  spatulas, 39
  timers, 41

wire whisks, 40
wooden spoons, 39
*Cooks Illustrated*, magazine, 50
cookware, 35-36
  baking pans, 39
  casserole dishes, 38
  fish poachers, 39
  frying, 25
  large cooking pots, 37
  pizza stones, 38
  saucepans, 37
  skillets, 36-37
  vegetable steamers, 38
  woks, 38
cores (fruit), 169
coriander, 18
corkscrews, 41
corn
  Black Bean and Corn Stew,
    206
  Corn and Red Pepper
    Mélange, 147
  Corn and Red Pepper
    Mélange, 147
Cornmeal Wheat Pizza Dough,
  86
cottage cheese, 74
Cottage Griddlecakes, 67
Country Potato Chowder, 220
couscous, 210
  Thai Couscous Salad, 210
crab, Dorst Family Crab Cakes,
  240
Crock Pots, 43
Crostini, 185
Crostini with Roasted Red
  Pepper, 185
crushed red peppers, 18
cucumbers, Quick and Cool
  Cukes, 33
culinary science, 24-25
Curried Rice, 246

**D**

Dad's Baked Fruit, 166
Delicious Decisions.com, 256

Delicious Whole-Wheat Bread, 157
Derek's Buffalo Wings, 105
Derek's Curry Ball, 236
Derek's Nutty Chicken Stir-Fry, 209
desserts
    Charles River Mud Pie, 174
    Dad's Baked Fruit, 166
    Easy Timesavers, 172-175
    Grammalane's Lemon Pie, 165
    Grampa Phil's Pudding Pie, 164
    Joe Frankenfield's Brickle, 172
    Lightning Strawberry Shortcake, 173
    Maple Sundae, 174
    Meringue, 165
    Muffy's Pumpkin Mousse, 229
    Oatmeal Chocolate-Chip Cookies, 171
    Poached Pears, 169
    Sabra's Meringue Kisses, 175
    Sara's Instant Chocolate Mousse, 167
    Strawberries and Thick Cream, 168
    Warm Apples, 170
    Whipped Cream, 167
Diana's Kitchen.com, 256
dill, 18
dinner parties
    appetizers, 235-236
    dinners, 236-240
    preparing for, 240-242
    throwing, 234-235
dollops, 245
Dorst Family Crab Cakes, 240
double boilers, 164
dough, pizzas, preparing, 84
Down Under Burgers, 211
dressings, salad, 142-143
Drumroll Chicken, 105

# E

Easy Mashed Potatoes, 139
Easy Timesavers, 56
    breads, 158
    cooked entrées, 56
    desserts, 172-175
    ethnic foods, 210-211
    ingredient mixes, 56
    key ingredients, 59-61
    making ahead of time, 57-58
    marinated entrées, 56
    pastas, 88
    pizzas, 88
    pre-prepared pizza crusts, 56
    pre-prepared salads, 56
    pre-prepared seasoning mixes, 56
    red meats, 117-118
    romantic meals, 228-231
    vegetarian meals, 128-130
    white meats, 108-109
EatDrinkDine.com, 258
eggplant, Garden Broil, 32
eggs
    Bacon, Eggs, and Rice, 211
    Colette's Bacon and Egg Buttie, 73
    Eggs for Two, Scrambled with Sun-Dried Tomato and Sweet Onion, 231
    Eggy Mess, 72
    Freddie's Spanish Eggs, 216
    Garden Herb Eggs, 71
    Highland Eggs, 202
    Lion Eggs Sandwich, 188
    Scrambled Eggs, 71
Eggs for Two, Scrambled with Sun-Dried Tomato and Sweet Onion, 231
Eggy Mess, 72
electric kettles, 43
Emergency Microwave Baked Potato, 137
enchiladas, 184

entertaining, 234-235
    appetizers, 235-236
    dinners, 236-240
    preparing for, 240-242
Epicurious.com, 51, 257
equipment, 35-36
    containers, 42
    cooking utensils, 39
    cookware
        bake pans, 39
        casserole dishes, 38
        fish poachers, 39
        large cooking pots, 37
        pizza stones, 38
        saucepans, 37
        skillets, 36-37
        vegetable steamers, 38
        woks, 38
    box graters, 40
    can openers, 41
    colanders, 40
    corkscrews, 41
    garlic presses, 40
    kitchen shears, 41
    knives, 41-42
    lime squeezers, 40
    machinery, 42-43
        blenders, 43
        bread machines, 43
        Crock Pots, 43
        electric kettles, 43
        food mills, 43
        gas grills, 43
        mixers, 43
        popcorn makers, 43
        rice cookers, 42
        toasters, 43
    measuring cups, 40
    measuring spoons, 40
    melon scoops, 41
    pasta spoons, 39
    peelers, 41
    rubber spatulas, 39
    salad spinners, 40
    sieves, 40
    spatulas, 39
    timers, 41

wire whisks, 40
wooden spoons, 39
ethnic foods, 201-210
Easy Timesavers, 210-211
expectations, setting reasonable, 7

**F**

family resources, 49
Fast and Easy Scalloped Potatoes, 138
fats
frying, 26
substitutions, 22
Feta and Black Olive Pizza, 86
Fettuccini Alfredo, 79
fish. See seafood.
fish baskets, 91
fish poachers, 39
Fitzgerald, Jim, 25
Fleisch Kuchle (Austrian Meat Cakes), 113
florets, 207
flour, 13, 267
floured surfaces, 84
Flower Bed Salad, 286
Fondue, 229
fondue sets, 229
food mills, 43
Food Pyramid, 8
Foodstyles.com, 258
Foodsubs.com, 257
Freddie's Spanish Eggs, 216
freezers, 44
French toast
Orange French Toast, 70
Quick and Healthy French Toast, 69
Fresh Herb Pizza, 287
fresh ingredients, benefits of, 46
Fresh Tomato Salad, 284
fresh-water fish, Whisker-Licking Catfish, 95
Fried Red Peppers, 198
Fried Tomatoes, 199
Friedkin Family Salmon Mousse, 241

friends, resources, 49
fruits, 75. See also apples; bananas; cherries; grapes; oranges; pears; rhubarb; strawberries
cores, 169
Dad's Baked Fruit, 166
maceration, 168
Orchard Fruit Mélange, 75
Pear and Walnut Salad, 144
Poached Pears, 169
Strawberries and Thick Cream, 168
Tropical Fruit Mélange, 76
Warm Apples, 170
frying, 25
cookware, 25
fats and oils, 26
sautéing, 26
stir-frying, 26
typical foods, 27
frying pans. See skillets
fusion cuisine, 202

**G**

Garden Broil, 32
Garden Herb Eggs, 71
gardens
benefits of, 281-283
easy-to-grow vegetables, 283
Gardiner, Ann, 25
garlic presses, 40
gas grills, 43
George Ames's Blueberry Muffins, 68
ginger, 20
Global Gourmet.com, 257
Gorgeous Seafood Stew, 94
grains, stocking your kitchen with, 16
Grammalane's Lemon Pie, 165
Grampa Phil's Pudding Pie, 164
Grampy's Barbecue Sauce, 104
grapes
Grapes Rockefeller, 267
varietal grapes
wines, 273

Grapes Rockefeller, 267
Greek Cucumber Dip (Tsatsiki), 130
green beans, Sautéed Green Beans and Scallions, 145
greens, growing, 283
Grilled Brie and Mushroom Sandwich, 196
Grilled Cheddar Chicken Sandwich, 196
Grilled Chicken and Sweet Onion Sandwich, 188
Grilled Ham and Swiss, 195
Grilled Pork with Cumin and Lime, 101
Grilled Salmon Steaks, 92
Grilled Sweet and Spicy Pork, 109
Grilled Zucchini, 29
grilling, 27-29

**H**

half batches, 247
halibut, Broiled Halibut Steaks, 92
Ham and Swiss Casserole, 239
hamburgers, Burgers with a Twist, 116
handfuls, 286
Healthy White Bread, 156
herbs, 17-18
basil, 17
caraway, 17
chili powder, 18
chives, 18
coriander, 18
crushed red peppers, 18
dill, 18
growing, 283
marjoram, 18
oregano, 18
parsley, 18
rosemary, 18
sage, 18
stocking your kitchen with, 15

tarragon, 18
thyme, 18
Hersheykitchens.com, 258
Highland Eggs, 202
hors d'oeuvres, 161
Hot Artichoke Dip, 192
Hummus Platter, 207

# I

I Love Pasta!.com, 258
ice cream, Maple Sundae, 174
ingredient mixes, 56
ingredients
    fresh, benefits of, 46
    baking accoutrements, 13
    condiments, 13
    flour and meals, 13
    grains, 16
    herbs, 15
    marinades, 14
    oils, 14
    pasta, 14
    rice, 15
    seasoning mixes, 15
    soups, 15
    spices, 15
    stocking your kitchen with,
        11-12, 16-17
    substitutions, 21
    sweeteners, 16
    vegetables, 16
    vinegars, 14
*Inquisitive Cook, The*, 25
Instant Mix Tune-Up, 74
instant mixes, breakfast, 73
Irelandseye.com, 257
Italian Farmhouse Vegetable
    Stew, 264
Italian Turkey and Sprout
    Sandwich, 187

# J

Jamie's Welsh Rarebit, 160
Jean's Mexican Dip, 235

Jean's Oriental Cabbage Salad,
    144
Jen's Potato Salad, 136
Joaquin's Tortilla and Scallion
    Pizza, 181
Joe Frankenfield's Brickle, 172
John Q's Mac and Cheese (with
    Slight Variation), 198

# K-L

kettles, electric, 43
kitchen shears, 41
knives, 41-42
    sharpeners, 41
Korean-Style Fried Rice, 209

*La Cucina Italiana*, 50
Labensky, Sarah, 25
lamb
    Easy Timesavers, 117-118
    Lamb and Feta Orzo, 250
    seasoning, 111-113
Lamb and Feta Orzo, 250
large cooking pots, 37
lasagna, 6
    Make-Ahead Lasagna, 58
    Make-Ahead Vegetable
        Lasagna, 124
leeks, Potato and Leek Soup, 125
leftovers, planning for, 48
light white wines, 272
light- and medium-bodied red
    wines, 272
Lightning Chicken Curry, 204
Lightning Seafood Stir-Fry, 57
Lightning Strawberry
    Shortcake, 173
lime squeezers, 40
Linguini with Hot Pepper and
    Oil, 80
Lion Eggs Sandwich, 188
Lo Cal Diner.com, 256
lobsters, Boiled Lobster, 30
low-fat meals
    Anya's Turkey Salad, 220
    Baked Acorn Squash, 216

Broiled Lemon Rosemary
    Chicken, 217
Broiled Zucchini, 221
Chicken and Paprika
    Cream, 217
Chicken, White Bean, and
    Vegetable Stew, 219
Country Potato Chowder,
    220
Freddie's Spanish Eggs, 216
keys to, 218-219
Pasta with Broiled Tomatoes
    and Garlic, 221
Whole-Wheat Penne with
    Summer Squash, Tomato,
    and Mushroom, 215

# M

maceration (fruit), 168
machinery, 42
    blenders, 43
    bread machines, 43
    Crock Pots, 43
    electric kettles, 43
    food mills, 43
    gas grills, 43
    mixers, 43
    popcorn makers, 43
    rice cookers, 42
    toasters, 43
machines, pasta machines, 78
magazines, 50
main ingredients, substitutions,
    21
Make-Ahead Lasagna, 58
Make-Ahead Vegetable
    Lasagna, 124
Maple Sundae, 174
Marcia's Shrimp Mold, 241
marinades, stocking your
    kitchen with, 14
marjoram, 18
Mayfield, Eleanor, 214
meals, 13
measuring cups, 40
measuring spoons, 40

mélange, 147
melon scoops, 41
Meringue, 165
methods, cooking, 24
Microquick Poached Salmon, 52
Microwave Poached Salmon, 97
Microwave Sliced Potatoes, 137
Minestra, 266
Minestrone, 265
Minestrone Pasta, 126
Minutemeals.com, 256
mixers, 43
molds, 241
Mom's Open-Faced Bacon and
  Tomato Sandwich, 186
Montereybayaquarium.org, 258
muffins, George Ames's
  Blueberry Muffins, 68
Muffy's Pumpkin Mousse, 229
mushrooms
    Grilled Brie and Mushroom
      Sandwich, 196
    Rotelle with Mushrooms and
      Spinach, 82
    Sautéed Greek Mushrooms,
      127
My Meals.com, 257

## N-O

Nachos, 183
nutmeg, 20
nuts, dishes, 208-209

Oatmeal Chocolate-Chip
  Cookies, 171
oils
    frying, 26
    olive, benefits of, 214
    stocking your kitchen with, 14
    substitutions, 22
olive oil, benefits of, 214
Onion Rings, 149
open-faced sandwiches, 186-188
oranges, Orange French Toast, 70
Orchard Fruit Mélange, 75
oregano, 18

orzo, 250
ostrich, Down Under Burger,
  211

## P

paella, 203
pairings list (wines), 270-274
Pan-Broiled Bacon, Scallops,
  and Rice, 230
pancakes
    Bay View House Sourdough
      Pancakes, 67
    Buttermilk Pancakes, 66
    Cottage Griddlecakes, 67
    Instant Mix Tune-Up, 74
pantries, 12
    stocking your kitchen, 11-12
    baking accoutrements, 13
    condiments, 13
    flour and meals, 13
    grains, 16
    herbs, 15
    marinades, 14
    oils, 14
    pasta, 14
    rice, 15
    seasoning mixes, 15
    soups, 15
    spices, 15
    sweeteners, 16
    vegetables, 16
    vinegars, 14
paprika, 20
paring knives, 41
Parmesan cheese, 5
parsley, 18
parties
    appetizers, 235-236
    dinners, 236-240
    preparing for, 240-242
pasta
    10-Minute Chicken and
      Herb Pasta, 60
    Always Delicious Pasta, 61
    Anya's Smoked Salmon
      Penne Pasta, 227

Baby Spinach and Feta
  Penne, 81
benefits of, 77-79
Bill's Arugula Pasta, 129
Black Tie and a Red Dress,
  248
Bowties with Sherry Pepper
  Cream, 225
Brendan's Penne Pasta
  Salad, 139
Chicken Chunk Pasta, 81
Easy Timesavers, 88
Fettuccini Alfredo, 79
Lamb and Feta Orzo, 250
lasagna, 6
Linguini with Hot Pepper
  and Oil, 80
machines, 78
Make-Ahead Lasagna, 58
Make-Ahead Vegetable
  Lasagna, 124
making, 78
Minestrone Pasta, 126
orzo, 250
Pasta with Broiled Tomatoes
  and Garlic, 221
Pasta with Chicken,
  Mozzarella, and Sweet Red
  Peppers, 5
Pasta with Herbs, 83
Penne à la Vodka, 197
Penne with Asparagus and
  Ham, 80
Penne with Sweet Sausage
  and Tomato Sauce, 249
Quick and Easy Angel Hair
  Pasta with Shrimp and
  Feta, 237
Romano Pasta, 248
Rotelle with Mushrooms
  and Spinach, 82
Sautéed Mushrooms, Olives,
  and Sun-Dried Tomato
  Penne, 148
Shrimp Shells, 82
Spaghetti Carbonara, 79
spoons, 39

stocking your kitchen with, 14

Tuna Broccoli Pasta Salad, 236

Whole-Wheat Penne with Summer Squash, Tomato, and Mushroom, 215

Pasta with Broiled Tomatoes and Garlic, 221

Pasta with Chicken, Mozzarella, and Sweet Red Peppers, 5

Pasta with Herbs, 83

Paul's Quick and Easy Mac and Cheese, 228

pea pods, Stir-Fried Teriyaki Beef, Pea Pods, and Rice, 245

peanuts, Za's Peanut Sauce and Rice, 208

pears, Pear and Walnut Salad, 144

peelers, 41

Penne à la Vodka, 197

Penne with Asparagus and Ham, 80

Penne with Sweet Sausage and Tomato Sauce, 249

Penzey's Spices.com, 258

Pepper Medley, 146

peppercorns, 20

peppers, Pasta with Chicken, Mozzarella, and Sweet Red Peppers, 5

periodicals, 50

pies, 164
   Charles River Mud Pie, 174
   Dad's Baked Fruit, 166
   Grammalane's Lemon Pie, 165
   Grampa Phil's Pudding Pie, 164
   Meringue, 165
   Sabra's Meringue Kisses, 175
   Sara's Instant Chocolate Mousse, 167

pinches, 46

pizza, 84

20-Minute Homemade Pizza, 85

Basic Pizza Dough, 84

benefits of, 83

Cornmeal Wheat Pizza Dough, 86

Easy Timesavers, 88

Feta and Black Olive Pizza, 86

Fresh Herb Pizza, 287

Joaquin's Tortilla and Scallion Pizza, 181

Roasted Red Pepper and Artichoke Pizza, 87

Shrimp and Basil Pizza, 87

pizza stones, 38

Poached Black Pepper Cod, 93

Poached Pears, 169

popcorn makers, 43

pork
   Bacon, Eggs, and Rice, 211
   Bacon and Cabbage, 147
   Bacon and Swiss Tortilla Melt, 181
   Colette's Bacon and Egg Buttie, 73
   Easy Timesavers, 108-109
   Grilled Ham and Swiss, 195
   Grilled Pork with Cumin and Lime, 101
   Grilled Sweet and Spicy Pork, 109
   Ham and Swiss Casserole, 239
   Mom's Open-Faced Bacon and Tomato Sandwich, 186
   Pan-Broiled Bacon, Scallops, and Rice, 230
   Penne with Asparagus and Ham, 80
   Penne with Sweet Sausage and Tomato Sauce, 249
   Quick Stir-Fry Medley, 27
   Rice with Mozzarella, Bacon, and Scallions, 246
   Rosemary and Garlic Tenderloin, 102
   Spaghetti Carbonara, 79
   Spiced Pork Loin Chops, 53

Potato and Leek Soup, 125

potatoes
   Boiled New Potatoes, 136
   Country Potato Chowder, 220
   Easy Mashed Potatoes, 139
   Emergency Microwave Baked Potato, 137
   Fast and Easy Scalloped Potatoes, 138
   Jen's Potato Salad, 136
   Microwave Sliced Potatoes, 137
   Potato and Leek Soup, 125
   Skillet Potatoes, 138

poultry, 100. *See also* chicken; turkey
   Easy Timesavers, 108-109

**Q**

Quick and Cool Cukes, 33

Quick and Easy Angel Hair Pasta with Shrimp and Feta, 237

Quick and Healthy French Toast, 69

Quick Cajun Kebabs, 114

Quick Chinese Cabbage Stir-Fry, 146

Quick Enchiladas, 184

Quick Grilled Cheese Dipping Sauce, 195

Quick Guacamole, 182

Quick Home-Style Barbecued Chicken, 103

Quick Menu Organizer.com, 257

Quick Seafood Stew, 98

Quick Stir-Fry Medley, 27

Quick Tacos, 183

**R**

Ratatouille, 288

Real Greek Salad, 205

red beans, Red Beans and Rice, 122

Red Beans and Rice, 122

red meat. *See also* beef; hamburgers; lamb; veal
Easy Timesavers, 117-118
seasoning, 111-113

red peppers, 18
Corn and Red Pepper Mélange, 147
Crostini with Roasted Red Pepper, 185
Fried Red Peppers, 198
Roasted Red Pepper and Artichoke Pizza, 87

red wines
light- and medium-bodied red wines, 272
rich red wines, 272

reducing heat, 10

refrigerators, stocking, 16-17

refried beans, 117

rendering, 186

resources, 49
cookbooks, 50
family and friends, 49
magazines, 50
restaurants, 51-53
World Wide Web, 51

restaurants, resources, 51-53

rhubarb, Rhubarb Sauce, 286

rice
Bacon, Eggs, and Rice, 211
Boiled Rice (Both White and Brown), 135
Chicken, Spinach, and Rice Soup, 193
Chicken, Tomato, and Rice, 244
Curried Rice, 246
Korean-Style Fried Rice, 209
Pan-Broiled Bacon, Scallops, and Rice, 230
Red Beans and Rice, 122
Rice Medley, 129
Rice Palao, 126
Rice with Mozzarella, Bacon, and Scallions, 246
Salsa Rice, 245
side dishes, 134
Stir-Fried Teriyaki Beef, Pea Pods, and Rice, 245
stocking your kitchen with, 15
Thai Couscous Salad, 210
Za's Peanut Sauce and Rice, 208

rice cookers, 42

Rice Medley, 129

Rice Palao, 126

Rice with Mozzarella, Bacon, and Scallions, 246

Rich Breakfast Bread, 156

rich red wines, 272

rich white wines, 272

Right-Brain Chicken and Apples, 62

Roasted Red Pepper and Artichoke Pizza, 87

Roasted Vegetables, 199

Romano Pasta, 248

romantic meals, 223-225
Anya's Smoked Salmon Penne Pasta, 227
Bowties with Sherry Pepper Cream, 225
Easy Timesavers, 228-231
Eggs for Two, Scrambled with Sun-Dried Tomato and Sweet Onion, 231
Fondue, 229
Muffy's Pumpkin Mousse, 229
Pan-Broiled Bacon, Scallops, and Rice, 230
Paul's Quick and Easy Mac and Cheese, 228
Romantic Veal, 226

Romantic Veal, 226

rosemary, 18
Rosemary and Garlic Tenderloin, 102
Rosemary's Quick Enchiladas, 123

Rosemary and Garlic Tenderloin, 102

Rosemary's Quick Enchiladas, 123

Rotelle with Mushrooms and Spinach, 82

rubber spatulas, 39

## S

Sabra's Meringue Kisses, 175

sage, 18

salads, 141-142
Barry's Taco Salad, 49
Brendan's Penne Pasta Salad, 139
Carol Ann's Tortellini Salad, 140
dressings, 142-143
Flower Bed Salad, 286
Fresh Tomato Salad, 284
Jean's Oriental Cabbage Salad, 144
Pear and Walnut Salad, 144
Real Greek Salad, 205
Spinach Salad, 145
spinners, 40
Thai Couscous Salad, 210
Tossed Salad, 143
Tuna Broccoli Pasta Salad, 236

salmon
Anya's Smoked Salmon Penne Pasta, 227
Broiled Soy Salmon, 91
Cold Poached Salmon, 242
Friedkin Family Salmon Mousse, 241
Grilled Salmon Steaks, 92
Microquick Poached Salmon, 52
Microwave Poached Salmon, 97
Sizzling Salmon, 93

Salsa Rice, 245

salt, adding to boiling water, 25

Sam Cooks.com, 255

Sandra's Easy Meatballs, 116

sandwiches. *See also* hamburgers.
Anya's Turkey Salad, 220
Down Under Burger, 211
Grilled Brie and Mushroom Sandwich, 196
Grilled Cheddar Chicken Sandwich, 196
Grilled Chicken and Sweet Onion, 188
Grilled Ham and Swiss, 195
Italian Turkey and Sprout Sandwich, 187
Lion Eggs, 188
Mom's Open-Faced Bacon and Tomato Sandwich, 186
open-faced sandwiches, 186-188
Tomato and Fresh Mozzarella, 187
Tuna Melts, 194
Sara's Instant Chocolate Mousse, 167
saucepans, 37
sauces
20-Minute Tomato Sauce, 54
Grampy's Barbecue Sauce, 104
Rhubarb Sauce, 286
Spicy Mayonnaise, 239
Sautéed Garden Beans, 285
Sautéed Greek Mushrooms, 127
Sautéed Green Beans and Scallions, 145
Sautéed Herbed Summer Squash, 284
Sautéed Mushrooms, Olives, and Sun-Dried Tomato Penne, 148
Sautéed Scallops, 267
sautéing, 26
typical foods, 27
*Saveur* magazine, 50
scallops, Sautéed Scallops, 267
science of cooking, 24-25
scissors (kitchen), 41
Scones, 152
Scrambled Eggs, 71

seafood
Anya's Smoked Salmon Penne Pasta, 227
Baked Sole, 96
Boiled Lobster, 30
Brewpub Fried Fish, 95
Broiled Halibut Steaks, 92
Broiled Soy Salmon, 91
Chicken and Shrimp Paella, 203
Cold Poached Salmon, 242
Dorst Family Crab Cakes, 240
Friedkin Family Salmon Mousse, 241
Gorgeous Seafood Stew, 94
Grilled Salmon Steaks, 92
Marcia's Shrimp Mold, 241
Microwave Poached Salmon, 97
Pan-Broiled Bacon, Scallops, and Rice, 230
Poached Black Pepper Cod, 93
Quick and Easy Angel Hair Pasta with Shrimp and Feta, 237
Quick Scafood Stew, 98
Sautéed Scallops, 267
seasoning, 90-91
Sizzling Salmon, 93
Sole Meuniere, 97
Tuna Broccoli Pasta Salad, 236
Tuna Melts, 194
seasonings
mixes, 56
stocking your kitchen with, 15
seafood, 90-91
substitutions, 21
vegetarian meals, 120-121
white meat, 100-101
setting tables, 165
shears (kitchen), 41
shrimp
Chicken and Shrimp Paella, 203
Marcia's Shrimp Mold, 241

Quick and Easy Angel Hair Pasta with Shrimp and Feta, 237
Shrimp and Basil Pizza, 87
Shrimp Shells, 82
Shrimp and Basil Pizza, 87
Shrimp Shells, 82
side dishes, 134
Boiled New Potatoes, 136
Boiled Rice (Both White and Brown), 135
Brendan's Penne Pasta Salad, 139
Carol Ann's Tortellini Salad, 140
Easy Mashed Potatoes, 139
Emergency Microwave Baked Potato, 137
Fast and Easy Scalloped Potatoes, 138
Jen's Potato Salad, 136
Microwave Sliced Potatoes, 137
Onion Rings, 149
rice, 134
Skillet Potatoes, 138
sieves, 40
Sizzling Salmon, 93
Skillet Potatoes, 138
Skillet-Baked Cornbread, 153
Skillet-Broiled Double Cheese Casserole, 247
skillets, 36-37
slow cookers, 43
sole
Baked Sole, 96
Sole Meuniere, 97
Sole Meuniere, 97
soups
Butternut Squash Soup, 123
Chicken, Spinach, and Rice Soup, 193
Country Potato Chowder, 220
Minestra, 266
Minestrone, 265
Minestrone Pasta, 126

Potato and Leek Soup, 125
stocking your kitchen with, 15
*Southern Living* website, 256, 259
Spaghetti Carbonara, 79
spatulas, 39
Spiced Pork Loin Chops, 53
Spiced Spinach, 47
Spiced Vegetable Kebabs, 127
spices, 19-20
    allspice, 20
    baking spice, 158
    cardamon, 20
    cinnamon, 20
    cloves, 20
    ginger, 20
    nutmeg, 20
    paprika, 20
    peppercorns, 20
    stocking your kitchen with, 15
Spicy Mayonnaise, 239
Spicy-cooking.com, 259
spinach
    Baby Spinach and Feta Penne, 81
    Chicken, Spinach, and Rice Soup, 193
    Rotelle with Mushrooms and Spinach, 82
    Spiced Spinach, 47
    Spinach Salad, 145
Spinach Salad, 145
sprouts, Italian Turkey and Sprout Sandwich, 187
squash
    Baked Acorn Squash, 216
    Butternut Squash Soup, 123
    Garden Broil, 32
    growing, 283
    Sautéed Herbed Summer Squash, 284
Steamed Asparagus, 31
steaming, 30-31
Stir-Fried Orange Beef, 238
Stir-Fried Teriyaki Beef, Pea Pods, and Rice, 245
stir-frying, 26
    typical foods, 27

stocking your kitchen
    baking accoutrements, 13
    condiments, 13-14
    flour and meals, 13
    grains, 16
    herbs, 15
    marinades, 14
    pantries, 11-12
    pasta, 14
    refrigerators, 16-17
    rice, 15
    seasoning mixes, 15
    soups, 15
    spices, 15
    sweeteners, 16
    vegetables, 16
    vinegars, 14
storage containers, 42
strawberries
    Lightning Strawberry Shortcake, 173
    Strawberries and Thick Cream, 168
Strawberries and Thick Cream, 168
striping vegetables, 285
substitutions, 21-22
summer squash
    growing, 283
    Sautéed Herbed Summer Squash, 284
Summer Tomato Platter, 47
Sun-Dried Tomato Canapés, 160
sweet red peppers, Pasta with Chicken, Mozzarella, and Sweet Red Peppers, 5
sweet wines, 272
sweeteners, stocking your kitchen with, 16

thyme, 18
Tienda.com, 259
timers, 41
timesavers. *See* Easy Timesavers
toast, 76
toasters, 43
Tomato and Fresh Mozzarella Sandwich, 187
tomatoes
    20-Minute Tomato Sauce, 54
    Chicken, Tomato, and Rice, 244
    Fresh Tomato Salad, 284
    Fried Tomatoes, 199
    Garden Broil, 32
    growing, 283
    Pasta with Broiled Tomatoes and Garlic, 221
    Summer Tomato Platter, 47
    Sun-Dried Tomato Canapés, 160
    Tomato and Fresh Mozzarella, 187
tools, 39
    box graters, 40
    can openers, 41
    colanders, 40
    corkscrews, 41
    garlic presses, 40
    kitchen shears, 41
    knives, 41-42
    lime squeezers, 40
    measuring cups, 40
    measuring spoons, 40
    melon scoops, 41
    pasta spoons, 39
    peelers, 41
    rubber spatulas, 39
    salad spinners, 40
    sieves, 40
    spatulas, 39
    timers, 41
    wire whisks, 40
    wooden spoons, 39
Tortilla Roma, 182

# T

"Tarragarlic" Chicken, 107
tarragon, 18
TastingTimes.com, 259
Thai Couscous Salad, 210

tortillas, 180
  Bacon and Swiss Tortilla
    Melt, 181
  Joaquin's Tortilla and Scallion
    Pizza, 181
  Nachos, 183
  Quick Enchiladas, 184
  Quick Tacos, 183
  Tortilla Roma, 182
Tossed Salad, 143
Tropical Fruit Mélange, 76
tuna
  Tuna Broccoli Pasta Salad, 236
  Tuna Melts, 194
Tuna Broccoli Pasta Salad, 236
Tuna Melts, 194
turkey
  Anya's Turkey Salad, 220
  Easy Timesavers, 108-109
  Italian Turkey and Sprout
    Sandwich, 187
Tuscan Chicken Breasts, 60

## U–V

U. B.'s Salsa Chicken, 106
Unbelievably Good Chili, 117
"Uncle" Marcia's Cheese Puffs,
  192

varietal grapes (wine), 273
veal, Veal Scallopini, 103
vegetables. See also artichokes;
  asparagus; beans; black olives;
  bok choy; broccoli; cabbage;
  chard; corn; green beans; leek;
  pea pods; potatoes; spinach;
  sprouts; squash; summer
  squash; sweet red peppers;
  tomatoes, zucchini.
    easy-to-grow vegetables, 283
    steamers, 38
    stocking your kitchen with, 16
vegetarian broth, 121
vegetarian dishes, 120
  Bill's Arugula Pasta, 129
  broth, 121

Butternut Squash Soup, 123
Corn and Red Pepper
  Mélange, 147
Easy Timesavers, 128-130
Fried Red Peppers, 198
Fried Tomatoes, 199
Italian Farmhouse Vegetable
  Stew, 264
Make-Ahead Vegetable
  Lasagna, 124
Minestrone Pasta, 126
Pepper Medley, 146
Potato and Leek Soup, 125
Quick Chinese Cabbage Stir-
  Fry, 146
Red Beans and Rice, 122
Rice Medley, 129
Rice Palao, 126
Roasted Vegetables, 199
Rosemary's Quick Enchiladas,
  123
Sautéed Greek Mushrooms,
  127
Sautéed Green Beans and
  Scallions, 145
Sautéed Mushrooms, Olives,
  and Sun-Dried Tomato
  Penne, 148
seasoning, 120-121
Spiced Vegetable Kebabs, 127
*Vegetarian Times* website, 256
vinegars, stocking your kitchen
  with, 14
vintages (wines), 275
Vivisimo.com, 51, 255

## W–X

waffles, Buttermilk Health
  Waffles, 69
Warm Apples, 170
web resources, 51, 253-259
Wheatena Bread, 157
whipped cream, preparing, 167
Whisker-Licking Catfish, 95
white meat
  Easy Timesavers, 108-109
  seasoning, 100-101

white wines
  light white wines, 272
  rich white wines, 272
Whole-Wheat Penne with
  Summer Squash, Tomato, and
  Mushroom, 215
Wilson, Sue, 25
wines, 269-270
  appetizers, 271
  dependable producers,
    274-275
  light- and medium-bodied
    reds, 272
  light whites, 272
  pairings list, 270-271, 273-274
  rich reds, 272
  rich whites, 272
  sweet, 272
  types of, 272-274
  varietal grapes, 273
  vintages, 275
wire whisks, 40
woks, 38
wooden spoons, 39

## Y

yeast breads, 154
  Banana-Oatmeal Breakfast
    Bread, 158
  Basic White Bread, 155
  Buttermilk Oat Bread, 155
  Delicious Whole Wheat, 157
  Healthy White Bread, 156
  Rich Breakfast Bread, 156
  Wheatena Bread, 157
yeasts, 25
yogurt, 74

## Z

Za's Peanut Sauce and Rice, 208
zest (peels), 70
zucchini
  Broiled Zucchini, 221
  Garden Broil, 32
  Grilled Zucchini, 29